4WD

SURVIVAL GUIDE

Driving Skills, Troubleshooting & Vehicle Maintenance

John Basham

Gregory's 4WD Survival Guide
Published in Australia by Gregory's Publishing Company
(A division of Universal Publishers Pty Ltd)
ABN 83 000 087132

Marketed and distributed by:
Universal Publishers Pty Ltd

New South Wales: 1 Waterloo Road, Macquarie Park 2113
Ph: (02) 9857 3700 Fax: (02) 9888 9850

Queensland: 1 Manning Street, South Brisbane 4101
Ph: (07) 3844 1051 Fax: (07) 3844 4637

South Australia: Freecall: 1800 021 987

Victoria: 585 Burwood Road, Hawthorn 3122
Ph: (03) 9818 4455 Fax: (03) 9818 6123

Western Australia: 38a Walters Drive, Osborne Park 6017
Ph: (08) 9244 2488 Fax: (08) 9244 2554

International distribution
Ph: +61 2 9857 3700 Fax: +61 2 9888 9850

Reprinted 2000, 2001
2nd edition 2005

The Publisher would be pleased to receive additional or updated material, or suggestions for future editions.
Please address these to the Publishing Manager at Universal Publishers Pty Ltd.

ISBN 0 7319 1828 2
Gregory's 4WD Survival Guide

Cartography, research and writing, photographic research, indexing, editing and project management by:
the staff of Universal Publishers Pty Ltd &
PlanBookTravel (http://www.planbooktravel.com)

Cover design and internal design by:
PlanBookTravel (http://www.planbooktravel.com)

Cover photographs: ARB Corporation Ltd and Offroad Images: left and 2nd from right (front), left and right (back); Geoff Higgins: middle (back); Land Rover Australia: middle (front); Nissan Motor Co (Aust) Pty Ltd: right (front); Universal Publishers Pty Ltd: 2nd from left (front); Waeco Pacific Pty Ltd: main photograph.

Printed by: KHL Printing Co Pte Ltd

Contents

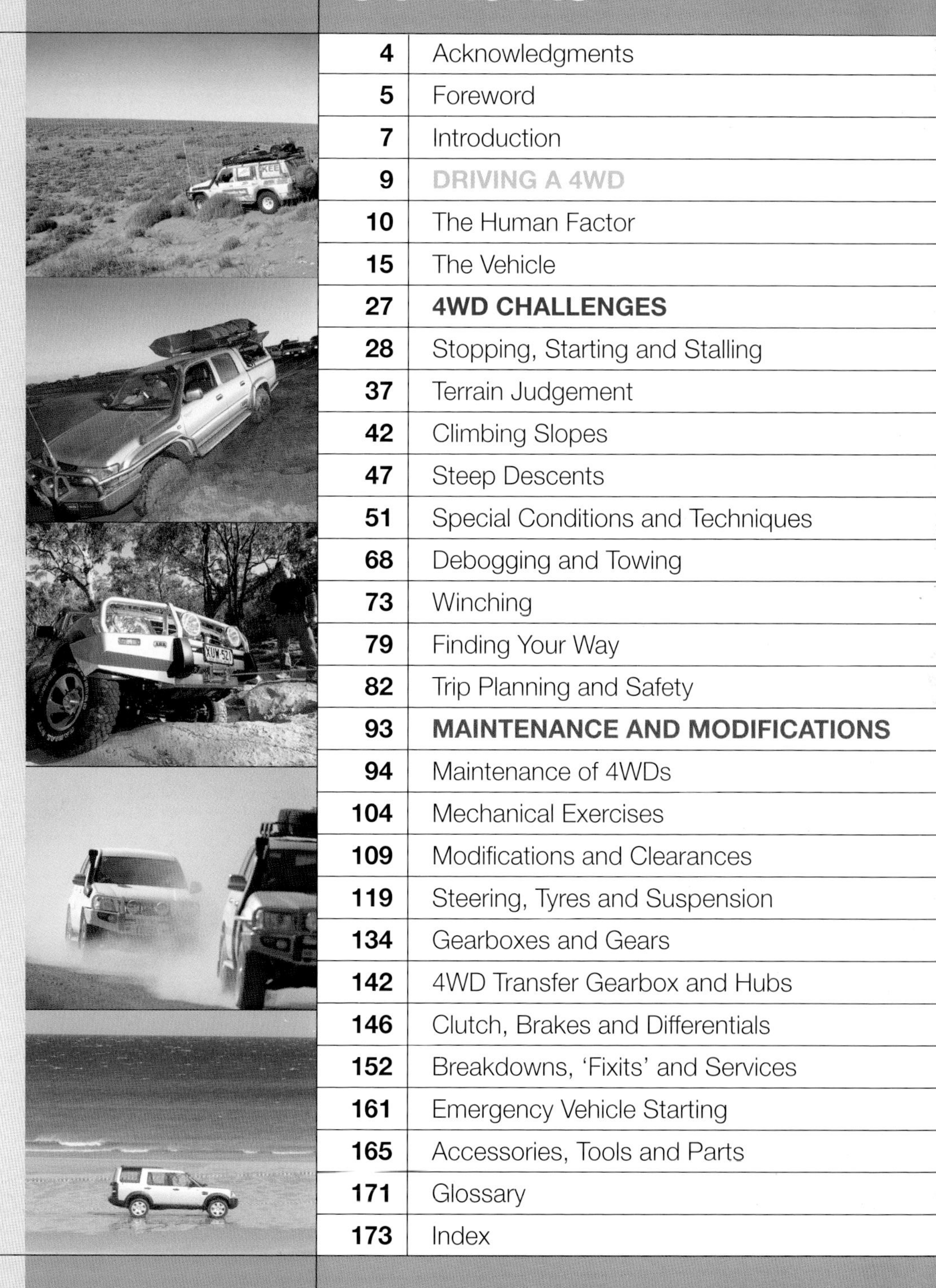

4	Acknowledgments
5	Foreword
7	Introduction
9	**DRIVING A 4WD**
10	The Human Factor
15	The Vehicle
27	**4WD CHALLENGES**
28	Stopping, Starting and Stalling
37	Terrain Judgement
42	Climbing Slopes
47	Steep Descents
51	Special Conditions and Techniques
68	Debogging and Towing
73	Winching
79	Finding Your Way
82	Trip Planning and Safety
93	**MAINTENANCE AND MODIFICATIONS**
94	Maintenance of 4WDs
104	Mechanical Exercises
109	Modifications and Clearances
119	Steering, Tyres and Suspension
134	Gearboxes and Gears
142	4WD Transfer Gearbox and Hubs
146	Clutch, Brakes and Differentials
152	Breakdowns, 'Fixits' and Services
161	Emergency Vehicle Starting
165	Accessories, Tools and Parts
171	Glossary
173	Index

ACKNOWLEDGMENTS

Author's acknowledgments

I would like to thank the following people for their advice and support:
Don, for the original suggestions and ideas, and for encouraging me to write the book. Steve, whose computer expertise saved me many hours of work. Squirrel and Mary, for their helpful ideas and support. Gary, Mike and Ken whose constructive comments at the time kept me on the right track. Sue, editor extraordinaire and friend, whose coffee I drank a lot. My family, whose capabilities and tolerance never cease to amaze me; they made it possible for me to "go play four-wheel drive" without too much worry, and made writing these words much easier.

Photographic acknowledgments

Gregory's would like to thank the following companies and individuals whose photography appears in this guide: ARB Corporation Ltd **www.arb.com.au** and Offroad Images pages 3 (2nd from top, middle and 2nd from bottom), 8, 10, 14, 15, 28, 29. 37, 42, 45, 47–49, 51, 52, 56, 59. 61, 68, 69, 72–75, 79, 82, 84, 88, 94, 99, 104, 109, 119, 120, 124, 129, 134, 139, 142, 146, 150, 151–153, 161, 165, 166 and front cover (top left and 2nd from right, back cover (left and right); John Basham page 167; Daihatsu Australia **www.daihatsu.com.au** page 40; Natasha Edwards page 131; Ford Motor Company of Australia **www.ford.com.au** pages 17, 97; Geoff Higgins pages 6, 92 and back cover (middle); Kincrome Professional Quality Tools **www.kincrome.com.au** page 89; Land Rover Australia **www.landrover.com.au** pages 3 (bottom), 19, 39, 41, 57, 63, 65, 117, 121, 133 and front cover (top middle); Macson Trading Company Pty Ltd **www.macson.com.au** page 80; Mitsubishi Motors Australia Ltd **www.mitsubishi-motors.com.au** pages 16, 81, 108; Nissan Motor Co (Aust) Pty Ltd **www.nissan.com.au** pages 26, 32, 66 and front cover (top right); Oppposite Lock **www.oppositelock.com** pages 3 (top), 23, 24, 50, 55, 62, 67, 71, 76, 112 (bottom), 164; PlanBookTravel **www.planbooktravel.com** pages 91, 103, 110, 118, 147, 155, 160; TJM Products Pty Ltd **www.4wdmegastores.com.au** pages 13, 78, 111, 112 (top), 113, 154; Toyota Australia **www.toyota.com.au** pages 20, 143; Universal Publishers Pty Ltd pages 34, 46, 96, 125, 126, 128, 144, 145, 148, 157 and front cover (top 2nd from left); Waeco Pacific Pty Ltd **www.waeco.com.au** pages 137, 170 and main front cover photograph.

FOREWORD

Four-wheel driving, now a popular recreational pursuit, has been important for almost fifty years in the exploration and enjoyment of remote places in this vast country. I have spent many pleasurable hours in a 4WD and have undertaken many both difficult and rewarding trips with my late husband Len (1923–1996), founding Patron of the Australian National Four Wheel Drive Council.

Len, whose pioneering work earned him the title of the last of the great Australian explorers, used his trusty Land Rover on many expeditions as surveyor and road builder in the opening of the heart of Australia. Together we experienced the adventure of the Outback, and enjoyed the warm friendship and benefited from the knowledge of many other four-wheel drivers.

Places otherwise inaccessible can be experienced using a four-wheel drive, and advances in technology mean that the average family can undertake some trips once only tackled by very brave people. But without the proper knowledge, planning and preparation, both short or long trips can end in discomfort or even disaster.

LEN AND
ANNE BEADELL

The network of experienced and dedicated drivers who belong to the hundreds of 4WD clubs around Australia is a valuable source of information and advice, and I join John in recommending that new drivers take advantage of the many benefits of joining a 4WD club. Training days and specially planned trips help increase driver skills and promote safe and responsible driving.

Gregory's 4WD Survival Guide is a valuable source of knowledge and information for four-wheel drivers, and contains advice which will help both new drivers and those with some experience improve their skills, understand the challenges and experience the pleasures that four-wheel driving has to offer.

Happy and safe four-wheel driving.

Anne Beadell
Patron
Australian National Four Wheel Drive Council

INTRODUCTION

Four-wheel driving is increasing in popularity, with growing numbers of people owning a 4WD – for recreation and transport. It also presents challenges that require drivers to act safely and responsibly.

Gregory's 4WD Survival Guide offers vital information to drivers wanting to prepare themselves and their vehicles to face various terrains and types of trips. It may even tempt those who normally avoid looking under the bonnet to take an interest in basic maintenance to help prevent breakdowns or unnecessary wear, or learn to solve problems that can happen in remote places where outside help is not available.

There are clear explanations of the mechanical and other special features of common dual-range transmission 4WDs, together with information about vehicle modifications. Methods and information that every four-wheel driver needs to know before venturing off-road are discussed and illustrated.

The combination of a 4WD vehicle and unfamiliar circumstances is a whole new world and there is much to learn for drivers only used to normal single-range two-wheel drive vehicles. This book provides practical advice aimed at those who want to understand the principles of four-wheel driving, as well as learning hands-on skills for all-round driving, maintenance, repairs and trouble-shooting. From learner-driver to expert, there are simplified descriptions, tips, real examples and suggestions that even experienced drivers will find useful. Better knowledge and skills will improve your chances of having more enjoyable and safer trips with less damage to your vehicle and the environment.

Learning by trial and error can be expensive, frustrating and dangerous. Four-wheel drivers should also seek advice from vehicle and recreational clubs, authorities and specialist magazines. For specific technical information, a genuine workshop manual is a source of valuable knowledge.

Almost forty years of experience and enjoyment are distilled in these pages. I have not set out to cover every possible topic, but instead concentrate on subjects that other books in my library perhaps do not cover in a straightforward and practical way. There is a lot of information in this book, simply because, to be a safe and competent four-wheel driver there is an awful lot to know. Good four-wheel driving should provide interesting, safe and enjoyable travel with minimal damage to your vehicle or the environment, and no situations that are unsolvable.

If this book provides useful answers to frequently asked questions, improves four-wheel driving skills and ability, and helps drivers enjoy their experiences with a 4WD, then my effort has been worthwhile.

John Basham, September 2004

IPF
IPF
IPF
IPF
IPF
VIC
ARBNTH

DRIVING A 4WD

IN THIS SECTION

- The Human Factor
- The Vehicle

The Human Factor

Advice

NOTHING MAKES A TASK HARDER TO DO THAN KNOWING THAT YOU DON'T HAVE SUFFICIENT EXPERIENCE TO COPE WITH UNEXPECTED OR SERIOUS PROBLEMS, ESPECIALLY WHEN YOU ARE ON YOUR OWN

Driver attitude

A four-wheel-drive vehicle often seems to have a mind of its own. Without knowing how to handle it you could work harder than needed. Driving a 4WD can be fun, and unlike driving a normal car. You need to feel confident and be competent as a driver in any motor vehicle, and particularly in a 4WD, if you want to take advantage of the places they are capable of going. Even if you are an experienced car driver, you may be in for a surprise when you first drive a 4WD. To many, the experience is almost a new state of mind.

Some 4WDs don't handle as easily as a normal car, and most lean over more in corners. They pitch front-to-rear in short-wheelbase (SWB) versions and the suspension, particularly in older 4WDs, lets passengers feel bumps in the road. Owning one for the first time often needs an appropriate driver mind change, an adjustment to accept the characteristics of a 4WD.

Because a 4WD is larger than an ordinary car it is easy to become an offensive, even aggressive driver. You may need to become even more tolerant of other drivers, including those who cut across in front of you to take up the extra cushion space you were allowing for braking or safety. There is one handy advantage — car drivers generally tend to give your 4WD a bigger space, especially if it is dirty or dented.

Driver safety

Using a 4WD vehicle "off-road" (i.e. not on bitumen or paved roads) for work or recreation can be very satisfying. It can also be mentally and physically demanding. It takes skill to negotiate the terrain, and at the same time minimise adverse effects on both the environment and the vehicle. Experience can make a difference between a safe and a risky 4WD action, but often it can be as simple as a state of mind. Drivers attending 4WD education courses at club or commercial level are taught the basic skills at an early stage and usually develop a responsible attitude, quickly learning the rules for off-road safety.

The surface you are driving on has a lot to do with driver safety. Hitting a patch of gravel or loose screenings on a bitumen road has brought many 4WDs undone. (Perhaps slower speed or better observation would have prevented this.) Anyone with basic 4WD experience driving on slippery hard clay tracks on a drizzly winter day can only blame themselves for damage resulting from failing to stop. (Sometimes chains are needed to make progress in such conditions.) Being too confident on a side-slope is one way to increase the chances of a rollover, causing injury and damage. On the other hand, getting through a delicate or really tough bit of driving safely is very satisfying.

Education

Trying to learn on your own through the school of hard knocks can be very dangerous, and can also be a waste of time. Dangerous, because a little knowledge gives a false sense of security, and a waste of time because it is difficult to get any better if you don't have new experiences, beginning with good instruction. Nothing makes a task harder to do than knowing that you don't have sufficient experience to cope with unexpected or serious problems, especially when you are on your own.

Most special-interest clubs run what are known as "beginners days" where skills can be safely learned. In a 4WD club, beginners days or new member days are usually times when experienced drivers take new members and their vehicles on an easy trip or for a series of activities to gain experience. If the new drivers get into difficulties, which is fairly common, help is given by the experienced members. If properly organised these training days can be most valuable to everyone concerned.

Things that experienced off-road drivers don't even notice can be a major problem for a beginner. Each of these quite different activities requires different skills. In time and with good instruction and practice, four-wheel drivers can learn advanced driving techniques to cope with specific, less common or more difficult situations. Even if you don't stay with the club, this initial and basic education is of great benefit.

Checklist

Questions to ask yourself before deciding to buy a 4WD

- Why am I buying a 4WD?
- Do I really need one?
- What percentage of bitumen driving will I do?
- Will I use it mostly as a towing or commuting, bitumen-road vehicle?
- What am I going to tow with it, and is this make and model suitable for my needs?
- Will a SUV with 'all-wheel drive' do the job I have in mind?
- Do I need a heavy-duty dual-range 'go-anywhere' four-wheel drive?
- How much money will I have to spend to make this vehicle exactly right for my purposes?
- How many weekends will I spend driving in the bush or desert each year?
- Will I really go out many times to find and explore new tracks?
- Which club should I join?
- What training or specialised driving skills do I need in order to do what I want?
- Am I a competent driver?

To learn about 4WDs takes effort, as there is a lot to learn and experience, particularly for "off-road" driving. As with most pursuits, you won't become competent unless you really want to, have proper instruction, experience a variety of situations and do the necessary practice. This takes a particular kind of driver commitment and attitude as well.

Checklist

Special-interest clubs provide valuable 4WD training

- Launching a boat on an open sandy beach for fishing can be quite dangerous, but with instruction from others experienced in this task, risks are reduced.
- Coping with the instability and movement of two horses in a horse-float on a long and tiring trip requires skill and concentration, but there are ways to make this easier.
- Towing a caravan on an interstate journey, particularly on rough or undivided roads, requires considerable skill and care.
- Backing a big caravan into and down a narrow driveway is not something that is easily learned in five minutes, and many drivers cannot do it efficiently.

Special interest clubs can provide you with many skills.

Hands-on practice and caution

Learning the capabilities of your vehicle as well as its limitations in a controlled situation is a major part of driver safety training. Learning the possible dangers of a particular 4WD activity or environment usually comes at the same time.

If the vehicle is used for family transport as well, the beginner tends to treat it with kid gloves. It is easy to do expensive damage to a 4WD, and knowing this can make new drivers even more tentative, but sometimes being too cautious can cause as much damage as being too bold. It usually takes a while before the worry about scratches and dents to the beloved 4WD wears off. Joining a club that has proper, sensible and realistic driver training as part of its activities is an excellent way of overcoming most of these worries.

Most 4WDs are not built for speed, and with a big load are not very fast at all, with diesels generally slower than petrol-engine vehicles.

It makes good sense to take it slowly and anticipate further than you can properly see on narrow, twisty and steep tracks. Think what could happen under full power when working your way up a nasty pinch in low-range second gear [L2] to the top of a razorback while the driver on the other side of the climb is doing exactly the same.

In the USA, the law requires vehicles being driven in sand dunes to display a brightly coloured flag on the top of a tall, flexible mast at the front. This is supposed to give a driver coming up the opposite side of the dune the opportunity and sufficient time to swerve to avoid a head-on collision.

What do you do if you are on a narrow track and there isn't enough room to swerve? On any twisty mountain track, particularly if it is in an area well away from normal traffic, there is a danger of head-on accidents on blind hairpin bends. Drivers often drift out over centre, away from their correct path, to get a better view of the track ahead. If it is a left-hander to you, it is a right-hander for the oncoming vehicle, who might well be cutting in to use the better road away from the edge. What may be worse, the oncoming vehicle could be a log-truck. Think safety, tread lightly and concentrate.

Physical limitations

Four-wheel driving can be enjoyable and a real mental challenge at the same time. But it can also be physically tough on your body. Backing a boat trailer or caravan usually means difficult twisting around in your seat, placing quite a strain on your back and neck. Lifting a heavy 4WD spare wheel back onto its mounting, or jerrycans of fuel onto the

Tip

THINK SAFETY, TREAD LIGHTLY AND CONCENTRATE.

roofrack can also be physically difficult. Climbing around underneath your vehicle to fix it is very uncomfortable on rocky ground. Using a Tirfor winch or highlift jack can be very hard work, and so can using an axe, shovel or chainsaw. Can you, the driver, survive a long and tough drive or climb, even if your vehicle is in good condition? If you have to drag a steel wire winch cable up a steep hill to an anchor point will your back stand up to the effort? How would your knees stand up to wading through deep water, tramping around in knee-deep mud, or scrambling down a slippery clay track? You do need to be in good physical condition, because nobody can really predict what kind of challenges you'll come across.

4WDs have tougher suspension than normal cars, and there is probably nothing more painful than being jolted about after you have been injured. Having to drive a 4WD with a bad back or any other painful physical condition can be very difficult. Concentration and clear thinking usually get thrown out the window, together with safety, in favour of basic personal minimum-pain survival.

If the driver is not well or has an injury, off-road driving can be very much harder. A headache, for example, combined with noise and rough off-road motion, can really make the going tough. One cause of headaches is fatigue from fighting a vehicle in hard-going conditions. Driving with a headache can reduce concentration, vital in difficult conditions, and cause dangerous driving mistakes.

Power steering is one of the best labour-saving devices ever invented. Driving a short-wheelbase vehicle without power steering, with oversize front tyres and running lowered tyre pressures for traction, can be physically exhausting. Adding a headache to physical tiredness can rapidly take the fun out of the day. Any kind of physical handicap can grow out of all proportion, when driving off-road.

Safety

Using a chainsaw, bow saw or axe to cut a fallen tree away to clear a track is a fairly common but potentially dangerous task. Despite protective clothing and powered recovery equipment, it is surprising the number of drivers who hurt their back or suffer other injuries doing this. Hand and eye injuries are also common. Learn how to do things the right way to reduce chances of personal injury. As for any other tool, a chainsaw can be dangerous if not used properly. Similarly, when learning to use a winch, another dangerous activity, the only safe way is to attend a recognised course, and learn from someone qualified to teach proper safety and user procedures.

USING A FLAG IN SAND DUNES INCREASES YOUR SAFETY BECAUSE OTHERS CAN SEE YOU COMING MORE EASILY.

Ego limitations

Unfortunately, many proud (read "foolish") four-wheel drivers won't accept the need for passengers to know how to drive the vehicle. Make opportunities for practice so passenger driving skills are at least sufficient to get you and your vehicle out of a bad spot.

Suppose you are sick or injured out in the desert or scrub, and are unable to drive your vehicle or even help with advice — what then? What happens if you have to get out in the mud or sand to use the winch, and the passenger has to drive but doesn't know how? Proper safety includes making allowances for these kinds of problems.

TRAVELLING WITH MORE EXPERIENCED FOUR-WHEEL DRIVERS IS A GREAT WAY TO LEARN THE SKILLS WITHOUT FEAR OF GETTING STRANDED.

If you are a beginner travelling with others who are much more experienced than you, ask for advice and don't take unnecessary risks. Attend a "new driver" day at your 4WD club, or do at least a basic course at one of the commercial schools. Some experienced drivers do not realise the strain, and maybe high-risk potential, put on new drivers on trips. Never be afraid to ask questions, or to let your trip leader know if you are having difficulty.

More than one potentially good four-wheel driver has unfortunately been scared off by unthinking companions, or from not asking questions or not listening to the answers of more experienced drivers. Be careful not to imagine your expertise is fantastic after driving for only six months. Nature has a way of trapping the unwary. Do several beginner-level trips until you really feel comfortable, then some intermediate trips. You'll know you've made it when a recognised expert club member asks you along on an advanced trip.

The Vehicle

Light-duty four-wheel-drives

There is much confusing data about "four-wheel-drive" vehicles. I feel we should briefly look at them, although apart from this mention, Sports Utility Vehicles [SUVs] and "Crossover" vehicles are not covered in detail in this book. On one side of the coin we have the "real" 4WD, the basis of this book. On the other side we find similar vehicles with new technology, commonly called SUVs and some are known as "Crossover" vehicles.

Gone are the days of the old three-speed gearbox, and almost of the four-speed as well. Welcome to Tipshifts, six-speed automatics, and five-speed manual gearboxes.

Some SUVs do have permanent four-wheel-drive. Some drive mostly via the front two wheels. Some have "all-wheel-drive", where the percentage of front/rear drive ratio changes depending "on demand", determined by how the on-board computer senses the road conditions

However, all come with one high-range of gears, not really suitable for off-road activities. Others have high-range only, but optional 4WD. None of them has a dual-range transmission. Many have automatic operation to lock front hubs in when four-wheel drive is selected. Doubtless, they have improved their "on-road" ability, with the safety of increased traction, and in some cases better driver-vision from higher seating positions.

Off-road limitations

On most of the new all-wheel-drive vehicles there are built-in off-road limiters. They include wheels and tyres not designed and not suitable for off-road use, limited ground clearances with minimal approach and departure clearances, suspension on a body platform simply not designed to cope with whatever off-road conditions might occur, paint finishes which would be prohibitive to touch-up — these and many other things contribute to making

Terms

TRACK TERMS:
UNIMPROVED
BASIC
ROUGH
POORLY PREPARED
NOT MAINTAINED
OUTBACK
DETERIORATED
NATURAL
UNSURFACED
UNFORMED

OUTLANDER IS ONE OF THE NEWER SUVs.

the majority of these SUVs unsuitable for "off-road" work.

With their trend towards "image" and car-like handling and driving, all SUVs and Crossover vehicles are compromised, some in major ways, for serious off-road work. Nonetheless, amazing progress has been made in the world of mechanical and technological things. Clearly, for many drivers these SUVs with their technical benefits and abilities satisfy their present needs

The Electronic Wizard can now give you Traction Control, Hill Descent Control, Antilock Braking Control, Active Suspension Control, Hill Ascent Control, Wheelspin Control and other kinds of vehicle technological "control" wizardry. Many of the top-class 4WDs have accepted the flow-on of some of this development.

Through technology and mechanical design, current SUV and Crossover all-wheel-drive vehicles are designed to get you up to the ski-field safely and easily, and through the typical gravel and muddy tracks into the Pony Club. Many would tow your ski-boat back up the steep boat-ramp well. Apart from being effective commuters and people-movers, I believe their proper purpose in life may well include a benefit not yet looked at in detail [in this book] — their on-road towing abilities, as a serious player in the growing world of ""Around Australia By Road" explorers.

Vehicle choice

Choice of vehicle can be quite complex. The same manufacturer may provide several combinations of the same vehicle. One model can be available in high-range-only permanent two-wheel drive, intended primarily for on-road driving, while the other has selectable four-wheel drive and low-range for hard off-road work.

4WD magazines are usually very up-to-date, and can provide intending four-wheel-drivers with current and well-considered information. From their figures, below is a compilation of 4WD, SUV and Crossover vehicles available for sale about mid-2004. Being fully aware of, and current with, this data should be an important part of your consideration if you are in the market for a 4WD of any type.

To show just some of the differences of vehicles included in this "four-wheel-drive" world, I broke them into these basic categories:

A: Part-time 4WD — Normally the rear two wheels driving, with the front two also available when selected.

B: Full-time 4WD — All four wheels driving permanently and equally.

C: All-Wheel-Drive — Four wheels driving, with the front/rear drive ratio dependent on road conditions as determined by an on-board computer.

D: Single-Range — Gearboxes, manual or automatic, with only one set of [say] five High-range forward gears.

E: Dual-range — Gearboxes, manual or automatic, using two sets of selectable gears — [say] five normal High-range gears plus five more Low-range gears.

Information was provided on a combination of 58 makes and models.

Of these, 24 were part-time 4WDs, where the option to select a low-range gearbox ratio was offered, with very few exceptions. There were 25 classed as full-time 4WDs, but in some cases these were full-time without the low-range transmission option. Nine had "on-demand" or "all-wheel" drive, in that they drove primarily with one set of wheels with part or no drive effort through the other axle, but four-wheel drive was available on demand via the less-driven axle, as the sensor-driven computer required. There was no low-range ability on 22 of the 58, so 36 vehicles listed had low-range gearboxes.

Some had all the electronic bells and whistles; some were simple, strong and effective workhorses. You really do need to be well aware of what you want to achieve, before you get too far into this fast-growing market.

Heavy-duty four-wheel drives

To return to this book's purpose, one thing that hasn't changed since the mid-1990s is the "off-road" environment in which many of us drive our 4WDs. I wrote this book for the person who likes driving a "real" 4WD. My definition of a 4WD, and what I originally based this book on, is the common understanding of a "go-anywhere" vehicle. It drives normally via two wheels, usually the rear two, when driving on good roads. It gives the driver the ability to select an additional two drive wheels into the drive system when needed. Through technical development many first-class 4WDs now have all four wheels permanently driving.

A 4WD has the ability to lock the drive chain solidly so that all four wheels will drive equally, regardless of terrain. It has sufficient leverage through the low range gear reduction to traverse any terrain where it can gain traction.

Perhaps a 4WD's most important benefit is to be able to go through the worst mud, the softest sand, the deepest water, the steepest hills up or down, and to give the driver an inherent sense of ability and safety, of

Terms

SOME 'OFF-ROAD' CONDITIONS HANDLED MUCH BETTER IN 4WD:

- SANDY
- WET
- MUDDY
- SIDE-SLOPES
- STEEP UP
- STEEP DOWN
- ROCKY
- BOGGY
- GREASY
- LOOSE
- GRAVEL
- GRASSY
- SNOW
- PADDOCKS
- SHALE
- ICY
- ROUGH
- UNEVEN

THE FORD TERRITORY IS ANOTHER SUV.

Checklist

4WD engine range

- Three-cylinder two-stroke Suzuki
- Four-cylinder Pajero
- Five-cylinder Mercedes
- Six-cylinder diesel Nissan
- Eight-cylinder Ford
- Ten-cylinder Dodge

knowledge that says "If you can do it, I will get you there". In general, only a real 4WD can do that.

What is a four-wheel drive?

A simple but accurate description of a "real" 4WD vehicle is "an effective means of getting further into the mud before getting bogged". To some people, a 4WD is mainly something to hang accessories on. Many owners add an electric winch, dual fuel tanks, driving lights, special seats, bullbar, roof rack, jerrycan-holder, aftermarket suspension, wide tyres, CB radio, antennae, GPS unit, laptop computer and Track-Maps, extra battery, fridge and air-conditioning. Perhaps the only thing missing is an electronic-funds-transfer machine!

Prices start at around $30,000. A new price of $55,000 is average, $85,000 is common and some cost much more than $120,000. Standard fittings and extra trimmings vary greatly. They range from the very basic vinyl seats, plastic floormats and no radio, right through to plush carpeting, ten-speaker stereo, all-electric monsters with a bottle-cooler between the front seats and two air-conditioners. It is easy to add more than $20,000 worth of accessories to a 4WD after purchase.

To some, a 4WD is simply a very expensive status symbol, and to others it is a security blanket. It is usually a safe vehicle, and will take a lot of mechanical punishment. In city traffic it provides a great view of other vehicles and the road ahead. Some 4WDs are like a truck to drive, with a heavy gearbox, large overall size and big tyres. The more luxurious vehicles, usually fitted with many extras, are not much harder to drive than a car. A 4WD can be the best freedom machine, a commuter, a sports or recreational machine, or a tough workhorse.

One of the things 4WDs have in common is the ability to go where a normal two-wheel-drive car can't, thanks to the extra two selectable driving wheels at the front, and extra ground clearance. One major difference between 2WD and 4WD vehicles is that a 4WD can also carry or pull loads, or travel through conditions impossible for any 2WD. A well-driven 2WD vehicle can go many of the places a 4WD can, but a 4WD can get to places many drivers simply wouldn't think possible.

4WDs come in all shapes and sizes, from the small Suzuki soft-top to the very big dual-cab Ford V8 diesels. There is a wide range of body types. There are two-door wagons, with vertical or horizontal rear doors. The five-door station-wagon configuration is common, and so are little soft-tops with two doors and a tailgate. Single-, extra-, and dual-cabin versions with standard tray, or utility backs with canopies are common, as well as normal utes and flat tray work vehicles. 4WD engines may run on petrol, gas/petrol or diesel, and manual or automatic transmissions are available. They are made in Australia, England, Japan, Russia, America, Germany, India, Korea and many other countries.

As a towing vehicle they are virtually unbeatable, and legislation on tow vehicles and weights makes them in some cases the only suitable vehicles for towing large boats, caravans and trailers.

The usual 4WD mechanical drive system consists of a front motor driving

Tip

REMEMBER — TAKE YOUR VEHICLE OUT OF 4WD WHEN YOU ARE DRIVING ON BITUMEN ROAD, UNLESS IT'S DESIGNED FOR FULL-TIME 4WD USE. IF YOUR VEHICLE IS FITTED WITH DIFF LOCKS AT THE FRONT/REAR, DON'T FORGET TO DROP THEM OUT AS WELL.

the rear two wheels via a manual gearbox. A major difference from a normal car is the selective option to engage the front axle so it can drive the front two wheels and, along with the normal two at the rear, then provide four-wheel-drive. Many new 4WDs are full-time (permanent) 4WD.

The number of combinations of differentials and drive systems is considerable. There are automatic, four-, five- and six-speed manual gearboxes. Quite a few early models are still going, many of these with three-speed gearboxes. For some manual vehicles overdrives are available. This makes the normal four forward gears into eight, or five speeds into ten, providing a gear for virtually any situation.

When to use 4WD

"If you are in 4WD before you need it, you often won't need it." When you realise the track is becoming hard going, in many cases if you are still in 2WD you've already dug a few unnecessary holes and left deep tyre tracks. Sharing the traction between all four wheels reduces wheelspin and skids considerably, therefore reducing environmental impact. A major advantage of being in 4WD is that the vehicle can do the job it is designed for, so the driver doesn't have to do it.

In any kind of uncertain off-road travel, it is appropriate to use 4WD. "Off-road" isn't sometimes the best word to use in the recreational sense. The term off-road doesn't only mean off any road, and driving across virgin land. It means not driving on normal, good quality hard-surfaced roads. Instead of off-road, you may come across a number of terms to describe a track. (See panels on pages 15 and 17.)

Pulling a boat and trailer up the boat-ramp or across the beach sand,

DRIVING THROUGH WATER THIS DEEP REQUIRES PLANNING AND CARE. NEVER JUST PLUNGE STRAIGHT IN.

Case Study

An expensive fire

A large 4WD vehicle belonging to a country Fire Brigade was driven along a bitumen road to fight a fire in a hay shed in a paddock. To get access to the burning hay 4WD was engaged at the road gate and the vehicle was driven across the grass paddock to the fire. On the return trip it was driven all the way back to town, still in 4WD.

One complete differential centre had to be replaced as a result of this incident, making it a very expensive attendance at the fire.

or towing a horse-float into the pony-club yards are typical places to use the advantages of better traction in 4WD.

I once met a Japanese 4WD engineer who could not understand why Australians paid extra money to buy a 4WD, but then didn't use the 4WD facility. In his opinion, whenever not driving on bitumen or hard-surfaced roads in a 4WD, you should be using it. With the front hubs already manually locked in, or engaging automatically with operation of the 4WD selector lever or pushbutton, it is just a matter of activating 4WD to have a much safer, better handling vehicle. There is very little intelligence or benefit in the "hero" attitude occasionally heard on 4WD trips, which causes some drivers to make a point of staying in 2WD as long as possible, as if this makes them better drivers. This damages the environment needlessly and puts unnecessary strain on the vehicle and the driver.

The advantages of all four wheels driving on a vehicle are obvious. Top rally cars are almost all full-time 4WDs. Steering is much improved, even if it does feel heavier. Suspension is evened out front to rear and the vehicle feels more stable and positive to the driver. Front wheels pull and back wheels push, giving increased roadholding and safety. Slips and slides across the road and in corrugated corners on roads with poor surfaces are much reduced. SUVs and Crossover vehicles have made use of these 4WD traction benefits.

When *not* to use 4WD

It can be a really expensive mistake to drive your vehicle very far in 4WD on a

TOWINGTOWING A HORSE-FLOAT INTO THE PONY-CLUB YARD IS A TYPICAL PLACE TO USE A 4WD

dry bitumen road unless it is specifically designed to be driven in 4WD all the time. Range Rovers, Discoverys, Lada Nivas, and various models of other makes including Toyota are some which are designed as full-time 4WDs. Some of the more recent vehicles offer the choice of full- or part-time 4WD, but at present most average 4WDs do not. Unless there is a differential of some kind in the transfer case, or somewhere else between the front and back axles to allow independence and variation in their speeds,do not use 4WD on dry hard-surfaced roads. The result is bad handling, usually excessive tyre wear and possibly mechanical damage.

Permanent 4WD vehicles usually have some method of locking the centre differential for difficult terrain. Do not drive one of these vehicles on hard-surfaced roads with the diff-lock engaged. If your 4WD has either front- or rear-axle diff-locks, the same rule applies.

Climb angles

Even though 4WD improves traction enormously, there are quite a few things a 4WD cannot do. Climb angles are a mystery to many, and claims are made by some drivers about tackling virtually impossible angles. Traction is based on the friction occurring between the tyres and the ground. Worn tyres or loose surfaces reduce climbing ability. And less experienced drivers usually assess a slope as much steeper than it really is.

Crossing water

Driving into water without caution or checking first can be dangerous. This may not apply to a rim-deep bog puddle on a bush track, but a creek, or even a clay-pan with water on it requires caution. Unless you have seen a vehicle in front get through all right, or take notice of where it got into trouble, it pays every time to take a walk and check it out for yourself.

While you are out of the vehicle before a creek crossing, use the chance to check for obvious signs of trouble. A simple check of the vehicle takes only a minute or two, but might save you hours later.

- Does the exhaust sound rattly, or is it hanging down more than normal?

Water entry

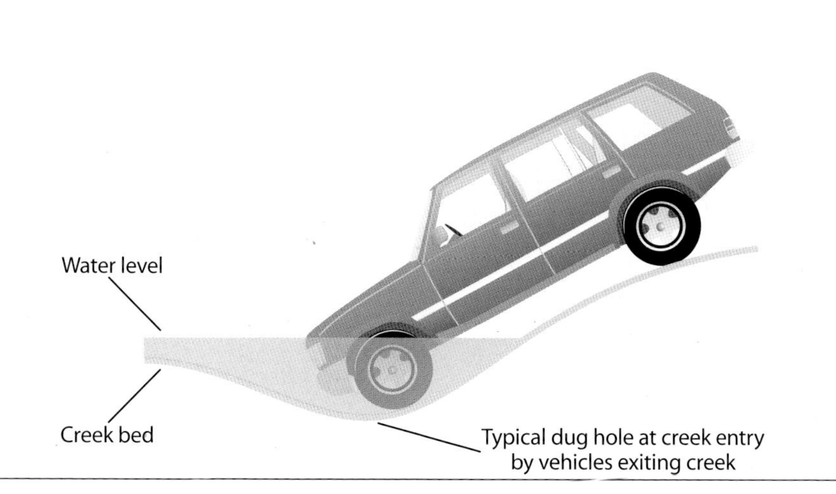

4X4 Advice

DRYING OUT BRAKES PROMPTLY AFTER A WATER CROSSING IS IMPORTANT. DISCS AND PADS WILL DRY WITH JUST A FEW QUICK PUMPS ON THE FOOTBRAKE, BUT TO DRY OUT THE REAR DRUM AND SHOES MIGHT TAKE A FEW MINUTES.

- Are any of the tyres noticeably down in pressure?
- Is the roof-rack loose, or one of the vehicle's lights broken?

Some points worth observing before entering water are as follows:

- Is the water running fairly fast and deep, perhaps even enough to sweep a vehicle sideways off the crossing?
- Is it better to try another crossing?
- Will it be necessary to waterproof the engine bay?
- Are there poles, stone cairns or other markers to indicate the safe track to follow?
- Do you have another option?

It is not safe to go barging down into a creek with steep sides. Previous vehicles may have dug a hole trying to scramble up the bank. It is easy to get stuck or drop your bullbar nose-down into a hole at the drop-off or entry point. This can make it difficult to reach down to the winch cable fairlead in the bullbar, for the cable to pull yourself out. In situations like this it really does pay not to drive further than you have checked.

If you think your 4WD is going under water, kill the motor immediately. It is far easier to dry out an engine than to repair the damage to a cylinder. And never try to tow-start a vehicle if there's a good chance water may have been taken into the motor. If it won't key-start within the first second or two, quit. Take out the spark plugs or glow plugs, and check for water in the cylinders immediately. Do it right the first time, because the result of getting it wrong could be very expensive. For information on emergency vehicle starting, see page 161.

Acceleration

Some of the newer turbocharged and intercooled common-rail direct injection 4WDs have good acceleration, but the average 4WD certainly doesn't. 4WDs will not out-accelerate a normal

Measurement of slopes simplified

Gradient (per cent)	Angle (degrees)
10	6
20	11
30	17
40	22
50	27
60	31
70	35
80	39
90	42
100	45

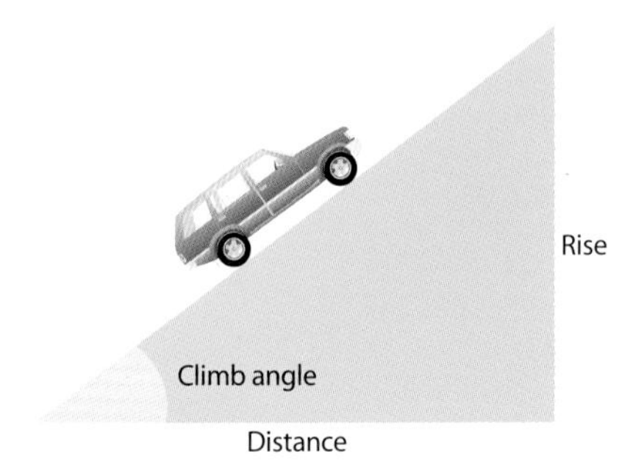

Slopes can be measured in two different ways — either in degrees from horizontal, or percentage of gradient. Some drivers get these a bit mixed up. If you go forward 20 m, and at the same time rise vertically 20 m, the gradient is 20/20 = 1.0 = 100 per cent gradient. The climb angle for this gradient is 45 degrees.

Specialised vehicles, with purpose-made tyres can climb a slope this steep in sand or dirt, but normal 4WDs cannot.

If you drive forward 50 m, but this time only rise 30 m, then mathematically that's 30 ÷ 50 = 0.60 = 60 per cent gradient, or a 31 degree climb angle. In loose soils, that's somewhere near the limit of most 4WDs.

car. They are not designed to do this; but then again, a normal car would not make it up the Canning Stock Route. The old saying, "horses for courses" is right. The new owner of a 4WD will have to learn to accept this and make allowances when overtaking and hill climbing. Most 4WDs respond better to a "steady as she goes" approach rather than being driven like a sports car.

Petrol-fuelled 4WDs are renowned for high fuel consumption. Diesel engines generally offer better fuel consumption figures. Towing or carrying heavy loads makes fuel economy even worse. Many drivers with large six-cylinder engines are delighted to make over 15miles/gallon (5.3km/litre) on bitumen roads. Flogging any motor through heavy acceleration will only push up fuel consumption and lead to wear and tear. Learn to accept the 4WD characteristics, and just cruise steadily along the blacktop.

Maintenance

4WDs are tough vehicles. They are designed to be driven over very rough terrain, and to cope with the strains placed on them they are made bigger and stronger than normal cars. But, like any other machine, in order to get the best from them they have to be properly maintained, and driven within their limits. A 4WD will not last very long if it is neglected.

Regular visual checks for breakages, leaks, dents, parts missing and general soundness is a part of proper maintenance. Regular cleaning of filters, greasing when and where it is needed, and changing of fluids is also an essential part. Without this, a 4WD vehicle can't sensibly be expected to

THE STRENGTH AND RELIABILITY OF A REAL 4WD, AND BELIEF IN YOUR OWN 4WD KNOWLEDGE AND PREPARATION, WILL HELP KEEP YOU SAFE IN THIS REMOTE AND HARSH ENVIRONMENT.

keep going, delivering reliable service to its owner. Thirty-year-old 4WDs in sound condition are fairly common, an indication that with proper and careful maintenance these vehicles will give good service for a very long time.

Driving skills

Some things 4WDs will not do on their own are get through bogs, climb steep tracks, cross creeks, and traverse rough country. On sandhills many drivers find it necessary to get out and curse their vehicle for its inability to make it up and over the top. The same thing often happens on boggy, steep or slippery sections of track. The answer is sometimes very obvious to onlookers — for whatever reason, the driver's approach or attitude to the obstacle was not correct, and it was not the fault of the vehicle at all. Sometimes, drivers won't accept this fact.

A different approach angle, lower tyre pressures or a more suitable speed is often the answer. Perhaps it needed more speed for momentum, listening to helpful advice from a more experienced driver, a different gear to give better control, or simply a more careful look at the situation. Often a successful result is as easy as that. A 4WD cannot be expected to go very far on difficult terrain unless it is skilfully driven. Driving skill alone is not the total answer. Skill, combined with appreciation and knowledge is what is needed, and this is best achieved through education and practice.

A 4WD CANNOT BE EXPECTED TO GO VERY FAR ON DIFFICULT TERRAIN UNLESS IT IS SKILFULLY DRIVEN.

Crossing Cooper Creek

4WDs can encounter trouble in water unless they are properly prepared, competently and intelligently driven, and a careful check of the intended path is made. A bridge spans the water now, but in the 1980s a driver from the Innamincka side who wanted to see the "DIG" tree had to do it the hard way, by driving through the creek.

The approach to the crossing at Cooper's Creek on the way out to Burke's grave was flat, and the creek entry on the Innamincka side was shallow and easy. Here the creek was about 150 metres across and at the time the water looked to be generally just below tyre depth. The group assessment was that it was not running fast enough for concern, but we marked the water height for safety. After careful observation for a time we agreed that there had been no rise in water level, so a crossing was attempted.

Two vehicles went safely across ahead of me, so obviously the water flow rate wasn't too strong, nor was it too deep to make a safe crossing. The path was clearly marked. From entry, I had to travel about thirty degrees upstream for 50 metres to where a tall pole had been placed. Passing left of the pole, the track continued slightly downstream left, obviously going between two more poles. They were fairly close to the bank, where the exit was square but looked a bit boggy, with a low jump-up right on the edge.

I made the crossing in low range second gear (L2), which gave me plenty of power if needed but was slow enough not to cause a big bow wave, or make a floating boat out of my 4WD. The next driver was relatively new, and was given careful instructions on the approach side by an experienced driver. Everyone watched in total disbelief as this person's diesel vehicle started to come almost straight across to us. About half-way the front dipped fully below water but came back out again. Within a few seconds the vehicle stopped dead and the rear windows on the wagon sank below water level. After some panic by the driver and help from other drivers the vehicle was winched out along with its load of water-soaked contents.

This was an expensive episode for a number of reasons. First, loss of time on the trip due to the driver not listening to more experienced drivers and not following directions on the safe path, marked with indicator poles. Second, time was spent on several attempts to tow-start the drowned vehicle after winching it out, without firstly checking the motor for water.

Much later, examination showed that water had been sucked in through the air intake, and had got above the pistons in several cylinders. Water isn't compressible, so the motor could not turn over to start. The tow-starting efforts destroyed the clutch plates, although fortunately another vehicle was carrying a spare set. It took almost a day and a half back at camp, with ample tools but no facilities, to fit the replacement clutch.

Later on, not far south of Tibooburra on the way back, the same vehicle had serious mechanical trouble. A connecting rod, which joins the piston to the crankshaft, broke, and exited the side of the engine block with a big bang. It is probable the conrod had been badly stressed or bent during the crossing, or from the efforts to tow-start the vehicle with water in the engine.

4WD CHALLENGES

IN THIS SECTION

- Stopping, Starting and Stalling
- Terrain Judgement
- Climbing Slopes
- Steep Descents
- Special Conditions and Techniques
- Debogging and Towing
- Winching
- Finding Your Way
- Trip Planning and Safety

Stopping, Starting and Stalling

Advice

IN SOME AWKWARD OR EMERGENCY CIRCUMSTANCES ON HILLS DELIBERATE STALLING IS A SAFE AND ACCEPTED PRACTICE.

Stalling a 4WD

Stalls happen for lots of reasons, the most common one being not enough power developed in the motor to drive the vehicle as required. Deliberately stalling a manual transmission vehicle on flat ground, that is, killing the motor while in gear and in motion, is not usually good driving practice, but in some 4WD situations stalling is quite normal.

For all intents and purposes, vehicles with automatic transmission cannot be stalled. Since the mid-1990s there seems to be a drift towards more automatic transmission or "auto" 4WDs being driven in the off-road area, and these vehicles can have some advantages.

It's apparent that many drivers see an automatic transmission vehicle as a miracle worker — put the selector in "D" and let the computer do the work. In off-road situations this is often not a good decision. Driving in hard going an auto box can and should be used as a manual, in that the driver selects the gear required depending on circumstances.

What to a manual 4WD driver can be a real challenge may be, to an auto driver, quite a simple effort. Hill starts are relatively easy in an auto. For an uphill stop, the auto driver merely has to take the foot off the accelerator enough so that that forward drive ceases, but sufficient revs are maintained to prevent backwards creep in the automatic transmission.

However, it's not all plain sailing, because autos can roll back on hill starts, just like a manual vehicle. In most cases an acceleration increase will bring the rear creep to a stop, to the point where a few more revs will make the vehicle creep forwards. In a difficult downhill situation, where a full-on stall-stop might make the difference between an awkward skid and a nasty collision, autos miss out.

The only way to practically stop an auto is by using the brakes, sometimes hard and often, on the four wheels. Odds even out though, if the track surface is really slippery, because without tyre traction it matters not what sort of vehicle you are driving.

Perhaps this is where relying on the braking technology wizard might be handy, but in general ABS is not really successful in hard off-road driving conditions.

Stalls can be planned or allowed to happen by the driver. In some awkward or emergency circumstances on hills deliberate stalling by braking the wheels hard enough so that they stop turning is a safe and accepted practice. It is an effective option to keep control of your vehicle and come to a stop without disconnecting the mechanical control of the vehicle. In sequence, when the vehicle is in gear, with the engine connected via the clutch to the manual gearbox, and thus to the drive shafts, axles, wheels and ground, if the engine stops then so will the vehicle.

A mechanical fault can be a reason for a stall. Fuel starvation or breaking an axle can also bring the vehicle to a stop. A puncture on a tough uphill usually makes the vehicle handle so badly that deliberate stopping is the only practical

Checklist

Stalling sequences

Manual Transmission

- Going uphill: Idle down and brake to an engine-stall stop, then turn the key off.
- Going downhill: Idle down and turn the key off to kill the engine, and then brake to a stop.

Auto Transmission

- Going uphill: Idle down and brake to a vehicle stop, engine idling.
- Going downhill: Idle down and brake to a vehicle stop, engine idling.

IN STEEP TERRAIN STALLS MAY BE EITHER DELIBERATE OR UNWANTED. LEARN HOW TO DEAL WITH THEM.

Caution

WHEN STALLING AND TURNING THE IGNITION KEY OFF, ONLY TURN IT BACK TO 'ACCESSORIES', NOT TO 'LOCK', OR YOU WILL FIND YOURSELF WITH THE STEERING LOCKED ON SOME 4WDS.

answer. Suddenly coming across an awkward situation without warning, or not assessing the track ahead well, or simply not paying attention are some reasons for making an immediate stall necessary. This point is often right on the edge of, or even in, a potential sticky spot.

In some conditions when approaching a major obstacle it may be necessary to stop and have a look at the situation. When restarting the climb, or reversing back down to a better position, the driver needs to be careful to keep control of the vehicle.

With a deliberate stall, there's no real chance of an unsafe gap in control. This would occur if the clutch is pushed in during a difficult uphill climb, and the driver is a fraction slow in then applying the brakes after pushing in the clutch. When going uphill and forward motion stops, some rollback occurs. The longer it takes to put the brakes on, the further and faster the rollback becomes. Gravity is something it doesn't pay to argue with, and obviously the faster the rollback is, the more difficult it will be to stop. It is clearly safest not to lose control in the first place.

Planned stalls are usually immediate. That is, when the vehicle is in a tight uphill spot, the driver just takes the foot off the accelerator pedal so that the engine revs drop to idle, and applies the brakes, hard. The result is a quick stall-stop. Another way of stalling is to actually brake the vehicle to a stop, forcing the engine revs to drop. This deliberately kills the motor by locking up the drive-train via the brakes. Once the engine has stopped, keep the footbrake on, pull the handbrake on hard and turn off the ignition key. What to do next depends on the situation.

Stalling places a considerable load on all the mechanical components in the drive-train, but when it is necessary for safety, just do it. Petrol or diesel, the method is just the same, but the vehicles may react slightly differently.

With LPG or petrol engines there may be some quite rough mechanical snatching or shuddering (and bad-sounding noises) as the motor dies. With diesels there is ample power at idle revs so unwanted stalling is normally less common than with a petrol motor. Diesels will still shudder quite a bit when being stalled, but occasional use of stalling doesn't seem to be very damaging.

Stop spots

Rain gutters or channels on hills are usually safe places to stop, as water generally washes any loose cover away. It is better to put up with rough but gripping surface under the wheels than to get stuck and possibly have to dig the vehicle out or winch it back onto the track. So, if there's a chance of having to stop on a hill, not only should you be looking for the tough spots coming up, but you should also work out a "fail-safe plan" — think ahead and keep your eyes open for safe stopping places.

If you have a choice about where to stall, try to find a hole in which a tyre could sit, or a rock or log that could be

Checklist

After a stall

- Wheels straight (or position known)
- Engine stopped
- Ignition off
- Foot on footbrake
- Foot off clutch [manual]
- Vehicle in gear [manual] or in 'Park' [auto]
- Handbrake on
- Rear wheel chocked (if going uphill)

Sequence for reversing downhill (after stalling)

Manual gearbox

1. Make the vehicle safe – keep the footbrake on.
2. Ease the clutch in slowly to unload the pressure off the drive-train.
3. Check where your wheels are pointing and get them in the right direction.
4. Check your path back downhill before moving.
5. Put the gearbox into LR (low range, reverse gear).
6. When you are quite ready to start, with engine idling, let the handbrake off gradually.
7. Let the clutch out, and don't touch it again until in a safe stopping position.
8. At the same time ease off the foot-brake, to place load back on the drive-train, so that only the engine and gears are holding the vehicle, and minimise braking until in a safe stopping position.

Auto gearbox

1. Make the vehicle safe – keep the footbrake on.
2. Drop engine revs to idle.
3. Select LR (low range, reverse gear).
4. Check where your wheels are pointing and get them in the right direction.
5. Check your path back downhill before moving.
6. When you are quite ready to start, let the handbrake off gradually, and ease off the footbrake sufficiently to allow the vehicle to creep backwards.
7. Ease off the footbrake to place load back on the drive-train so that the engine and gears are holding the vehicle, and minimise braking until in a safe stopping position.

Start sequences

Manual gearbox

- Going downhill: with the engine off and the vehicle in the appropriate gear, simply turn the ignition key on without acceleration and start.
- Going uphill: with the engine going, a handbrake start (or perhaps combined handbrake/ footbrake and hand-throttle start) will be needed.

Auto gearbox

- Going downhill: with the engine started and running at idle speed and the vehicle in the lowest appropriate gear, release hand-brake and ease off footbrake enough to allow steady vehicle movement.
- Going uphill: with the engine going, and a gear selected suitable for conditions, increase engine revs sufficiently to drive uphill, but not enough to break traction. A hand-brake start can be helpful.

used to help hold the vehicle on the hill by resting a wheel in, behind or against it. Natural obstacles like this are real bonuses. The chances are that if you get stuck in a particular place, someone else has as well, and they may have placed a rock or log you could make use of. This is where passengers earn their keep — while the driver keeps the vehicle stable on the hill, the passengers may be able to find a rock or something to chock the wheels with, or run out a winch cable to a fixing point

Stall starts

Getting going again safely in a bad spot after a stall is one of the more challenging parts of four-wheel driving, but doing it correctly can also be one of the most satisfying parts. Whether the vehicle is facing uphill or downhill, there is considerable risk.

Let's assume a manual vehicle has stalled facing uphill, and to get out of bother it is necessary to reverse back downhill. The engine is not running. Mechanically, the vehicle is still in L2 gear used to climb the slope, your foot is not on the clutch, and the footbrake is hard on. The front wheels are pointing straight ahead. At this stage you are relying on the gears and footbrake to prevent your 4WD from moving backwards. (Without brakes, if it is only holding in gear and you depress the clutch, the vehicle would immediately roll back down the hill.) **Nothing moves until everything is fully in control**. The engine should be stopped, the ignition key off and the handbrake and footbrake on, hard. The sequence of actions for reversing downhill is important.

DIESEL ENGINES ARE GREAT BECAUSE THEY OFFER BETTER, MORE CONTROLLABLE ENGINE BRAKING.

Before you even touch that start key, look around and be sure of the best possible safety factors for yourself, your passengers, any observers and the vehicle. Turning the key on to the start position allows electrical current to reach the starter solenoid, which then operates the starter-motor. This causes the engine to spin over and start. In this case, if your foot is not depressing the clutch, and the vehicle is in gear, the end reaction will be that the vehicle will move, driven solely by the starter-motor. There is ample power in the starter-motor to do this, even with the 4WD in gear. The direction will depend on whether your 4WD is in a forward or reverse gear.

During starting and moving in this situation, do not touch the accelerator, and do not touch the clutch. Don't touch either of them at all until you are satisfied that the vehicle is sufficiently far away from the danger spot and that you could stop in safety. If things go wrong, stall the engine again. Use low range gears, the slowest and strongest possible ratio for vehicle control.

Engine RPM for key start (downhill)

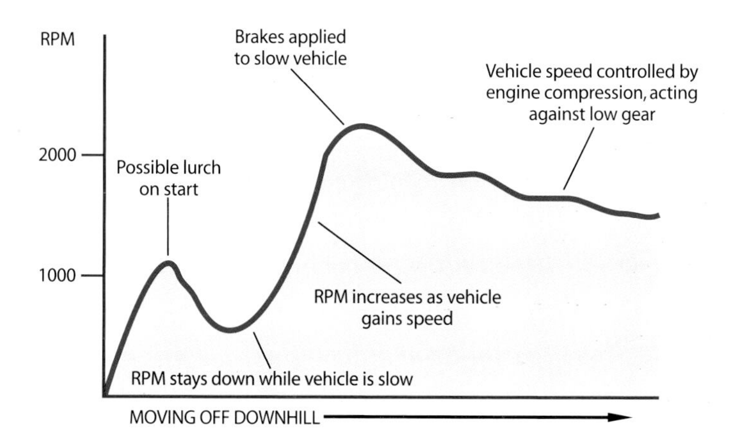

When you are satisfied about all the safety conditions, (follow the checklist) and you are looking where you are going, simply turn the key to start the vehicle engine. The moment you turn the key to start, the engine will fire and the vehicle will move in reverse downhill. When it starts, the vehicle might take off with a lurch, but it will quickly settle down as it becomes controlled by the idling engine. The speed will be kept down largely by engine compression alone, although light braking might be needed to help keep it slow. Going back downhill, there is no real load on the motor, other than it being in gear and holding the vehicle against the slope of the hill. Remember to turn the air-conditioning off in case the idle-up solenoid increases the engine revs. Any form of rev increase can become very difficult to handle.

With auto transmission, unless you have modified your vehicle, it will not start in gear, only in "P" or "N" positions. Start your vehicle, be certain you are in low range for minimal speed, select "R" for a reverse downhill, do your safety checks and ease off the brakes. Feather the brakes to help minimise any engine over-run. Although it is destructive, pulling the handbrake partly on can be helpful. Always be aware that braking a fraction too hard can be an easy way to break tyre traction and induce a skid.

Engine braking

Diesel engines are more strongly built than petrol engines, and in a downhill situation they are usually more controllable. This is due to the very much higher compression ratio required in a diesel (see page 107). Many semi-trailers rely on this "back compression" ability to assist with braking. (This is known as a "Jake Brake", after its inventor, the man who developed Cummins diesel truck engines.) The same kind of effect happens with a diesel 4WD.

When your foot is off the accelerator, new fuel doesn't get injected into the diesel engine to burn because the injector rack shuts down. It makes no difference if the ignition is turned on or off, in most diesels. If it can't get fuel, it doesn't run at all. In effect, it becomes a compressor, drawing in air, compressing it and exhausting it. The effort of compression at very high pressure causes strong resistance through the engine and into the drive-train, so the revs don't build up very much and this slows the vehicle very effectively.

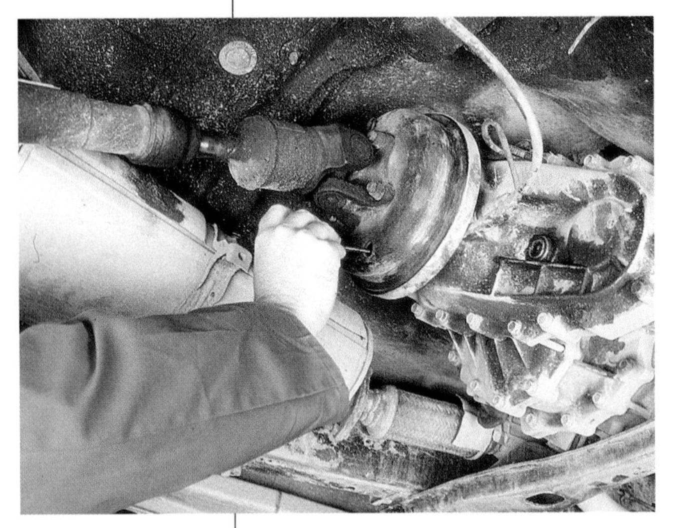

A TAILSHAFT DRUM BRAKE IS VERY EFFECTIVE BUT IT MUST BE KEPT CORRECTLY ADJUSTED.

Petrol engine 4WDs normally don't have the positive fuel shut-off like diesels because they rely on suction of fuel into the inlet manifold, supported by external air pressure, to get the mix from carburettors into the cylinders. Even at complete idle, some fuel is being drawn into the engine, and unless the ignition is turned off, spark-plugs will ignite this mixture, so the motor is still trying to run.

In general, petrol engines can rev much higher than diesels. They are proportionately lighter, more powerful overall and more responsive to acceleration. They don't have the same ability to maintain low revs and keep the 4WD at slow steady speed when being pushed downhill by vehicle weight and gravity. Revs build up a bit, so the vehicle usually has to be braked down more often than a diesel to keep the speed low on descents.

Engine RPM shown on tachometer

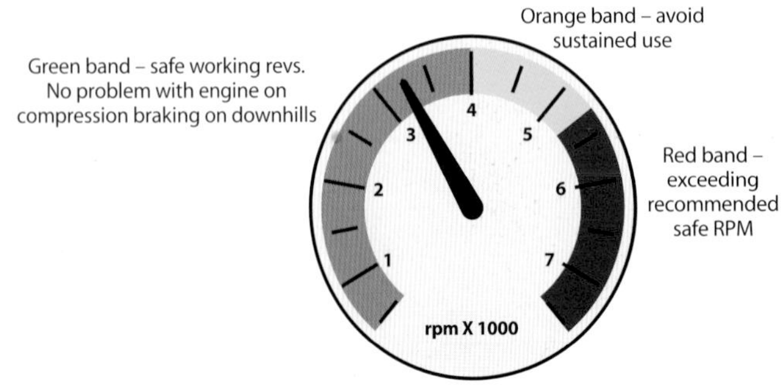

Engine over-run

While driving down any steep hill, because of the steepness and the load of the vehicle pushing from behind, the engine can rev up quite a bit. The steeper the hill, the more gravity pushes the vehicle against the engine, forcing it to increase in rate. Being in a very low gear will help keep the speed down, as the vehicle can only travel at a certain speed depending on the engine revolutions. You can't directly control those revs because you are not touching the accelerator, but indirectly you can, by braking and forcing the vehicle to slow, which will slow down the engine, therefore the vehicle.

If you feel your 4WD is not going too fast down the hill, resist the temptation and keep your feet off the pedals. The revs might sound horrible, but for the short time involved, it won't matter much. If the tachometer needle goes up into the red zone it might be wise to brake the vehicle down a bit. When the speed does get too high, even with the over-run of the engine revs, use a little bit of brake. Do it very cautiously. Don't brake hard — feather them and let the engine do as much work as possible. Keep the vehicle as slow as practical, and even more so in reverse gear, because of the rapid-reaction steering effect. Steer as slowly and as little as possible until you are in a safe position.

Power braking

If you stall your engine, remember that you could only have two or three brake pedal operations remaining, or a few seconds, before the vacuum reservoir for the power-assisted brakes runs out. Then you will be back to person-powered brakes. Although they will still be useable, disc brakes don't work well without power assistance. Going forward, about 85 per cent-plus of braking is on the front wheels, which are commonly disc-braked. Drum brakes can still be used, but you need strong leg muscles to hold the vehicle stationary on a hill. Quite a lot of extra pedal pressure will be needed to stop the vehicle without engine-driven power assistance; likewise, the handbrake will need to be pulled on really hard to hold the vehicle.

Vehicles spend almost all their operating time going forwards, so brakes are designed to be most effective in that direction, and drum brakes in particular. You may have noticed that it takes less handbrake pressure to hold the vehicle when it is facing downhill, than it does if facing uphill. This is because of the mechanical design of the rear drum brakes.

Hand throttle

Almost all 4WDs are fitted with a hand throttle. Don't confuse this with the choke on a petrol-engine vehicle. The symbols on the knob are different — check them. The hand throttle is another form of accelerator, but instead of being foot-operated, the linkage is managed by the driver via a hand-adjusted cable. Pulling on the knob for the flexible cable increases the engine speed, and releasing the pressure drops the revs. Usually this device is located somewhere beside the steering column on the right-hand side down near the bottom edge of the dash. Some cables pull out, locking in any desired position when the cable knob is rotated; some pull out and notch into place in several preset positions. One type works by winding the knob out like a screw thread, and can be slow-acting, even though it is exactly adjustable.

To warm up an engine, simply push the choke in quickly after starting and set the engine revs up at a fast idle with the hand throttle for a few minutes. When electric winching, hand throttles can be used to set the engine revs at the preferred speed to ensure the alternator is charging vehicle batteries against the high current drain of an electric winch. Power-take-off and hydraulic winches driven by the vehicle engine can also benefit from a constant, adequate and manageable fixed rev rate. On a difficult uphill start, a combination of footbrake and hand throttle might be needed to move off.

In sticky situations, for example a difficult climb out from the bottom of a valley on a rough track, steady engine speed can be important. Steady revs in a selected gear over rough terrain helps keep the working load on transmission components at as even a pressure as practical. This is when a hand throttle can be used very effectively, minimising accelerator snatch. Nothing strains the mechanical components of a vehicle drive-train more than irregular or uneven load-on/load-off pressure. The unevenness is very often caused by the driver's unsteady accelerator pedal control. This can be aggravated by the very rough terrain, a poor driver seating position or unusually light or heavy throttle linkage spring pressures. A throttle-rest for the accelerator foot can help solve this problem.

Keep the revs as steady as practical and try to keep the vehicle moving smoothly, so the suspension can do its job of keeping the wheels following the

Tip

A TAILSHAFT DRUM-HANDBRAKE MAY BE OLD-FASHIONED BUT IT IS VERY EFFECTIVE, AND WHEN IT IS ADJUSTED PROPERLY IS USUALLY MORE EFFECTIVE THAN A REAR-WHEEL DRUM-HANDBRAKE.

Typical symbols

Choke knob

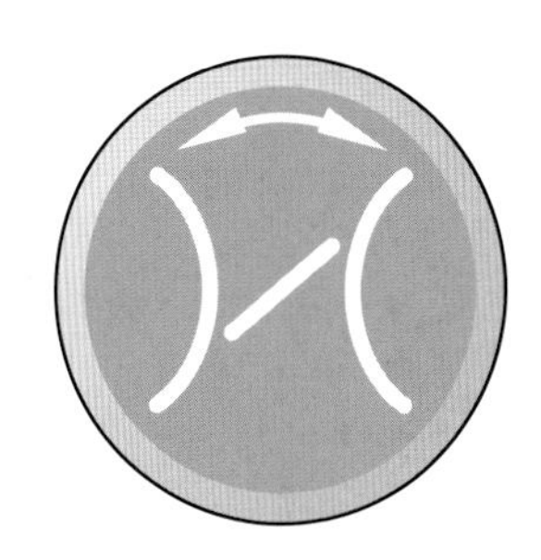

Hand throttle

Accelerator snatch

Accelerator snatch is a common fault, particularly at low speeds in powerful gears over corrugations or fairly rough ground. One place to expect corrugations is on the inside of an uphill corner where previous vehicles have accelerated and made ripples or braked and cut up the surface. Snatch is caused by almost a "wind-up" or "domino" effect where the vehicle bounces over a short sharp bump, so the driver's accelerator foot also jerks. This causes a snatch or jerking effect on the accelerator, which makes the vehicle lurch, jerking the driver. The accelerator foot jerks again, and the cycle repeats, often increasing in severity.

Big powerful engines with high torque can damage transmission or drive-train components through the on/off/on load imposed by the on/off/on accelerator. The same effect will usually cause a break in tyre/ground traction, often ending up in bad wheelspin. Concentrating on preventing this snatch means the driver isn't fully attending to driving the 4WD, not a desirable situation at all. Lifting the foot quickly and completely off the accelerator pedal until the 4WD slows breaks the cycle and stops the immediate situation. By fitting a simple foot-rest to stabilise the driver's foot, the potential snatch can be cured.

Throttle footrest

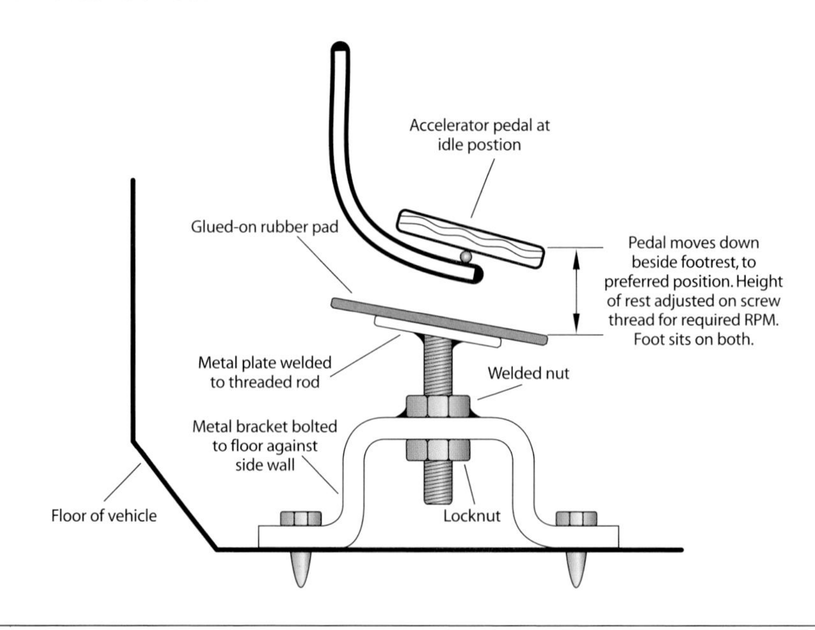

ground. A sudden increase in revs when climbing up a hill usually encourages vehicle body bounce with considerable suspension movement, resulting in wheelspin or slip. Even down around a 1,200 rpm fast idle, tyres will often keep biting all the way up a climb. Constant revs are much less likely to cause a break in tyre-ground contact. By selecting the appropriate gear and the right engine revolutions to produce power and flexibility, then setting the hand throttle, the vehicle can be allowed to make steady progress up a climb. The wheels will then tend to roll or drive smoothly and more consistently, giving even contact pressure wherever possible.

Terrain Judgement

Useless climbs

There are hills that no 4WD can climb or descend. In a really desperate situation, it could be possible to winch your 4WD up the impossible hill, but the obvious question is "Why?" Go back the way you came; find another route to your destination. Doing this takes a lot of willpower, to abort what shows promise of being a challenging section of the trip. You have to make a judgement about whether there is a reasonable alternative. If you have no other practical option than to try, and you are a very experienced driver, you may be able to get one vehicle up or down the hill, and then use it to assist the other vehicles to minimise effort and damage.

Climb limits

In general, a well-driven 4WD is capable of steadily climbing a hill with as much as a 30-degree up angle. Successfully driving up a much steeper angle than this on a continuous climb is not very common, even though lots of momentum will often get you up and over a steep little pinch. Climbing ability should be judged on a vehicle's maintained rate, or capacity to stop then start off again, on the climb. Remember, a 45-degree climb means that you go up one metre vertically for every metre you travel forward. This is a 100 per cent gradient, where the horizontal and vertical distances are the same (1:1). To do this needs a friction coefficient of 1.0 between tyres and ground. On a clean concrete ramp with good tyres and ample power, it can be achieved. In rocks, dirt or sand, without a good run-up or momentum assistance, 45-degree sustained climbs for a 4WD are virtually impossible. For an explanation of climb angles, see the diagram on page 22.

Advice

THERE ARE LOTS OF USEFUL POINTS YOU CAN LEARN FROM PRACTICE AND INSTRUCTION, AND EVERY INTERESTED FOUR-WHEEL DRIVER GRADUALLY PICKS UP SKILLS OVER TIME. ONE OF THE CHALLENGES OF OFF-ROAD DRIVING IS THAT IT CAN TAKE A WHILE TO LEARN.

Checklist

Before attempting a climb

- Have you assessed the climb properly?
- What are the real risks, or what could go wrong?
- Is your need to make the climb even realistic?
- Is there a practical and minimal-damage path?
- Is it simply ego/macho to continue driving?
- What will happen if your plans don't work?

Your view changes with the different aspect, and so too does the perceived difficulty. What may look like a fairly simple climb or descent from inside your 4WD can have quite a different perspective when you actually walk the section. A steady climb itself would be okay, but inspection might reveal a steep jump-up or lip, or a bad hole or edge in the middle of the section will cause difficulty. What you can judge from the driver's seat while mobile is never the same as a careful view when you are standing in the middle of the climb.

Evaluating the terrain ahead

Let's presume that there has been no rain on a bush track for three weeks, but there is still 300 mm of water in a fair-sized puddle across the track. Two questions to ask are:

- How solid is the bottom?
- Would you expect trouble driving through it?

As a general rule, if the puddle holds water the bottom would probably be solid enough to drive on. To make this little exercise more difficult, suppose by looking around carefully you find a small spring-fed trickle that keeps the puddle full. What about the probable condition of the bottom now?

Terrain judgement has an essential place in all driving, especially in off-road conditions. It may involve working out land contours on a topographic map or from a satellite mosaic on a computer-based map and terrain program (see page 80). When driving on mountain tracks, watching ahead for tricky sections is important, because where you look is where you go, and the further ahead you look the more time you have to make driving decisions. Anticipation is important in making a judgement about a particular section from some distance, so that you can base your approach actions on that assessment. Following indicators or marker poles is logical, as they have usually been placed for guidance.

Some tracks up in the Great Divide have marker sticks placed along them indicating a hole, washaway or broken edge. Up in the Snowy Mountains from Cooma down to Khancoban, and in many other alpine areas, driver survival can depend on the orange marker poles outlining both edges of the road in heavy snow. Looking ahead for the shiny and soft boggy patches in a saltpan helps

Careful vehicle placement

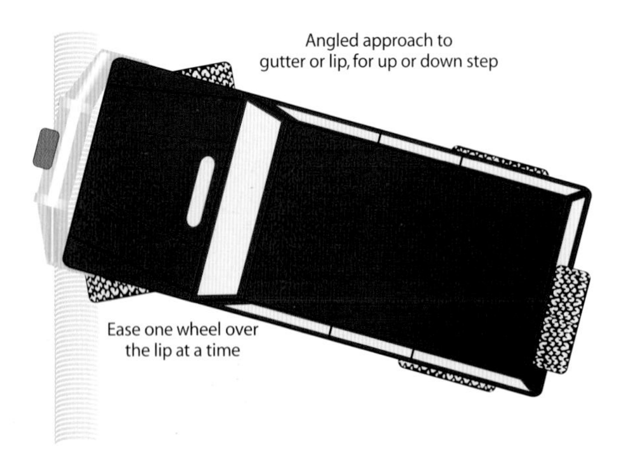

CRESTING DUNES REQUIRES PRACTICE. YOU NEED ENOUGH MOMENTUM TO REACH THE TOP WITHOUT GOING BLINDLY OVER INTO THE UNKNOWN.

keep you out of the bog. Checking for oncoming traffic over the other side of a tight hairpin bend before you get to it will help give you an indication of how much of the road you can use.

Dune crests

Crossing sand dunes from west to east in the Simpson Desert, the prevailing wind often makes a sharp, triangular wave-like crest in the sand, facing you at the top. Although the fine sand might only be 300 mm deep, this lip has to be broken through by the front wheels because it blocks the wheel-tracks. The risk with getting up speed to help push through the crest can be that the track commonly has an unexpected dog-leg at the top, before heading down the east side. In this case, it can certainly be risky to travel forward so quickly you don't have enough time for corrective steering or braking at the top, or when starting on the down-side if needed. Learning just when to kick the clutch in, or when to deliberately lose power in the sand and reduce vehicle speed quickly, takes a bit of practice. Knowing when to decelerate sharply at the right point on top, to let vehicle momentum gently break the sand down for a wheel track, can be critical terrain judgement. It is certainly a driving skill, and mastering this is a satisfying achievement for most drivers.

Vehicle placement

One of the most repeated (and potentially very damaging) traps is hitting a washout or deep rain-gutter square-on and also with considerable impact, with both the vehicle's front tyres at the same time. Quickly dropping off a lip or climbing up onto a step can have the same effect on the wheels and suspension. Instead of this damaging approach, the vehicle can usually be rolled more smoothly at a diagonal over the edge. By angling across the gutter, one wheel can be eased through first, then the other wheel on the same axle, repeating the sequence for the rear axle. Each wheel

Advice

IF YOU ARE DRIVING UP OR DOWN A HILL SIMPLY TO PROVE YOU CAN DO IT, THINK CAREFULLY FIRST.

THE DRIVER OF THE FOLLOWING VEHICLE CAN MAKE ALTERNATIVE PLANS TO AVOID GETTING STUCK IN THE SAME SITUATION.

contacts the edge at a different time and different angle, reducing the impact and hopefully keeping three wheels on the ground at the same time. That way, you shouldn't get hung up when the front end drops sharply into the hole, or if the rear end drags the towbar over the edge and takes some driving effort or load off the rear wheels. Where you place your vehicle before entering and traversing a tricky bit depends on good judgement as well as driver ability. To get it right most times takes practice. Getting it wrong may involve extra time, effort and expense. As well as looking after your vehicle, learning more about vehicle placement should lead to some rethinking of your driving skills. For information on vehicle placement see the illustration on page 38.

Checklist

If you are following another 4WD

- Make use of its movements to help you assess the track ahead.
- Did it have a difficult time crossing a bog or rock?
- Which grooves did it travel in, up the clay-surfaced hill?
- Did it drag through the black soil mud, or maintain momentum?
- How much clearance did it have around the cut-off tree trunk?
- Does the track it took look slippery, boggy or loose?
- Would a different approach give your 4WD a better passage?
- Based on what you've seen the other vehicle do, which gear will give you the best result?

Case Study

An expensive boghole experience

A long-wheel-based late-model Nissan 4WD entered a 100-metre-long, two-wheel-grooved boghole along a narrow, scrub-lined slippery clay track. There was an alternative track but it added about half a kilometre and meant back-tracking several hundred metres before the bog. The driver used a fair amount of power to push through the water, as it looked to be just a straight, wheel-grooved water-filled puddle. A number of other drivers were watching for the Nissan's result before doing it themselves.

About 50 metres into the boghole, it was obvious the ruts were getting deeper, floorboard-deep in fact. Suddenly a noticeable and metallic dragging sound was heard, rapidly followed by the vehicle lurching and a definite "clung", so the driver quickly stopped the vehicle. Reverse attempts failed. Forward attempts failed. Exiting via his window, the driver asked if someone would snatch him out. As no other 4WD could practically get past, it was decided to drag him out backwards.

Chains, cables and snatchem-straps made up the length, and a diesel Toyota pulled the Nissan back. During this, even louder noises came from under the water near the front of the vehicle. It was finally towed right out backwards, because it could not reverse unaided. The driver eventually found that a previous driver had placed a great big rock virtually in the centre-hump of the bog, and it was this that had done the damage. Inspection showed that the bashplates under the Nissan were all missing. We finally recovered them. They had been badly dented as it drove forward along the puddle, and were then ripped off by the rock when the vehicle was towed back. The first noise was the bashplates dragging over the rock going forwards, and the "clung" was the rock driving up into the gearbox, damaging it. The second and louder noise was the bashplates being torn off during the tow out, because the rock was immovable and the bashplates were not.

EVEN THOUGH DRIVING ON THE BEACH MAY BE RELAXING, PAY ATTENTION. HITTING ANY OBSTACLE AT SPEED COULD SEVERELY DAMAGE THE VEHICLE.

Climbing Slopes

Caution

SOME DRIVERS SEEM TO THINK THAT THE BEST METHOD OF GETTING THROUGH A BOG-HOLE IS TO CHARGE, PRAY A BIT, AND RELY ON THE BASHPLATE AND MOMENTUM. THIS WORKS SOMETIMES, BUT IF IT FAILS IT CAN BE EXPENSIVE.

Power

On a steep climb, accelerating in a gear that is too low and powerful usually results in digging holes in the dirt with the downhill tyres. There is a kind of vicious circle with losing all forward traction on a hill, and therefore losing momentum; if you lose one, you lose the other. On the other hand, if the gear you've selected is too high for the same climb, then the mechanical effort of climbing may limit or overcome the engine's revs. Sometimes the selected gear would be correct to make the climb, but the limiting factor is the driver not being prepared or experienced enough to really use the engine to develop power at its designed maximum.

If the engine simply can't (or is not encouraged to) rev high enough to develop adequate power, sufficient to propel the vehicle forward and also overcome the resistance of gravity on the hill, it will probably stall. The engine may shudder and fight to keep going, but unless something is done to reduce the engine load, or multiply the power advantage, eventually it will stall. Deliberate stalls can be useful (see page 28). After you stall a petrol-engine vehicle, don't leave the ignition key on any longer than you really need to, because there is a chance of damaging the ignition coil. With a diesel, as it doesn't have electric ignition, this is not as important.

Clutch

The clutch controls the lifeline in a manual 4WD, being the main connection between engine and wheels. On any hill, if the connection is broken, drive and traction are immediately lost along with power. The vehicle is then not really under control, and the driver will need very fast reflexes to regain

Case Study

An expensive clutch lesson

Here's an example that's hard to forget — the sound of a breaking spider gear, inside a differential. This happened when a new driver didn't do as instructed on a hill at the Toyota Club (Vic.) property at Yarck. He was driving a twin-cab four-cylinder diesel, and lost traction on a short, straight climb out from the bottom of a gully.

As the vehicle's engine slowed under the load of the climb, the driver obviously pushed the clutch in quickly, not wanting to stall the vehicle. He should have stalled it according to instructions given beforehand in how to do so. The engine was revving loudly and the gearbox was still in second gear. When he then dumped the clutch back out to try to stop the vehicle rolling backwards down the hill, a quite loud clunk was heard.

What had happened mechanically was quite straightforward. Climbing the hill, the mechanicals were working properly under the designed load. When the steady load was taken off suddenly by the driver depressing the clutch, the vehicle lost drive and naturally began to roll back. As the engine was revving quite a bit and the clutch was then just dumped, combinations of the peak mechanical load became overload, which was simply more than the diff component could take, so it broke.

The gear breakage meant the twin-cab was immediately reduced to two-wheel-drive only. Had it not been a practice area with good access, the situation could have been quite a problem because it is sometimes impossible to get back out to a good road unless all four wheels are driving.

Fortunately, the practice drive was videotaped, so one benefit was that the video was replayed many times afterwards in slow motion, as an instructional tape on what not to do.

control before gravity takes over. One vital reason for not touching the clutch in this situation is the probability of the vehicle lurching out of control when the pressure suddenly comes off the drive-train. Not putting the brakes on quickly or hard enough at this point can cause loss of control.

If the clutch is depressed while climbing, and the driver realises the risk and by reflex action immediately drops the clutch again, the short and very severe load dumped back onto the drive-train can easily do damage, particularly if the vehicle has begun to move back down the hill. Dropping the clutch to stop the vehicle moving can easily result in broken drive-train components. As well, the judder and sudden jolting stop to the vehicle tends to break tyre–ground contact, which can result in a skid.

Broken parts

Effects of a broken drive-train part can be more than just loss of forward motion or driving ability. You may well need all wheels locked up to keep the vehicle in the preferred place, holding on a hill. Often the handbrake which locks just two wheels on the one axle is not enough. With a broken drive-train component, even if your vehicle is in 4WD and all four wheels are locked in, relying on leaving it in gear would be risky. Chocking several wheels may be the only way to stay stationary on the slope. The vehicle might have to be towed to a safer or flatter area where it can be worked on or repaired.

To complicate matters, if a rear axle shaft or diff parts break, it might mean having to take out the broken shaft and its opposite number in order to get home. Leaving broken parts in place

Tip

SOMETIMES BEING TOWED IS HARDER OR WORSE THAN THE MOST DIFFICULT DRIVING.

Clutch control

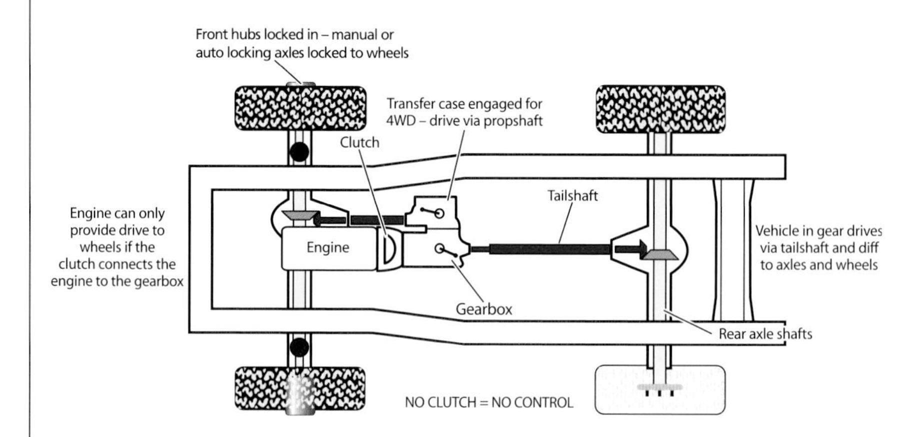

can really cause trouble. There is a good possibility the remaining broken diff parts or axle stub could get chewed up inside the axle housing or create more damage. They may even jam or lock up solid, so that the wheels on that axle will not turn. In some vehicles, a broken axle shaft can drift sideways out of the differential housing, even to the extent of letting the wheel fall off.

Skilful driving

One 4WD training school puts students at a very steep, clay-covered face in a quarry to teach driver and vehicle capabilities. The instructors prove that a 1,200 rpm engine-speed maximum in L1 will not only climb the face, but will give enough power for a handbrake start after a deliberate stall-stop half-way up the face. Exactly the same happens in low reverse also, with a descent to half-way with a stall-stop, then a 1,200 rpm handbrake start for a full reverse back to the top. This is skilful driving, not brute luck; carefully using the clutch, brakes and steering are all vital when doing this. Steady throttle control means less likelihood of breaking traction, and lower revs often mean the tyres will grab again quickly. Just to make it sound harder, these moves are done in absolutely stock six-cylinder vehicles running manufacturer's standard 7.50x16 dual-purpose tyres. It may seem difficult, but with practice it is not difficult to do at all. Less can be more.

Most four-wheel drivers seem to prefer power-on climbs to power-off descents. Maybe it is psychological. Whether going up a steep pinch, where you are using a lot of power to control the vehicle, or trying to maintain control where the downhill slope provides unwanted momentum, the chances of bother are not much different.

Uphills can be one place where often, less is more. Less power usually means a lot less wheelspin, and that often means a lot more track climbed more easily. Providing the tyres have traction and can keep it, quiet and steady power will mostly produce good results on a climb. At the same time, it is a lot less difficult to control the 4WD, and very often it is also less damaging to both the vehicle and the environment. That's not to say that using more power doesn't have a place, because it sometimes takes sheer power and momentum to get up or over a steep pinch. Overall though, picking the right path, having ample power in the

4X4 Tip

UPHILLS CAN BE ONE PLACE WHERE OFTEN, LESS IS MORE. LESS POWER USUALLY MEANS A LOT LESS WHEELSPIN, AND THAT OFTEN MEANS A LOT MORE TRACK CLIMBED MORE EASILY. PROVIDING THE TYRES HAVE TRACTION AND CAN KEEP IT, QUIET AND STEADY POWER WILL MOSTLY PRODUCE GOOD RESULTS ON A CLIMB.

right gear and letting the vehicle do the work is the best way.

Rather than hard and slow driving, quite often winching a short distance is well worth considering. It could be quicker and less damaging where there are a few obstacles together, such as a pile or section of rocks or a bad washaway, keeping in mind the time, effort and possible damage from several unsuccessful attempts. Don't forget to try less tyre pressure to get a bigger footprint for more grip and traction, but remember to reinflate the tyres with your recovery-kit compressor or pump as soon as practical afterwards.

Assessing the way ahead

If the section ahead looks bad, it might be, so a walk to pick the best line is usually worthwhile. Use something to mark your intended path such as a little pile of stones or a stick. Remember the trouble spots, commit yourself and stick to your chosen line, even if it does look different from the driver's seat. With ruts and grooves, pick the grooves that hopefully won't jam or wedge tyres. Make sure there is a driveable exit, not a dead-end lip, or that you can cross up out of one groove into another if needed. If it will help, before driving get out the gloves, shovel and axe. Build up ramp approaches or exits to potential trouble spots with rocks, logs, dirt or whatever is at hand. This is another form of terrain judgement. Spending a little time doing this early often saves a lot of time later, especially where there is a group of vehicles or a wide difference in driver ability.

If it has been wet and the climb is slippery, for extra traction try to keep the wheels in the main grooves that have had fine gravel washed into them. Likewise, the very outside edges of the track are often rougher, have bigger stones or may be less slippery on the climb. Sometimes it might be necessary to put a wheel up on one of the centre humps and the other along the track edge. Each washed-out section has to be judged on scene at the time, but unless the tops of the humps are very rounded and your vehicle is likely to slip off down into the grooves, driving on top of the humps is often effective, even though it can be nerve-wracking.

Keep your thumbs outside the steering wheel, in case the steering

Tip

RATHER THAN HARD AND SLOW DRIVING, QUITE OFTEN WINCHING A SHORT DISTANCE IS WELL WORTH CONSIDERING.

IF IT HAS BEEN WET AND THE TRACK IS SLIPPERY, FOR EXTRA TRACTION TRY TO KEEP THE WHEELS IN THE MAIN GROOVES THAT HAVE HAD FINE GRAVEL WASHED INTO THEM.

WHEN DRIVING ON ROCKS, IN GROOVES OR WASHOUTS, OR ROUGH GROUND BE AWARE OF THE POTENTIAL FOR SERIOUS KICK-BACK FROM THE STEERING WHEEL. GRIP THE WHEEL FIRMLY AND KEEP YOUR THUMBS OUTSIDE THE RIM TO PREVENT INJURY.

kicks back and the steering wheel hits them. If a wheel is deflected into a groove by vehicle movement, even if you have not steered into it, enormous mechanical pressure is placed on the wheels and steering system. This is one situation in which power-assisted steering is indispensable.

For a long climb, consider using the hand-throttle for steady control. A throttle footrest (illustration page 36) is an excellent investment, helping to reduce fatigue and improve driver concentration. You must be physically comfortable in the driver's seat, and in a good position to control the vehicle.

Momentum

The faster you are going, or the heavier your vehicle is, the more brake effort it takes to slow down. This is due to kinetic energy which is commonly referred to as momentum. The same energy can work for or against you. If you need to climb a steep sandhill, for example, but don't build up enough momentum (because you didn't get up enough speed), not only will the hill surface and gravity work against you but so will your own lack of momentum. It is possible to drive a 4WD over a very steep little climb with momentum working for you, whereas without ample speed to help carry it up and over, the vehicle could not climb it. The longer the steep climb, the more time there is for momentum to be lost. The mathematics and calculations in this subject can be quite complex. Learning and knowing how much accelerative effort it takes to develop enough momentum to get or keep a vehicle moving in differing off-road conditions is a rewarding and interesting process, as it can be applied in just about every type of four-wheel driving.

Momentum applies to things falling as well. Be sure to check for items in the vehicle that might distract you from concentrating on driving. It can be distracting and dangerous if gravity pulls the CB radio and maps from the overhead console down onto the driver during a steep climb. Make sure that before a tough climb or steep descent there are no loose items that may dislodge inside the cabin or in the rear storage section.

Driving over rocks and rock slabs can be tricky, but you can use momentum to help. If rocks are dry and give good traction, inching or idling up works well; if they are wet and slimy, it might need a run-up to get sufficient momentum. When approaching a rock step, or log, one good method to get up and over is simply to give the engine enough power to get the front wheels up onto the obstacle, then quickly back off the accelerator and let momentum carry the front of the vehicle up and on. Finally, add a little power to help pull the back wheels over. Keep your foot off the clutch, use the accelerator and let the engine do the work. If traction breaks, a quick off/on of the accelerator pedal will often help the tyres bite again.

Steep Descents

Options

One very good reason to learn some of the skills that good 4WD clubs teach is for driving down steep hills. Going down bad hills can be a psychological worry for some four-wheel drivers. It takes a bit of nerve, or experience, to remember that as you can easily stop at the bottom of the descent, there's probably no real need to stop part-way down.

You can't escape going downhill, because for every climb on your trip, somewhere there will be a descent. Gravity is not a good enemy, so it pays to know as much as possible about how it behaves, and what it can do to a vehicle. It is quite possible to drive a 4WD down the face of a sand dune so steep you could not physically climb back up, but there is absolutely no room for error if you do this. Getting off line almost always means pain — physical or financial or both. The same rule applies to a bad rocky downhill, or a clay or shale spur in the mountains. In some cases, the trees along the side of the track might minimise the amount of damage if you spear off the wheel grooves onto the edge, but this is not something to rely on in normal circumstances.

If you get out to check the descent, make your vehicle safe, chocking the wheels if necessary. Don't forget the vehicle position and occupant safety check. Think about whether it is better to try to continue down, or to go back and start again, or could you bypass the track altogether? Remember about downhill braking, low and slow gears, never touching the clutch and so on. If the engine stalls, there's no power for the power steering or power brakes, so don't forget to allow for the considerable difference in physical effort that will be required. See page 31 for what to do after a stall.

The first question is, "Do I have to go down here?" The answer requires exactly the same logic as for steep uphills. Alternatives and those other considerations really should be applied.

Caution

IF YOUR 4WD HAS A TURBO-TIMER, CHECK HOW IT OPERATES AND IF AN IMMEDIATE OVERRIDE FUNCTION IS INCLUDED. PRACTISE HOW TO STALL WITH IT, JUST IN CASE.

DRIVING DOWN A STEEP DESCENT REQUIRES A COOL HEAD AND KNOWLEDGE OF HOW TO HANDLE YOUR VEHICLE.

If there is only one way out, the hard way, then minimise the risk and walk the section. A few minutes of walking is better than risking disaster, every time. This is one place where knowing your vehicle dimensions (see page 115) can be critical, especially when placing a wheel beside or over a rock on the edge of a bad drop-off. The view over the bonnet changes with angle, and the short nose of a Suzuki is usually much easier to judge for placement than a Ford F100. Get to know your vehicle.

Braking

Engine braking can be very useful, reducing wheel-braking effort and giving steady speed control. Rely on the engine. If the downhill is steep enough to cause you bother, then definitely use L1, and let the vehicle do the work. Gentle steering, smooth lines if possible and minimal braking unless you can find a straight bit of track to brake a bit harder — these are essential.

If you have to brake, do it very gently so that traction isn't lost. Don't lock up the wheels, because a non-rolling or skidding wheel doesn't steer. Skidding on solid downhills in the dry is usually not too bad. But when tracks are wet, or you are driving on loose surfaces, or on clay or rocks or loose shale, it is easy to get sideways quickly, making regaining control a lot more difficult. Never kick the clutch in on a descent unless you already have the brakes applied to maintain vehicle control when you disconnect the clutch. If you do snap the clutch in, the vehicle could rocket away, even for just a short distance before you can get the brakes on and working. If it does accelerate because of the downhill, getting control back via applying brakes or letting the clutch out again will be much more difficult. The probable result will be loss of traction and steering, skidding, and maybe serious trouble.

Technology has brought many different kinds of wizardry into the 4WD area. Uphill or downhill, wet or dry, the genius of on-board computers has doubtless helped many off-road four-wheel-drivers. However, not all 4WD vehicles have these electronic aids, and many drivers prefer the off-road challenge of driving their own 4WD vehicles. Electronic aids are not substitutes for driver experience gained through 4WD club training days and activities, and through simply doing the kilometres.

ABS, or Antilock Braking System, has been available for quite a few years, and without doubt it is one of the most valuable functions you can have on a vehicle for everyday driving. Considerable experience has shown that it can have limited value in many off-road conditions, and the option to switch its operation off would be very handy. Drivers who have come to rely on ABS benefits on-road are usually very surprised when the ABS results off-road are not as they expected.

Basically, ABS has sensors at the wheels which determine if a wheel has too much brake effect, and is slowing so much that it is likely to skid. If so, the on-board computer limits the amount of hydraulic braking pressure which the driver can apply to that wheel, and instead it pulses the brake on/off perhaps ten times per second. In some off-road conditions wheel-skidding is simply not avoidable, or it is desirable, and ABS limits this.

Traction Control can be essentially the opposite of ABS — if a wheel begins to increase speed and spin up from lack of traction, the brake to that wheel is computer-applied many times per second, to reduce its speed and help regain traction.

Mechanical maintenance is vital. Keeping the footbrake in good order and adjustment really pays off. The handbrake is just as important, because without it, uphill starts can be difficult; on a bad downhill, if it is pulled slightly on it can be used to help as a drag. It works on the tailshaft or rear wheels, acting as a steadier behind the steering wheels, and assisting engine braking and low gearing to keep the vehicle stable and slow. For information on using the engine to assist with braking, see "Engine over-run", page 34.

Emergency stopping

To stop on the way down, stall the vehicle if necessary (see page 28). Turn the ignition key off and brake steadily, enough to pull the vehicle up. For safety, be careful to only turn the key back to the "accessories" position — if you turn it all the way on some 4WDs the steering could lock and leave you unable to turn the steering wheel.

Remember that when you kill the engine, you also lose the power-steering function as well. Look for ready-made buffers to help slow you down

WINCHING DOWNHILL IS A SAFE BUT SLOW DESCENT TECHNIQUE.

Caution

ALTHOUGH IT SOUNDS A BIT GRIM, IF THE GOING IS REALLY BAD THEN YOU DO NEED TO HAVE A FAIL-SAFE PLAN IN YOUR MIND.

and secure your 4WD when stopped. A blade-cut, a drainage channel, soft earth bank, protruding rock, rain groove, washaway or built-up track edge can all be used as a slowing point or a final stopper. When all else fails and you have to crash into something, plan for a soft stop. Body panels along the side can be replaced. Ripping out a wheel and mudguard by grinding along a bank or edge is cheaper and less dangerous than writing off a 4WD.

Winching downhill

Winching downhill, probably the least-used descent technique, is usually quite safe, even if it is slow. For a particularly nasty section, winching downhill may be your only safe option. Consider one vehicle securely rear-anchored lowering another, with the cable attached from the front of the winching vehicle to the rear anchor-point of the descending vehicle.

With two vehicles face to face, one of them can be lowered down a hill for the combined length of both winch cables. A single vehicle can easily lower itself by anchoring the winch cable at the top and reversing down the hill, chocking the wheels and re-anchoring the winch cable, if needed, then repeating the process.

Problems with turbo-timers

There may be hidden traps with some aftermarket accessories. A turbo-timer is a timing device that switches off the 4WD engine after a preset time, allowing the vehicle's turbocharger to cool down properly without load. Not all turbo-timers have a positive, total over-ride button to make the normal "key-off" immediately kill the engine.

With a turbo-timer set on one-minute delay, if you turn the key off and brake to slow for a stop, the question is, will the engine stop unless you do dead-stall it? If you have a turbo-timer with a push-and-hold over-ride button, you might have to take one hand off the wheel to turn the key, and then another to find and hold the over-ride button. If your 4WD has one, check this function. As well as this, remember that in some awkward driving situations you may have to kill your engine in a hurry. Perhaps the turbo-timer should be turned off before going into terrain where an immediate stall might be needed.

VARYING DRIVER ABILITY LEVELS OCCUR IN ANY GROUP TRIP REGARDLESS OF THE TERRAIN.

Special Conditions and Techniques

Experience and ability

There are so many hints, clues and points to remember about driving in off-road conditions, it is probably worth a book on its own. Thousands of drivers have discovered different ways of handling the various interesting or challenging situations found in driving off-road. Some become experts in their preferred fields such as beach or desert sand, rocks or clay hills. Many of the driving techniques that work in one environment also work well in quite different situations. No two vehicles are exactly the same, and neither are their driver's attitudes and approaches to an obstacle. When you add the different experience and ability levels of drivers to that, it creates a big set of possibles. Varying driver ability levels occur in any group trip, no matter what the terrain.

Skimming the surface

Think of a vehicle as similar to a boat on a lake. Sitting there, the boat is low down in the water; trying to push a large amount of water ahead of it would not be possible for a small outboard motor. But with a sharp burst of power, the front lifts. The boat rises up virtually out of the water as it accelerates, until it is sitting almost flat on the top in what is called a planing position. It skims over the surface with only a small part of the hull in the water.

It is kept there by speed or momentum. When the power is cut off, the boat sinks down until the hull is again sitting well down in the water. If it doesn't have the power applied it can't get to the planing position. This principle also applies to a 4WD in various situations.

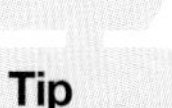

Tip

ONE LESSON TO BE LEARNED IS THAT WIND DRIES OUT A TRACK SURPRISINGLY QUICKLY, AND WAITING CAN SOMETIMES BE THE BEST COURSE OF ACTION.

Dry sand

A 4WD is just like a skimming boat, in dry sand. To get moving in sand can take a lot of power, because some sand has to be pushed ahead of the tyres and some displaced out to the side before the tyres can ride up over the sand and virtually float on top.

Momentum can be critical. Four tyres don't have much surface area in contact with the sand, and have a lot of weight to be supported by those footprints. So, when it is going slowly or stopped, a 4WD tends to sink down into the sand, and the softer the sand is the further the vehicle can sink. This is one situation where bigger footprints will help, because this reduces the point-loading (see page 132).

So when you get stuck or bogged part-way up a dune, it can be very difficult to continue forwards. Not only is there the gravity effect, but there is also the additional resistance of the sand in which you are stuck. By reversing, at least you have gravity helping you get back downhill for another attempt. If you can stick to the same wheel tracks on the next attempt, the sand will have been compressed a bit, and may not sap out so much energy from the engine. You may have to play "road-roller" for a few passes, to get the sand compacted enough to let you over the top. If you can get a good run-up, the built-up energy in momentum of the vehicle will help you reach the top.

There can of course be a risk using speed because it is harder to see traps ahead of you, or take evasive action. Checking out each sandhill before making an attempt on it can take hours of walking time, and may not be worth the effort. Climbing a sandhill in a 4WD in an untracked area is a calculated risk, and driving skills are vital in this situation.

4X4 Tip

QUICK, SMOOTH GEAR CHANGES ARE IMPORTANT TO AVOID BOGGING DOWN, AND PLENTY OF POWER TO KEEP MOMENTUM WILL HELP YOUR TYRES STAY ON THE SURFACE RATHER THAN DIGGING IN. AUTOMATIC TRANSMISSION IS OFTEN HELPFUL IN SAND BECAUSE OF QUICK, SEAMLESS GEAR CHANGES.

Sand handling

Driving at high speed in dry sand can have a peculiar effect on handling — it can largely disappear. With plenty of power on, in most cases the front of a 4WD will steer where it is pointed. Attempts at tight turns in this situation

DROPPING TYRE PRESSURE TO ABOUT 15–20 PSI MAY HELP WHEN DRIVING UP SANDHILLS. BE EQUIPPED TO REINFLATE TYRES AFTERWARDS.

are not effective and the vehicle's turn arc greatly enlarged. It doesn't take long to find out how effective steering is at different speeds in sand. The rear end often gets a strange side-to-side wobble, similar to a "flat-tyre" feeling. There is nothing you can really do about this wobble. In 4WD, all four wheels should be providing traction, so as long as the front is steering adequately, learn to accept what the back end does.

Braking needs to be minimal; to come to a planned stop just means backing off the accelerator until almost stall point, then kicking in the clutch to avoid the stall. When you stop on sand, try to have the vehicle on the hardest surface available or at least pointing downhill to make starting off as easy as possible. On sandhills or dunes when the first attempt doesn't work, dropping tyre pressures down to about 15–20psi for the retry might help. Be careful with tubeless tyres. Don't deflate them too low. They can move on the rim and they may fully deflate, or not

Case Study

Waiting often works!

Sometimes the only or best practical way out of a long slippery climb can be as simple as waiting a short time for the track to dry out.

Four 4WDs travelled along steep, clay-based and sometimes rocky tracks through the centre of the Great Divide, and made several successful creek crossings early in the day. Progress was good, then it began to rain. By late afternoon it had lightened off to a fine drizzle, and there was no wind. Radio transmission was poor from the bottom of the valley. Some members of the group were very concerned at the late hour. The only way out was via a long and known steep climb, all clay, although with plenty of trees for winching anchors. Going back was considered by all to be a worse alternative.

Two vehicles had winches – one PTO, one electric. Despite best efforts, none of the vehicles made it very far up the slippery climb, and closing darkness and the still-drizzling rain did not make it any easier. The 4WD with the PTO winch went first, towing one of the vehicles that had become disabled. In the process, it snapped the shear-pin in the winch drive shaft, then slid sideways, well down into the edge drain.

This effectively blocked the path, stopping progress for quite some time until the vehicle could be hand-winched sideways back onto the track. It was unlikely the group would get out that night. When the drizzle had stopped at about 9.00 pm, a couple of the group carried a radio, antenna and vehicle battery the several kilometres up to the top of the hill, and made contact with their base. Prearranged recovery plans were put into place, and two well-prepared vehicles with powerful winches and plenty of cable and chains set out to rescue the four stuck vehicles. Meanwhile, the wind had begun to blow, and it lasted all night.

The two recovery 4WDs arrived around 6.30 am, and relatively easily drove down to a bend just above the stuck group. Turning around to face uphill, they parked hard over to the inside, leaving the track clear enough for a climbing vehicle to pass. The more experienced drivers in these two vehicles then walked down to the stuck vehicles. They guided them to reverse well back down the climb to a good spot for starting off. After giving some advice to the drivers on the best way to make the climb, they watched as the three operational vehicles, not without some difficulty, made it all the way up. The broken-down vehicle was towed up to the top as well, and then A-barred home.

Preparing a ramp

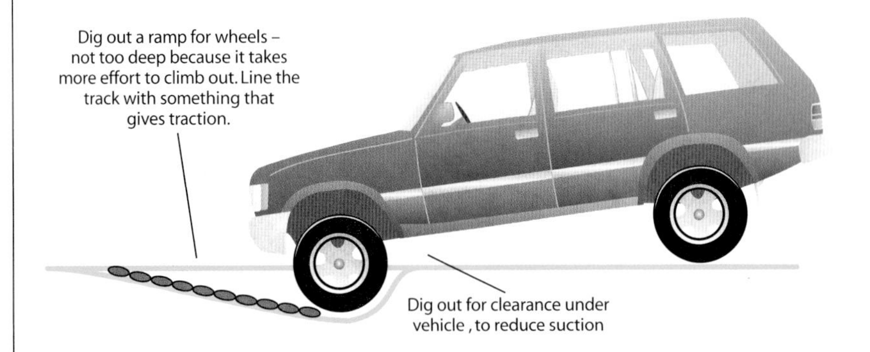

seal again properly. If forward traction is almost lost when clawing your way up a sandhill, try swinging the front wheels sharply from side to side, to get a fresh and bigger bite of sand. Use plenty of power. But in dry sand, the same as for mud, if the 4WD stops going forward and starts going down, consider yourself stuck. Don't make matters worse by digging an even bigger hole.

Wet sand

Wet sand can be just as smooth to drive on as the best highway. Recent rain on sand dunes makes progress much easier, and the number of retries at climbs is usually greatly reduced. Hard-packed sand is excellent to drive on, and the long runs on some Australian beaches can be really magnificent from both the driver's and the passenger's point of view. On the other hand, beaches can be an absolutely treacherous place to drive, requiring you to really keep your wits about you. Washouts come up without warning. There can be a danger with what is almost "quicksand" in places where water run-off from higher ground channels down to the beach edge. Specialised beach driving experience is best first learned with a recognised 4WD club, or in company with several other experienced drivers and vehicles in a careful "exploration" drive.

Note the "several other vehicles". The odds on getting stuck are usually against a lone 4WD. Perhaps this is part of the personal challenge that makes some people buy real 4WDs. Tide knowledge can be critical, and "sweeper" waves can catch you out. There are many 4WDs barely showing above the sand on Australian beaches, and even in tidal creeks and rivers, proving the danger and power of tides. At least with several other vehicles, you will probably have a winch anchor point available. If not, you may need a fast shovel and a lot of physical effort to bury the spare tyre as a winch pull-point, or to use some other kind of anchor or pull-point.

An alternative to digging an anchor point for winching is an earth anchor, an auger that digs itself into the ground as you twist or pull against it, with a wide load-sharing plate or assembly on the top to prevent it sinking into the sand, soil or mud. There are various sizes available, and they work very well. On the top is an eye, to which you D-shackle the winch cable. Include an earth anchor with your recovery equipment along with those other two great labour-saving inventions, the chainsaw and the bull-bag.

Tip

DIGGING A RAMP OR TRENCH AHEAD OF THE WHEELS, SLOPING FORWARD UP TO THE SURFACE MAY BE NECESSARY ONCE YOUR WHEELS HAVE GONE DOWN IN THE SAND OR MUD.

Clay

Dry clay is not difficult to drive on, but when wet it can be slippery and fairly messy. Clay can vary from almost rock-hard to oozy and clinging. Some kinds of clay will just not wash off with a hose, and take hours of rubbing and scraping to clean off. Most clay surfaces seem to repel water, or develop a fine slurry on the top after a few drops of rain.

On a steep downhill there is very little a four-wheel driver can do once a vehicle starts sliding down a hard, slippery clay track, other than remember the fail-safe plan (see page 48). Lowered tyre pressures can help, by giving a bigger and softer footprint in any slippery going. Deliberately steering into a washaway will often help regain traction or steering. Look for a rain-groove where pebbles and other rough material have been washed down, or steer hard along an edge where the coarser dirt hasn't been washed away. Dropping the wheels into a groove might collect a lot of mud, or maybe dent a few lower panels, but it is usually the lesser of two evils. Once the vehicle has picked up speed in a slide it is much harder to stop. Being vigilant to detect the instant the slip happens can be critical, as it gives the best possible chance of corrective action.

Jacking

Digging a ramp or trench ahead of the wheels, sloping forward up to the surface may be necessary once your wheels have gone down in the sand or mud. Jacking the 4WD up enough to fill in the holes dug by tyres is also an option. Doing the jacking is a physical challenge, and may not be realistic with the basic wind-the-handle jack. A highlift jack or similar, lifting from the bullbar, a wheel or towbar, is easier to use. The footplate or jacking-plate needs to be big and tough enough so

A BULL-BAG IS AN EASY WAY TO LIFT THE VEHICLE.

A HIGHLIFT JACK CAN BE HANDY IN CERTAIN OFF-ROAD CONDITIONS BUT USE CARE AND BE AWARE OF THE STABILITY OF THE JACK.

that it won't break or sink down in the sand instead of lifting the vehicle.

Jacking and packing can be hard work. Jack the vehicle up a little, pack some traction under the wheels and go forward a little, then repeat the process. Almost anything a 4WD can drive over is useful to put ahead of your wheels to help get out.

Sometimes it is the only choice, unless there is another 4WD with a snatchem-strap or similar to pull you out. An easier way to lift a 4WD is by using a bull-bag, quickly and easily inflated by vehicle exhaust gases. The bull-bag inlet hose nozzle is fitted to the exhaust pipe with the engine running and held there until it pumps up the bag. Bull-bags are tough, and there are several sizes available, from small 50-litre drum size up to bigger than a 44-gallon drum. These can almost effortlessly lift the tyres and body on one side of a fully laden 4WD well clear of the ground in a few minutes.

4X4 **Tip**

MAKE SURE THAT THE FOOT PLATE OR JACKING PLATE IS BIG ENOUGH, SO THAT THE JACK WILL LIFT THE VEHICLE INSTEAD OF SINKING INTO THE SURFACE.

Chains

Most four-wheel drivers think tyre chains are for use only in snow, but they can also be very useful in hard-surfaced, slimy clay as well. On a track with a pronounced camber, that is, with a high centre and deep gutters, sometimes the only way to make progress is with very bitey tyres. Snow chains will work, but they are not good for the track and should only be used as a last resort. For flat ground, chains on the front wheels give the best result. If you have only one pair of chains, fit them to the back wheels going uphill, as most of the weight transfers to the rear end on a climb. The reverse applies on a descent, but they can tend to make steering less effective.

Less speed using wheel chains often results in more progress. Chain ends can fling out and damage body panels with increasing vehicle speed. High engine revs and low gearing can combine to dig bad gouges in the track surface. By travelling as slowly as practical, the chains will bite, imprint and drive, instead of biting and being torn out or clogging up.

Wet bitumen

Tread designs on tyres with adequate tread depth usually handle smooth wet bitumen safely. On a medium-use country road, wet bitumen isn't too bad to drive on with 4WD tyres. Some concrete roads are a bit like smooth bitumen, although the newer concrete roads seem generally well designed for rapid drainage. In larger towns and cities with heavy traffic, the picture changes altogether in drizzle and/or rain. Airborne matter of all kinds, oil and other materials continually drop onto the road. In dry conditions, these deposits remain in the rough road surface, and braking effectiveness isn't reduced much, if at all.

When it begins to rain, the water droplets pass down through the deposited junk onto the non-porous bitumen surface, so the junk virtually floats on top of the water. After a few tyres churn up the mixture, the result

AUSTRALIA DOES NOT GET MUCH SNOW COMPARED WITH EUROPE BUT MOST DRIVERS TREAT IT WITH A LOT OF CAUTION, AND RIGHTLY SO.

is a thin and slippery slurry on top of the bitumen. Safely braking can then become quite hazardous. It is not uncommon to see the back end of a vehicle hanging out when it goes around a corner on slippery bitumen. As the rain increases, the slurry tends to wash off the road surface and the road usually becomes easier to drive on; that is, unless a large amount of rain falls, sufficient to fully coat the roadway surface. Then the road becomes slippery again.

A lot of rain on bitumen changes the situation, perhaps to the point where the front wheels can actually skate down the road on a film of water. Sometimes if you hit a deep puddle of water on a roadway the front tyres can skid and not steer the way you want. This is known as "aquaplaning"; it isn't that common or usual, and speed too high for the circumstances is the cause. On slippery bitumen roads, some wide 4WD tyres can actually work against grip, due to the larger surface contact area and relatively inflexible tread. Because of the reduced point-loading per square inch or cm, in some situations such as cornering they can slip more easily, especially if too much speed is used.

Greasy surfaces

Bald or wide tyres and incorrect tyre air pressures can contribute to slides on wet and greasy roads. Tyres fitted to 4WDs are larger, usually have heavier tread and are not generally as flexible and adaptable to road surfaces as most car tyres. Unless the driver makes allowance for the chances of skidding, or reduced steering and braking effectiveness, a 4WD with its high centre-of-gravity and large body weight can slide around far worse than a car on some slippery roads. Higher vehicle speed increases the possibility of poor handling, and poor tyres can make it into a probability.

When you react to something and apply the brakes, the vehicle will still keep travelling for whatever distance it takes for you to physically react, plus whatever distance it takes for the vehicle to stop. Even with quick physical reactions, the average shortest distance

Tip

WHEN IT BEGINS TO RAIN THE WATER DROPLETS PASS DOWN THROUGH THE DEPOSITED JUNK ONTO THE NON-POROUS BITUMEN SURFACE, SO THE JUNK VIRTUALLY FLOATS ON TOP OF THE WATER.

Braking distances

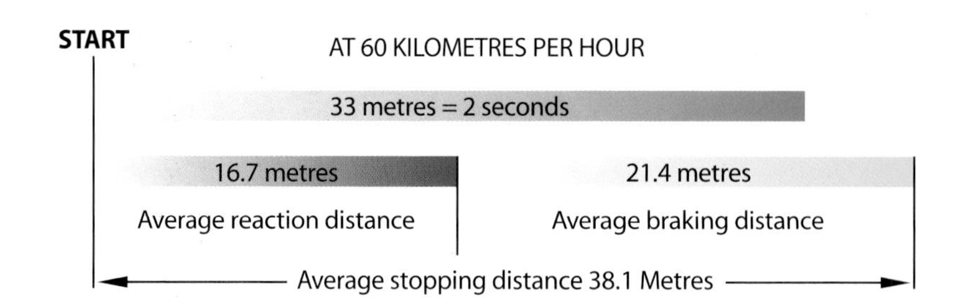

Tip

WHEN YOU REACT TO SOMETHING AND APPLY THE BRAKES, THE VEHICLE WILL STILL KEEP TRAVELLING FOR WHATEVER DISTANCE IT TAKES FOR YOU TO PHYSICALLY REACT, PLUS WHATEVER DISTANCE IT TAKES FOR THE VEHICLE TO STOP. EVEN WITH QUICK PHYSICAL REACTIONS, THE AVERAGE SHORTEST DISTANCE OVER WHICH YOU CAN BRING A VEHICLE FROM 60 KILOMETRES PER HOUR TO A STOP IS ABOUT 38 METRES.

over which you can bring a vehicle from 60 km/h to a stop is about 38 metres. This distance is based on driving on a dry road, with good tyres and vehicle braking efficiency of 65 per cent. Thinking about this stopping distance, it is not difficult to understand why nose-to-tail vehicle collisions happen, as almost every driver underestimates the distance really needed to stop. This is one situation where ABS fitted to your vehicle can often make the much-needed difference.

At 60 km/h your vehicle is covering about 16.7 metres per second, or just over 33 metres each two seconds. The "keep away from me for about two seconds" rule is very sensible, and more so on a slippery or greasy surface. This idea simply needs each vehicle to keep at least two seconds apart when driving. In most cases on flat dry ground in general traffic flow, that's about enough following distance, giving a reasonably safe amount of road in which to either swerve out of trouble's way, or brake to avoid a collision. On greasy roads a sensible idea is to at least double your normal following distance, and brake half as hard for twice as long. It doesn't matter whether you are driving over slick clay on a track, or along a bitumen road. Giving yourself and your vehicle more time to react will help reduce the likelihood of skidding and/or accident.

Snow and ice

In Australia, roads with snow on them tend to be of three types: bitumen or hard-surfaced roads up to alpine areas, formed access roads, or tracks out in the surrounding Great Divide areas. We don't get much snow compared with Europe but most drivers treat it with a lot of caution, and rightly so. It can be great fun to drive through but at the same time it can be very challenging, and dangerous on some terrain. Those roads that are hard and swept by snow plough often still present an ice problem, particularly black ice. Gravel roads may not have the ice difficulty as much, but they do have a drawback: if you go off the formed surface edges it is quite likely you'll bog. Snow ploughs don't often visit the kind of tracks many four-wheel drivers like and use, so caution is necessary when driving in snow.

The same rule for wheel chains applies in snow as for mud. With only one pair, on flat ground put them on the front wheels. Carry and use a full set for all four wheels, if you are out driving seriously in snow. A few minutes practice at home putting chains onto your wheels in the driveway, or learning on an organised trip, could save many embarrassing moments in the cold. On alpine roads there is a often a legal requirement for chains to be carried in a vehicle, and in some areas signs

CARRY AND USE A FULL SET OF CHAINS ON ALL FOUR WHEELS IF YOU ARE PLANNING SERIOUS DRIVING IN SNOW.

advise of parking bays where they must be fitted before proceeding any further. 4WDs are not exempt from this requirement. In most cases their grippy tyres and 4WD capability will take a 4WD much further than conventional cars. But they are still subject to physical and mechanical laws of sliding, wheelspin and reduced handling ability.

Perhaps the greatest 4WD challenge in snow is not the ground you may be travelling on, but the personal challenge of successfully and safely driving through the snow. It is wise to use a track you know when first learning about snow driving.

In axle-deep snow on a track, the basic rule is that you will get stuck if you go off the wheel-grooves. If at all possible keep to the crown of the road. Gutters are for water, ice, mud and slurry, not 4WD tyres. As in dry sand, vehicle momentum in snow can be important. The highest practical gear giving flexibility for the needed speed is the one to use. As for any other slippery surface, low gear ratios and high engine revs cause wheelspin.

Use the engine and gears for braking in snow driving and be gentle with the accelerator and clutch. Keep off the brakes, and keep the vehicle moving as smoothly as you can. Where possible, drive the vehicle quietly and don't let it coast or over-run. While you keep power on, you usually control the vehicle, instead of the terrain controlling it, even with very gentle throttle. Always try to stop in a place where you can easily get going again. Look for bare patches, crests or a place where the ground shape will help you get mobile.

Tip

4WDS ARE NOT EXEMPT FROM RULES ABOUT USING CHAINS IN SNOW.

It is quite surprising just how much engine effort is needed to move off in new and untracked axle-deep snow, compared with following in someone else's wheel tracks.

On a slippery or snowy climb, if traction is reducing, try the same trick as in loose sand — swing the front wheels quickly and continuously from side to side, lock to lock. The edges of the tyres tend to bite more, helping with steering as well. It is important to keep the engine revs steady so that wheelspin is minimal. Remember that the back wheels have to keep driving as well as the front wheels. You may have a fair bit of power on to try to find bite for traction with the front tyres, but the back tyres may be slowly travelling in a relatively straight line. They could be sitting in an already compressed groove of snow, and will spin if too much power is used.

Snow problems

Snow can short-circuit 12volt electrical equipment. After driving for sometimes only a short distance, it is common to find a build-up of snow in parts of the engine bay. When heat melts the snow it can run downwards or be blown all over the engine bay by the fan. While this might not be too bad on diesels, it can cause problems in the ignition systems of petrol-engine vehicles. When you get a chance to stop, check for snow build-up around the steering box and various other low-mounted mechanisms. Driving in plenty of snow in a straight line for a few kilometres, using minimum steering travel, can allow build-up of icy hard packed snow. This can limit movement of steering components.

The usual warnings in automobile association handbooks, on alpine resort signs and in 4WD magazines to "use radiator antifreeze" are not put there for fun. It is surprising how many drivers don't heed this advice. Frozen engines can cause problems, from simple non-starting through to cracked metal engine castings from ice expansion. Do not use the handbrake in snow or freezing conditions when you are parking the 4WD for any length of time, and certainly not overnight. The inner cable can easily freeze up with ice. Gearbox in gear, wheels to the gutter, chocked wheels — combine these three points for a safe park. Lift the wiper blades off the screen as well.

Slush or melting snow can become ice when it is carried on a moving vehicle. Slush on the ground can also become ice, a perfect substance for causing a 4WD to slide sideways into the table-drain, gutter, or worse — nothing. A chainsaw is a great device for cutting trees, but a good sharp axe is often better for trimming off some scrub to make a quick track surface to help get the vehicle back onto the crown of the road.

The old rule of "uphill traffic has courtesy right-of-way" definitely applies in snow, but the efforts of restarting one vehicle uphill can sometimes be no worse than the downhill one trying to stop. Keep a very careful eye out for oncoming or other traffic in snow conditions, and allow much more stopping and turning distance than usual.

Although it might at first sound like an unnecessary step, proper preparation for a full-day snow trip should include vehicle spares, survival-clothing and recovery equipment for the worst-case scenario. Food and drink sufficient for an overnight stop should be carried, just in case. A warm jacket, a thermos of hot drink and some food to eat may well make the difference between "miserable and totally awful", and "cold but enjoyable".

Shaley rock and scree

Shaley rock, scoria and pebbly scree surfaces can give very poor traction. In

Tip

IF THE TRACK IS WET, DOESN'T HAVE A FIRM BASE AND YOU CAN SEE YOU ARE LEAVING OBVIOUS TYRE MARKS, PERHAPS YOU SHOULD CONSIDER IF YOU REALLY HAVE TO BE THERE AT ALL.

dry conditions they break up and roll about easily, and in the wet they slip and slide. Even the best diff lock is no help if tyres simply can't get enough surface to hang on to, and on some shaley spur tracks the rock breaks away under very little pressure. On a bad shale or pebbly climb it may be worth using a shovel to clear some grippable track to make headway. Because of the softness of the surface, if there isn't an alternative track, consider steadily winching up rather than chewing up the surface. In dry conditions wheels create a lot of dust, and a shaley downhill is certainly not a good place to be when visibility is limited. As with most sand, the less steering and braking in scree or shale, the better. Widely spacing out vehicles on a loose-based climb or descent, to allow a distance buffer for different vehicle speeds and driver abilities, can be very important.

Bulldust

Northern Australia has a unique problem for the four-wheel driver on some roads and tracks. It is known as bulldust. If you haven't experienced it, you are in for a surprise. Because it is so fine, it coats and disguises the track surface, making it impossible to tell just what is under the smooth-looking blanket. Twenty centimetres or more of dust on top of the wheel tracks is quite normal. The dust is so light that it does not affect vehicle handling itself, but to the downfall of many drivers, hidden potholes are also common in the hard roadway, some 300 mm deep, so these can be very damaging areas to drive through. With

IN VERY DUSTY CONDITIONS IT IS NECESSARY TO KEEP A SAFE DISTANCE BETWEEN VEHICLES.

GETTING BOGGED IS JUST ONE OF THE POSSIBILITIES WHEN FOUR-WHEEL DRIVING.

lowered speeds, the impact from hitting a bad pothole is obviously reduced. Tyre and mechanical damage can easily happen on these roads.

In very dusty conditions it is obviously necessary to keep a substantial distance between vehicles, and for safe visibility, sometimes this can mean being several kilometres apart.

On a still day, a vehicle driving through bulldust can be seen from many kilometres away as the dust haze lifts into the air. If you spot an oncoming vehicle still some distance off, the safest action is to use your advantage and pick a good place to pull over early. Close off all the air-vents and windows. It is worth trying to pressurise the vehicle cabin by using the heater or air-conditioning fan, to keep the dust outside, but this is not of much benefit unless you have some way of filtering the incoming air.

If the dust-stirrer is a road train, remember the driver is sitting up much higher than you, can probably see much better, and will not normally give way to you, or move to give you more track. Quit while you are ahead and pull over, because a road train can stir up enough dust to totally blank out all visibility for quite a few minutes; you could drive a long way off the road in that time.

Advice

IF THE DUST-STIRRER APPROACHING IS A ROAD TRAIN, QUIT WHILE YOU ARE AHEAD AND PULL OVER. A ROAD TRAIN CAN STIR UP ENOUGH DUST TO TOTALLY BLANK OUT ALL VISIBILITY FOR QUITE A FEW MINUTES; YOU COULD DRIVE A LONG WAY OFF THE ROAD IN THAT TIME.

Just because you are well off the beaten track doesn't mean there are no other vehicles around. It can be a major surprise when you are rapidly overtaken by a road train you didn't realise was anywhere near you, because you relaxed and didn't keep a watchful eye on the rearview mirror.

Bulldust is only a problem in the dry period, and it isn't a problem on all tracks, thankfully. At least as fine as talcum powder, a thin film of bulldust gets everywhere. This includes inside zippered-up bags, the closed ashtray and glove-box and even inside your mouth. Masking tape can be used to seal around vehicle windows and doors, and lightly smearing vaseline or silicon on rubber door seals will help them to seal out the dust. One simple way of helping keep dust outside the vehicle is to wait until the swirling dust from outside has dispersed and settled before opening the doors.

Pressurising the inside of a 4WD will help minimise dust entry while driving along, but nothing will completely stop it getting in. Use the heater or air-conditioning fan to push air and pressurise the cabin, but there is a catch-22 here. Pressurising the inside of the vehicle requires air from outside. In your vehicle preparation for dusty areas, don't forget to put filters on the fan air inlets. On most vehicles they are below the formed slots in the scuttle, just ahead of the windscreen near the windscreen-wipers. Check the vehicle service and repair manual or with the manufacturer for exact locations.

Air vents into the cabin can be filtered and sealed by using a "Chux" or similar thick paper towel. Fold it a few times, make sure it covers the vent by a good margin and stick it down all the way round with wide duct tape or similar. Remember to wipe off or wash the paintwork carefully before using the tape, or the fine film of dust will not let anything stick. Air outlets at the rear of the vehicle for the flow-through ventilation should be treated the same way. Even if the cabin air is pressured by a fan, dust still gets back into the rear side panels through the air outlets.

Areas of bulldust tracks are certainly one place where an oiled-foam engine aircleaner really earns its keep. Air-intake raised snorkels have proven their benefits, and in dusty conditions they could be considered essential equipment. Some are available with top-mounted pre-cleaners, helping greatly to limit the damaging dust which may enter your engine.

Mud

Mud driving can be great fun, a real challenge, or tiring. As nobody can see what is under the surface, if the muddy section is unknown it pays to be very careful. The basic rule, "If you don't know, you don't go", is worth remembering. Walking every difficult bit of track before driving it would rapidly take the enjoyment out of the trip. Obviously, practice will make traversing sticky bits become very much easier but experience will also teach that measuring the depth of a mud hole with a stick from the edge is much simpler than debogging a 4WD. Other drivers who have been through the mud ahead of you may have put rocks or logs in to fill holes in the track to help them get through, so be careful.

Letting tyre pressures down a little in mud usually improves the footprint, allowing the tyre tread to distort or flex more to grip and provide traction in slippery or soft muddy driving. Tyres can be let down so they look almost flat, somewhere around 20psi or even less for short periods, but they should be reinflated as soon as possible after the difficult section. To minimise wheelspin in mud, use the highest gear possible, providing it still gives enough power to drive. Unless the mud is almost liquid, chances are that the vehicle through ahead of you may have compacted the mud just enough to make your turn easier. On the other hand, it might also have almost broken through the crust, so that your vehicle really does go down in the bog. That is one of the joys or

MUD DRIVING CAN BE FUN, BUT BE CAREFUL OF HIDDEN DANGERS.

Tyre dangers with rocks

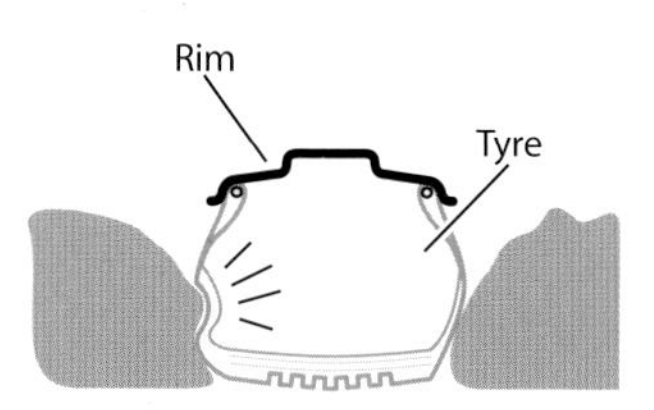

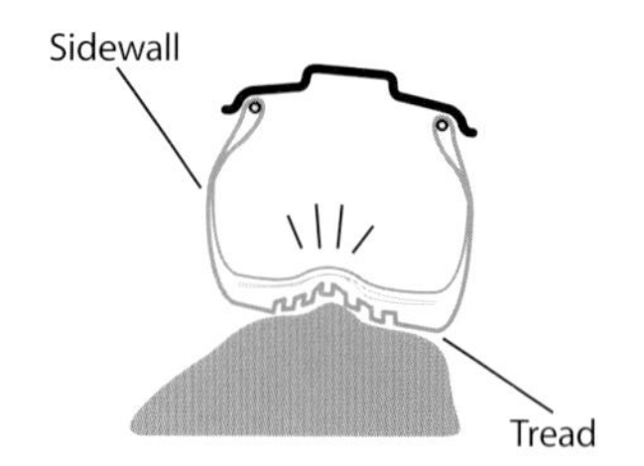

frustrations of mud driving — no-one really knows what's coming next.

In deep and/or serious mud, sometimes even an earth anchor (see page 54) will not be enough to winch against. Without substantial trees or similar really solid anchor point, another vehicle and a very long cable may be the only way to drag yourself clear. Sometimes drivers stuck in really bad bogs or floods on outback roads have to walk out, or make camp and wait for the mud or road to dry sufficiently to be able to drive out, or may even have to be evacuated by air. In some outback mud, there really is no other way so if you have a choice, don't go anywhere near it unless you like digging or waiting.

Rocks

Driving cleanly over rocks in dry conditions is often an interesting challenge, and the benefits of a lockable rear differential are very obvious in really tough rocky going. Driving over average rocky tracks is usually straightforward, providing the 4WD is driven steadily in a gear low enough for flexibility. Rocky tracks can do damage to tyres, panels, sills and underbody, if you get it wrong. Many drivers are reluctant to use peak engine revs for a short time to get over or through a difficult strip of rock, but occasionally the only way up a big sheet of hard rock, apart from winching, is sheer momentum and power. Although sometimes lots of revs and a hard charge is a very effective way to get over a big and loose rocky section, steady climbing is often better. Using the hand-throttle or a throttle rest for the driver's accelerator-pedal foot (see page 36) can be valuable in helping keep a steady engine rev rate in this kind of situation. Crawling over rocks on the way up a bad hill, in a flexible gear at not much above idle revs, produces surprising results. For a start, lower speed and power doesn't usually try to spit the rocks out from under the wheels; it tends to move the vehicle forward over them, unless the rocks are very loose.

Keep your foot off the clutch and let the engine, gearbox, suspension and tyres do the work when crawling down a nasty rocky hill. Engine braking is very effective at controlling descent speeds. Most times, all you need to do is steer

Advice

IF THERE IS A CHOICE, ALWAYS DRIVE ONTO A ROCK SQUARELY WITH THE TREAD RATHER THAN PUT LOAD ON THE TYRE SIDEWALL, AND TRY TO PLACE THE TYRE ONTO THE ROCK SO THAT IT WILL NOT SLIDE OFF.

Courtesy costs you nothing

Driver courtesy is sadly lacking in some off-road situations. It is commonly accepted that when two vehicles meet on a narrow track, the vehicle climbing uphill has the right of way over the one going downhill. There's a good practical reason for this. Assuming the descending vehicle is under control, it can stop relatively easily, and restart quite simply. Moving off and regaining traction for the ascending vehicle after a forced stop might be very difficult and time-consuming.

and maybe brake a bit, quietly and carefully. It is quite possible to gently brake-on, brake-off, almost down to a virtual stall, to pick your way through rocks on many downhills. Gravity will help keep the engine in a manual vehicle from stalling.

On rocks or rock steps you have to climb over, jumping the front wheels up onto the rock often works. Doing this in a vehicle with a poor approach angle, that is, a lot of front overhang, is likely to damage the bullbar or front body panels. If the front wheels don't roll up onto the rock easily, the end result will usually be a bigger hole for the rear wheels to drive out of, making the step up even more difficult. Against this, a few minutes bridge-building an approach ramp out of some smaller rocks or logs leading up onto the big rock might be necessary. It may also be necessary to build a drop-off ramp for the down side as well, rather than letting the back end drop off, crunching the rear panels and tow-bar.

If there is a choice, always drive onto a rock squarely with the tread rather than put load on the tyre sidewall, and try to place the tyre onto the rock so that it will not slide off. Treads are designed to cope with this load; sidewalls are not, and can get pinched between the rock and the wheel rim. This pinching often causes a split in the sidewall, even to the extent of jamming and puncturing the tube. On a tubeless tyre, a fractured sidewall can become porous and leak pressure, making it unsafe or useless. Ideally a lowered-pressure, bagged-out tyre should adapt to the shape of rocks for better grip and traction. Before dropping tyre pressures, to minimise chances of damage it may be worthwhile trying the tyres on the rocks at normal pressures, only letting them down if traction can't be gained.

If ever there is a good reason for really knowing the vehicle dimensions and tyre placement of your 4WD, driving among rocks is certainly one. The passenger can help from outside, by advising you on clearance and wheel placement as you negotiate a tricky section of track. Sometimes there is a decision to be made before driving the awkward bit. Will it be easier for the passenger to guide you through and then walk to where you can safely stop the 4WD after the obstacle? Or will it actually be quicker to spend time making several unguided tries at the awkward section? Driving experience and terrain judgement are important in making this kind of decision.

Environmental damage

There are some places where 4WDs are not permitted. Water catchment areas are restricted and there are usually hefty fines if you are caught there. Some park and reservation areas are restricted, but a permit to pass through is usually available. Most Aboriginal land is subject to permit approval. One well-known permit area is the

ALL IT TAKES IS A ROCK IN THE WRONG PLACE TO BRING A TRIP TO A STOP. **LOOK BEFORE YOU GO.**

LOOK AFTER THE ENVIRONMENT BY STICKING TO EXISTING TRACKS.

Simpson Desert which requires a South Australian "Remote Parks" pass.

Official closures of tracks for winter seasons or wet conditions is done to minimise damage. Increasing numbers of 4WDs using smaller amounts of track must equate to greatly increased wear rates on those tracks. Obviously, the more tracks available for use, the less likely any particular one will be subjected to heavy use, and the less the overall pressure will be. Environmentally conscious drivers use their vehicles in such a way as to minimise damage, and reduce the probability of more track and area closures.

Some thoughtless four-wheel drivers congregate at "playgrounds", and use the same areas over and over, creating considerable damage. Planning a trip during winter, which includes the probability that you'll have to do a lot of winching, is usually a great way of contributing to the environmental damage score. So is using 2WD and clawing your way up a hill, when by using 4WD your vehicle could make the climb much more easily and with less impact on the track. Driving in wet weather has a much more pronounced effect on off-road tracks, and should be kept to a minimum. Stick to formed roads and well-defined tracks, and leave the exploration on smaller, more fragile tracks for the better weather.

Ordinary red desert sand or white beach sand is not really affected by vehicle tyres. But the vegetation which has managed to grow in sand is easily affected and a few years worth of growth can be wiped out in an instant by a tyre. This also applies in some alpine areas and on steep hillsides along the Great Divide. In dry conditions, a 4WD can roll along and barely leave a tyre print, hardly affecting vegetation, but in wet conditions the picture may change totally. In the alpine high country, which often has a skin of dirt over poor clay or rock base, tyres can easily damage tracks and leave deep grooves, in some cases hastening erosion activity. Stay on defined tracks in these areas.

Whether you should make a by-pass track or not is often a difficult decision if you balance the potential damage to the vehicle versus probable damage to the environment. After floods along an outback road a long stretch of mud can be totally impassable one day and quite driveable the next after drying-out time. Detouring around the bog section might be a choice, and in many cases this could be quite practical, even if it means cutting a track to do it. However, there is sometimes no detour outback because the formed road is quite likely the only surface really hard enough to drive on. The cost of getting repair equipment to the outback to resurface soft roads in many cases is prohibitive; if you force your way, the tyre grooves you leave in the mud may well still be there a year later. Sometimes the choice of detouring or not is made for you, as in some parts of the mountains with hills on one side and a drop-off on the other, there is no option.

Nobody wants to give up a good trip part-way through, but there are sometimes very practical reasons why doing so may be the lesser of two evils. Sooner or later, every four-wheel driver gets caught in a sticky situation, as far as potential to damage the environment is concerned. For example, half-way through a Sunday trip, consider what happens when it begins to rain. The choice is often a difficult one, with several options. Would it be better to continue, although the track in front is not known, or, knowing the track, continue despite the few difficult bits ahead? Should you go back over your own tracks, or perhaps detour and get out of the bush or sand onto solid tracks?

There may well be an alternative route, or the only way out could be the hard way. The choice is usually not easy, and it often requires experience and willpower to make the best decision in the circumstances. Track damage is track damage, and if it is unavoidable, then that must be an acceptable situation. When damage can be prevented by using an alternative, any damage done must be labelled "irresponsible".

There is a saying among the many responsible drivers which neatly expresses the right idea: "Take nothing but photographs, leave nothing but footprints". Thoughtless drivers have left a disgusting legacy of rubbish at many places, so a logical answer may well be the provision of rubbish bins, bought from the fees charged to enter these areas. The old saying of "burn, bash and bury" your rubbish is not in favour any more. In many instances, feral animals can smell the rubbish and will dig it up. The preferred idea now is: "You carry it in, you carry it out."

Advice

ENVIRONMENTAL DAMAGE WILL RESULT FROM MAKING A NEW TRACK, SO ANY DECISION TO CREATE A DETOUR SHOULD NOT BE MADE LIGHTLY.

BIG RED, THE LAST REAL SANDHILL CHALLENGE BEFORE BIRDSVILLE.

Debogging and Towing

Debogging

When debogging another vehicle, be sure to use a low and flexible gear, steady acceleration and ample power. If a 4WD gets bogged, the ground around the bog is likely to be soft, so using 4WD, low range and even diff locks is logical for the towing vehicle. Depending on circumstances, the bogged vehicle may be able to use its own driving power to help extraction by the towing vehicle. If so, the tow cable may become slack and get run over, if the towed 4WD suddenly gets traction, but the towing vehicle does not accelerate enough to keep the tow cable tight. Agree between drivers on some kind of signal to indicate when to stop, or that the job has been done.

Make sure to tow far enough out for the debogged vehicle to be properly clear of the sticky area.

With the appropriate rescue equipment, freeing a bogged 4WD in many cases is usually just a mental challenge that takes a certain amount of time to solve. Getting seriously bogged may not be great fun, but being bogged on a hill is even worse. Dropping a wheel into a soft spot, or a deep wash-out or bad hole on a downhill and coming to a total stop can create a real challenge.

If you can't reverse back uphill, or easily dig a path downhill, this is often an indication that the "Jack Absalom Principle of Debogging" is applicable. Reach over into the back and get the gas cooker and kettle, or the thermos, and take a break. While you are doing this, think about the best sequence or options for getting unbogged. After a few minutes break, things may not seem such a mess.

Using another vehicle for debogging assistance is always preferable, but not always possible. With a power winch or a hand winch, debogging can be relatively

Tip

AGREE BETWEEN DRIVERS ON SOME KIND OF SIGNAL TO INDICATE WHEN TO STOP, OR THAT THE TOW JOB HAS BEEN DONE.

straightforward, and just a matter of finding an anchor point to pull to, ahead or behind as necessary. As you winch or make progress, the passenger can help by chocking a relevant wheel with a log or rock to keep the vehicle going in the required direction. Make use of the passenger as an extra set of eyes and hands. Digging will probably also be needed to make run-up exit ramps for the bogged wheels.

When you have cleaned out the slowly sloping ramp in front of the wheels, you'll have to put something in place of the mud or whatever you dug out, for the tyres to grip on. Newspaper, carpets, tarps, branches, leaves, logs, floormats, sheets of plastic, the tailgate from your trailer, proper wire-mesh sand mats, the roof-rack — all of these things will help you get out of a hole if your need is bad enough.

Most four-wheel drivers would have seen or heard about the Malcolm Douglas or Jack Absalom "Outback Survival" series on TV. Their videos demonstrate some good ideas. Debogging is one subject covered, and there are two ways of doing it — the thinking way, and the hard way. The satisfaction from successfully debogging a vehicle is worth the effort.

Jacking is often needed to get the wheel (or more often, both wheels) high enough to pack some timber or rocks underneath, to allow driving out, especially if you are stuck in a narrow deep wash-out. It may even be necessary to first secure the vehicle from behind, back to an anchor point, to prevent it sliding further into the hole before working on getting it out. When there's no tree or rock or other natural fixing point, or no other securely located vehicle for an anchor, digging out of a bog on a hill can be difficult as well as dangerous, and needs a lot of careful thought and considered actions. For more information on jacking see page 55.

Saltpans

It is easy to become bogged in a desert saltpan because the purple-blue-

DEBOGGING NEEDS TO BE DONE CAREFULLY AND STEADILY WHERE WINCHING IS USED.

Case Study

A saltpan saga

A driver was heading east on his own, and crested a sand dune to find a large saltpan below. It was late afternoon and the sun was low in the sky behind him. The sun's rays from behind were partly blocked by the dune, lowering the light level and putting the saltpan and corridor into shadow. It was difficult to distinguish between soft and harder spots from on top of the dune because of this, but he took the risk and tried to cross it anyway. It didn't work, and he bogged down, badly. Walking kilometres to cut scrub to pack into the tyre grooves, digging, jacking, cursing and working at it until nearly 11.00 pm, he finally gave up. What he did, entirely by accident, was discover another way of getting out of a saltpan bog.

It turned out to be the coldest night for years. Early on in the night, he had shovelled long gentle ramps or run-out grooves for each of the tyres, and laid cut scrub in to fill the grooves. He'd also cleared ample space under the vehicle, to minimise underbelly suction. By waiting, and by default, the night froze the saltpan almost solid. He drove out and off the pan fairly easily at first light, well before the day began to soften the surface again.

grey-white colour does not give much indication of soft spots. As a general rule, the shiny surface is soft and the duller part is a better chance for gaining traction. Most of it is treacherous, and the whitish crust can hide wet spots.

Saltpan bog can be deep and soft enough for anything you put down for wheel traction to be pushed under the surface by vehicle weight, and an ordinary jack will sink instead of lifting the vehicle. In any really sticky bog, as well as shovelling good ramps, be sure to dig clearance space out under the vehicle to release the suction, or nothing short of a Caterpillar dozer will be able to pull your 4WD out.

A-bar components

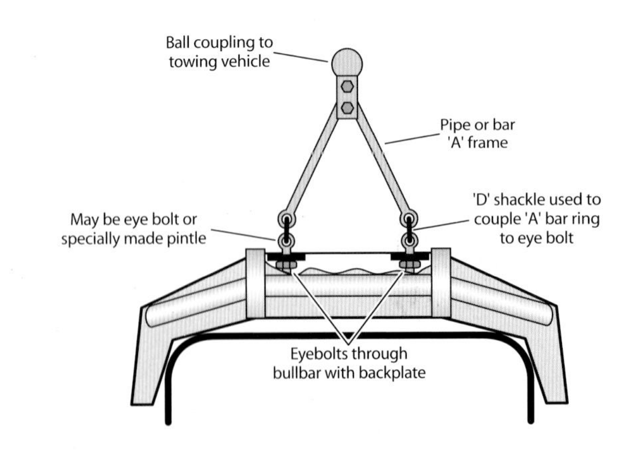

Towing a dead vehicle

Towing a dead vehicle home or out to safety on a cable is rarely fun for either driver, so if at all possible, use an A-bar. Most 4WD clubs have a list of minimum equipment to be carried on certain types of trips, and many of these require either A-bar pintles, tow eyes or a tow-ball to be fitted securely on the front of the participating vehicles. With a towbar and ball coupling fitted at the rear of the majority of 4WDs, a rigid and safe tow of the undriveable vehicle is relatively easily done.

The idea of carrying an A-bar may seem pointless to some, but it is sensible. Even the best maintained and driven 4WDs can become mechanically damaged. Faults in braking systems can happen anywhere, and with an A-bar, it is practical for the tow vehicle to do all the braking for both vehicles on the slow trip home. Multi-coupling is also an option. I've only seen it done once, but it worked perfectly — three vehicles coupled together with rigid bars, with the drivers communicating on CB radio, successfully crossed several hundred metres of shallow floodwater over a sandy and soft interdunal corridor. The rest of us had to wait for a couple of days, until the water level dropped.

Using a snatchem-strap

If the towing vehicle has reasonable ground to drive on, and the bogged vehicle has had run-up ramps dug for each wheel to help lift it up out of the glop, towing a vehicle out of a bog with a snatchem-strap is not very difficult. Digging ramps can't be done where the bog is a great liquid puddle, but should be done if possible.

Snatching works on the same principle as a strong rubber band, and usually works very well. The loop at one end of the soft and flexible strap is securely attached to the bogged vehicle, laid out slack in a few flat and unkinked s-shapes at the towed end, then safely coupled to the tow vehicle. The tow vehicle drives away, steadily taking up the slack on good ground. While the snatchem-strap is being stretched in one direction, the increasing pulling pressure on the strap (and therefore the stationary vehicle) tends to make the towed vehicle follow in the same direction. The more severe the bog or heavier the stuck vehicle, the more the strap stretches. When the load comes on the snatchem-strap between the two vehicles, the strap stretches to the point of maximum needed tension. Then it more-or-less catapults the stuck vehicle out of the bog, due to the combined effort of the towing vehicle pulling, and the strap stretching but wanting to resume its normal shape and size.

There are naturally risks with a snatchem-strap. Onlookers should be kept well away from a snatching operation, because tow can be multiplied over 300 per cent with the stretch effect. Despite their strength and well-earned good reputation, a snatchem-strap can be overstretched, and if that happens, it loses elasticity, becoming relatively stiff. In this case, rather than waste it you might as well take it to a cable and sling dealer and have it made into several tree-protectors or strops. A snatchem-strap is made of nylon webbing or similar, and if it breaks it will scythe. It is relatively light weight, and so it loses energy fairly quickly but can still do physical harm. If they are attached to irregular anchor points with D-shackles, and if one of those breaks or slips off, it will become an instant missile from the rubber-band effect of the strap. The safe way is to loop the strap ends through proper tow points

Caution

ONLOOKERS SHOULD BE KEPT WELL AWAY FROM A SNATCHING OPERATION, BECAUSE TOW CAN BE MULTIPLIED OVER 300 PER CENT WITH THE STRETCH EFFECT.

MAKE SURE BOTH VEHICLES ARE EQUIPPED WITH PROPER TOW POINTS BEFORE ATTEMPTING TO USE A SNATCH STRAP.

Advice

THE BEST AND THE ONLY SAFE TOW POINT IS A SOLIDLY BOLTED CHASSIS-MOUNTED ANCHOR.

or over tow hooks. Good snatchem-straps have a protective or sacrificial cover over the inside of the end-loops to minimise wear.

Tow points

If you have to tow with an ordinary rope or steel wire cable, or even chain, put some kind of padding around the anchoring point to minimise damage to both parts. Incorrect tow points can do quite a bit of damage to the cable or rope, or worse, to the towed vehicle if they go wrong. The best and the only safe tow point is a solidly bolted chassis-mounted anchor. Tow hooks, proper tow eyes, tow bars, tow loops — all vehicles should have correct tow points.

Cables and chains

With anything but a snatchem-strap, load should be lightly taken up on the tow device before any real load is applied to it. Hard acceleration, resulting in a sharp take-up jerk, is the easiest way to break the tow rope, cable, chain or strap. Keep onlookers well clear. When using a cable, place a wet bag or similar on it to deaden it if it breaks; a broken steel wire cable will scythe, and can do tremendous damage. If a chain breaks under load, it quickly loses energy and usually drops to the ground. Technological developments have introduced a new kind of synthetic winch-cable, with a breaking strain claimed to be about 40% higher than steel wire cable. This thin, nylon-look plaited cable known as "plasma" rope acts the same as light rope, losing energy very rapidly if it breaks.

Padding

The edges of a spring shackle are sharp and can damage a steel wire cable or strop. If you must use them, always put some kind of padding around awkward shaped tow points. There is one typical kind of damage on a winch cable that shows that someone using it has not been careful. It is usually just a metre or so in from the cable-end eye or tow-hook — an obvious kink, or damaged or flattened section of cable. This indicates that someone has hooked the winch cable around an object, and then looped the tow hook or eye back to the steel wire cable and placed load on it. Depending on the purpose, a short length of chain with a bag to pad it, or a tree protector or steel wire cable should be used for that job, not the winch cable. Winch cables are for hooking to things, not for being hooked.

A TREE TRUNK PROTECTOR PREVENTS DAMAGING TREES WHEN THEY ARE USED AS WINCHING POINTS.

Winching

Dangers

Winches and winching are an integral part of four-wheel driving, but many drivers are uncertain of how they work and how to use them correctly. Understanding how they work is not very difficult, but using them safely can take a lot of thought, practice and care. For further reference, there are books that deal specifically with winching.

Because winching can be risky, learning to reduce the dangers should be a systematic process. It is best learned properly from experienced instructors in controlled circumstances. Not much specific detail on winching operation is included here, although some of the uses and benefits of winches are discussed elsewhere in the book.

A winch itself is not usually dangerous, but the cable spooled onto its drum certainly can be. Cables under load should be treated with the utmost respect — take no chances, and keep away unless you really have to be there. The winching situation itself compounds the risk, as any winching job has danger potential. For example, you probably wouldn't be winching unless a vehicle is stuck. Bogged on flat ground, a vehicle won't run away downhill if the winch cable or something else breaks. Even though the 4WD might not be damaged in such circumstances, people could be injured. The risk changes on an uphill or downhill winching job, because the vehicle itself could become lethal if something goes wrong during winching. In either case, the winch cable is dangerous, but during steep hill winching, the danger potential is greater than on flat ground.

Learning

Winching with a load on the cable is definitely not a task to teach yourself,

Caution

BECAUSE WINCHING CAN BE RISKY, LEARNING TO REDUCE THE DANGERS SHOULD BE A SYSTEMATIC PROCESS.
IT IS BEST LEARNED PROPERLY FROM EXPERIENCED INSTRUCTORS IN CONTROLLED CIRCUMSTANCES.

POWERED WINCHES COME IN DIFFERENT SIZES SUITABLE FOR A RANGE OF VEHICLE WEIGHTS.

because one mistake could prove very expensive. The combination of safe and consistent operation, drive methods, external clutches, roller fairleads, cable tension, snatchblock use, safe pull angle and many other winching considerations is not easy to learn by yourself, and it is unlikely you would master it safely without help.

Consider learning through 4WD club practice days, a 4WD school or at a dealer's demonstration or field day. Learn from experts with safe winching knowledge, or in a managed situation such as one of the 4WD magazine "readers trips". The physical operation of the winch fitted to a 4WD or the hand-operated puller in the recovery kit should be learned from someone who has had proper hands-on practical experience. There are very specific regulations governing operators and use of winching equipment in any industrial area, obviously because it can be dangerous. 4WD winching operations are no less dangerous.

Warning

KEEPING WINCH CABLE CLEAN ALLOWS YOU TO SEE DAMAGE MORE EASILY AND HELPS IT LAST LONGER.

Powered winches

A winch is simply a mechanical means of winding a cable, typically steel wire, onto a spool or drum. A winch can be power-driven or manually operated. It can wind in, or it can pay out. Regardless of the method of doing it, the operator directs what it does.

There are three types of power-driven winches on 4WDs. Two are engine driven. One is driven via a gearbox and dedicated shaft, and known as a power-take-off (PTO) winch. The second type of engine-powered winch is hydraulic, and uses the vehicle's own power-steering pump to operate a small hydraulic motor to turn the winch drum. The third type is an electric winch, powered by the vehicle batteries through electrical cable, driving a low-geared electric motor.

There are several different internal drive systems in winch bodies. The most common system uses planetary gearing, in some ways similar to the gears in an automatic gearbox. Another system uses a worm-drive, which is usually slower and stronger than planetary gearing. Heavy-duty versions are available. Various makes have good and bad features and comparison is important before buying.

Pulling or load capacity varies with winch size. The rated capacity of a winch (how much weight it will pull) is determined by the cable on the first layer of the drum. The more layers spooling onto the drum, the more the pulling capacity reduces. A snatchblock (single-sheave pulley) should be used whenever possible to reduce the load on the winch. Several blocks could be used to multiply the pulling power. For safety, it is important that the diameter of the winch cable or rope is suitable for the groove in the pulley sheave.

Regardless of the operating means, all power winches have the same objective — to wind cable on to a drum or spool, either in or out, at a rate controlled by the operator. They are usually mounted at the front of the vehicle, but can be mounted wherever the need is, provided strong mounting points are available. The usual place is in, on, under, above or behind the bullbar or front chassis rails, depending on the type and size of winch. Most winches have mounting kits, so it can possibly be transferred to your next vehicle, simply by using a different mounting kit.

If it is necessary to winch up or down a bad hill, and the vehicle is fitted with a PTO winch or hydraulic winch (both of which require the vehicle's engine to be running to operate), then with a dead motor you are in trouble. With an electric winch the vehicle is still moveable, at least until the batteries run flat. With a hand-winch, even if it takes all night, you could still probably get out of trouble.

Hand-operated winches

Hand-operated winches are often called "pullers", and all pull two things together in some way. They are powered by physical effort on a lever. Some types could be compared with a fishing-reel, which winds line in onto a spool when you turn the handle. There are other devices that can be used or adapted for winching, like the well-known highlift jack.

Small "come-alongs" can be quite similar to a chain-block used in mechanical workshops to lift engines out of car bodies. They can be a fixed chain, pulled by a combination of gears inside a small housing, and driven by a ratchet handle or lever, or by an endless pull-chain. Smaller pullers often have a small drum or spool that is turned by a ratchet handle, with the cable effort multiplied via a system of parallel pulleys to wind the cable onto the holding drum.

The most common hand-operated winch or puller is usually called a "Tirfor", which is a well-known brand, although there are several makes. They do the same job as a little "come-along", but in a scaled-up and much more sophisticated way, and are very tough and quite reliable, using cable instead of chain. Smaller ones weigh around 10 kg, and the large ones are very heavy. A Tirfor is something like a fence-wire strainer. It is a mechanical cable-grabber, which walks along a steel wire cable inserted through the mechanism body, rather than winding it onto a drum.

A cable is fixed to the 4WD to be winched, the rear of the Tirfor is securely anchored, commonly with a tree-protector strap to a big tree, and then when the actuating lever is moved back and forth the cable is pulled through the Tirfor. The excess cable

Advice

CARRY SPARE SHEAR-PINS AND KNOW HOW TO CHANGE THEM.

ON A STEEP TOW LIKE THIS, A SNATCHBLOCK WOULD HALVE THE PULLING EFFORT WHEN THE WINCH CABLE WAS RUN THROUGH IT AND BACK TO THE VEHICLE.

GLOVES SHOULD BE WORN DURING ANY WINCHING OPERATION.

passes out the back, and can be coiled behind the winch body. Tirfor cables are usually supplied and kept on a separate reel. Cable diameter, therefore load capacity, varies with the size of the puller. Operating a Tirfor can be very hard work, and snatchblocks are usually necessary to increase manual mechanical leverage. Compared with the usual 30 metres of steel wire cable stored on a power winch drum, Tirfors have the capacity to pull through an unlimited length of steel wire cable. Again, for both safety and efficiency it is important that you use the correct and matching cable diameter for the puller you are operating. Incorrect diameter may allow the cable to creep or slip under load.

Mechanical knowledge

Winches are tough, and generally quite reliable, although some components can suffer from abuse. When the winch is overloaded, usually what breaks is a designed-in weakness on a shaft, where a "shear-pin" snaps, and then the shaft won't provide drive any more until the pin is replaced. Sometimes electric winches overload and start smoking a bit, but they generally work again once they have cooled down. Hydraulic winches seem to have a very high duty-cycle. Use the handbook for the particular winch to become familiar with the way to operate it, and to have a basic idea of its mechanical and/or electrical system. With your knowledge, and perhaps someone else's mechanical skills, you shouldn't get stopped by winch trouble very often.

Handling winch cable

Leather rigger gloves or similar are an absolute must. All winch cables take a punishing. When just one tiny steel wire cable strand breaks, and it will, if it sticks up just five millimetres, without gloves you will get a five millimetre deep slash across your hand or fingers. Gloves eliminate or reduce damage to flesh, so include them in the kit, like safety eye protection, and make sure you wear them.

Warning

NO MATTER HOW AWKWARD IT MIGHT FEEL AT FIRST, THERE IS ONLY ONE WAY TO HANDLE WINCH CABLE: WEAR GLOVES EVERY TIME.

To prevent skin burns or abrasions, gloves should still be worn with a new type of synthetic winch cable known as "plasma" rope, even though it feels much like nylon rope, and it has nothing hard to snag or cut your hands.

A boilersuit, or one-piece overalls, is another important item to include. Apart from keeping clothing worn underneath them cleaner, if overall cuffs and other press-studs or zippers are kept done up your clothing generally won't snag or get caught up in scrub or equipment.

When pulling out steel wire winch cable from the drum to the anchor point make sure there are no kinks or twists in the cable. If you use a tree for anchoring, it should have bark protection around it so that winching does not damage it. A wide nylon tree-protector sling is best, but several heavy bags wrapped around the tree inside a chain or cable strop will do the same job. The ends of a tree-protector have heavy loops stitched in them, similar to a snatchem-strap, and a D-shackle is effective to couple it to a winch cable. To increase leverage on a difficult operation, consider running the vehicle's winch cable out to a snatchblock attached to an anchor, then back to the vehicle. Recovery speed will be halved, but so will the pulling effort needed. It is quite practical to add a third pulley into the system for even more purchase, and with a Tirfor or similar, sometimes a multiple pulley-system is really useful, and sometimes it is the only way to save your back.

All winch cable should ideally be wound evenly onto the drum on a power winch, like cotton spooled onto a cotton reel. Sometimes this is simply not possible, and the cable gets kinked, flattened, and bunched up one end of the cable drum. Never leave it like this. Unspool it when you have the chance, clean it and respool it back onto the drum properly. The strand-plaiting in plasma rope does not seem to be affected by shape deformation. Where a flat spot has been squashed in a steel wire cable but the individual strands are not damaged, it can be almost beaten back into shape using a copper or plastic hammer on a block of wood. To avoid damage to the winch cable end, and give more flexibility, use a hammerlink to join several metres of top-quality proof-stamped chain onto the cable eye, then replace the original hook onto the end of the new chain. Apart from normal care, plasma-type rope doesn't need any end protection, nor does it seem to be easily damaged.

Winching loads

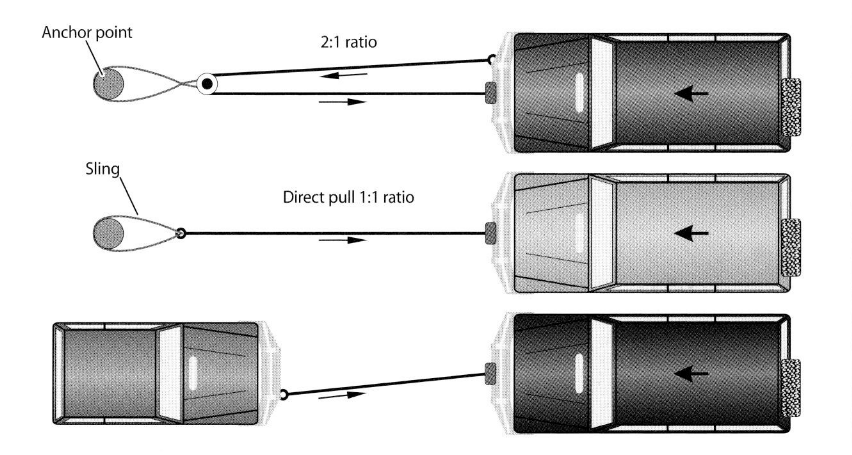

Tip

TO PREVENT LOSING THE PIN FROM A D-SHACKLE: TIE THE PIN WITH ONE END OF SOME LIGHT NYLON CORD, LEAVE ABOUT 300-MM SLACK AND TIE THE OTHER END TO THE D-SHACKLE. IF THERE'S NO HOLE IN THE PIN, DRILL ONE IN THE NON-THREADED END, SUITABLE FOR THE CORD.

Checklist

Buying a winch

These are some of the things to take into consideration before buying a winch:

- Need for a winch
- Winch physical dimensions
- Cable drum types
- Mounting requirements
- Manual or powered type
- Electrical drain on batteries
- Possible modifications to vehicle to allow fitting
- Speed of cable winding out and speed of cable recovery
- Cost of the complete job
- How much are you willing to spend
- Additional batteries needed
- Other accessories required

Each type, make and model of winch has points for and against it; a sensible way to learn more is to compare them at a reliable 4WD accessory outlet. Most staff at accessory shops are there because they are experts, and are happy to provide useful information.

If a section is considered unsafe, it is relatively simple to cut and safely rejoin the rope by splicing.

Pulley systems

Pulley systems reduce the effort to pull, but in proportion also reduce the effective overall winch cable length. Using a snatchblock or more than one, a small 4WD can relatively easily pull a much larger vehicle from a bad bog, even if it does take time.

Using a winch cable in direct-line pull (1:1 ratio) can overload the winch's pulling capabilities, but running it through a single snatchblock (a pulley giving a 2:1 ratio) halves the effort. Snatchblocks often are fixed direct to a tree protector so that the anchor-point tree is not damaged while winching.

A spare length of cable or chain can come in very handy for spacing out the snatchblock from the anchor point or towards the stuck vehicle to give a better direction of pull. Using one vehicle as an anchor point for the snatchblock, so that another vehicle can pull on a difficult angle to help extract a third vehicle from a bog, is quite practical. The possibilities for recovery are almost as endless as the ways to get stuck or bogged in the first place.

A SNATCHBLOCK IS HANDY WHEN THE PULL ANGLE IS NOT DIRECT OR THE PULLING POWER NEEDS TO BE MULTIPLIED.

Snatchblocks

When buying a snatchblock, check that the pulley sheave has the appropriate diameter groove for the winch cable to pull around. In general, the bigger the pull-capacity of the winch, the bigger the diameter of the steel wire cable supplied with the winch. A snatchblock that fits a Tirfor hand-winch cable might not be right for a power-winch cable. Many snatchblocks are made of stainless steel to cope with the heavy loads often applied to them, and the axle the sheave rolls on usually has a protected grease nipple.

Using a snatchblock is easy. Every snatchblock needs its own shackle, and to save trouble it pays to store the two linked together. If the clevis pin from a shackle falls in the mud, it is very frustrating. To help stop this see the "4WD Tip" on page 77.

Finding Your Way

Map reading

If you are considering serious off-road or outback driving, it is important to learn how to use a map. A good map is invaluable and could be a life saver. It is equally important to make sure the map you use is current. Special-interest clubs and companies such as Gregory's publish maps and books, and there are some hard-to-get maps published by government departments.

Map use and contours

Maps show physical features such as creeks and landforms, as well as man-made features including towns and roads. They come in various scales and physical map sizes. Maps with a larger scale (e.g., 1:25 000) show more detail such as buildings and fences, but the area covered is smaller. Here are examples of different scales:

- 1:1 000 000 scale, (one cm on the map represents one million cm or 10 km on the ground) — only basic detail for four-wheel driving.
- 1:100 000 scale map (one cm on the map represents one km on the ground) — more useful for four-wheel driving, with buildings and creeks usually shown.
- 1:25 000 (four cm on the map represents one km on the ground) — good maps for bushwalking, but in a 4WD this may be too detailed.

Topographical or "topo" maps show terrain in a "relief" or more-or-less two-dimensional form. This involves contour lines, which give a fairly reliable indication of what the country is like. It can be quite confusing looking at all those lines and symbols at first, and there are several ways to learn about this interesting and important subject.

Advice

ORIENTEERING, SCOUTING, BUSHWALKING AND OTHER ORGANISATIONS RUN CLASSES IN MAP READING. DOING A COURSE CAN BE REALLY WELL WORTH THE EFFORT AND SMALL AMOUNT OF TIME INVOLVED. CORRESPONDENCE OR DISTANCE EDUCATION COURSES ARE AVAILABLE.

WHERE CONTOURS ARE CLOSE TOGETHER, SLOPES ARE STEEP. WHERE CONTOURS ARE WIDELY SPACED, SLOPES ARE GENTLE.

Topographic profile, showing contour lines and elevation

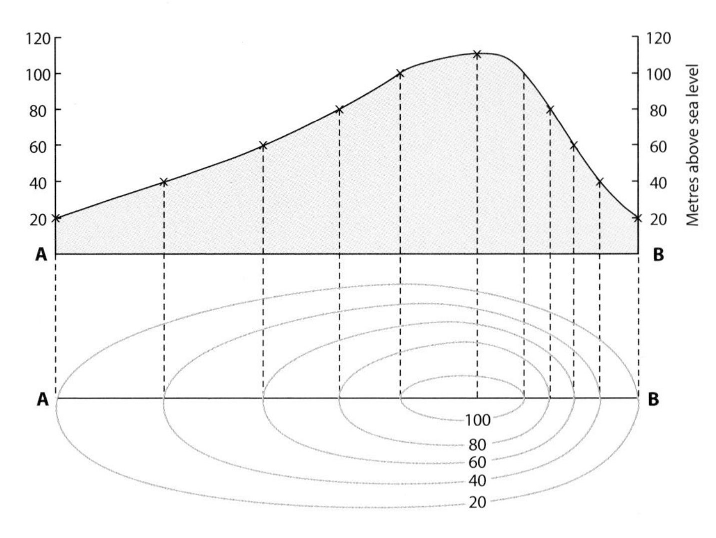

On a topographical map, don't plan on driving where the contour lines are shown close together — that means it is steep. The closer the lines, the steeper the terrain, and in a 4WD that equals more difficult and riskier travel, or more likely, completely undriveable conditions.

A GPS IS GREAT FOR FINDING YOUR EXACT LOCATION ON THE GROUND.

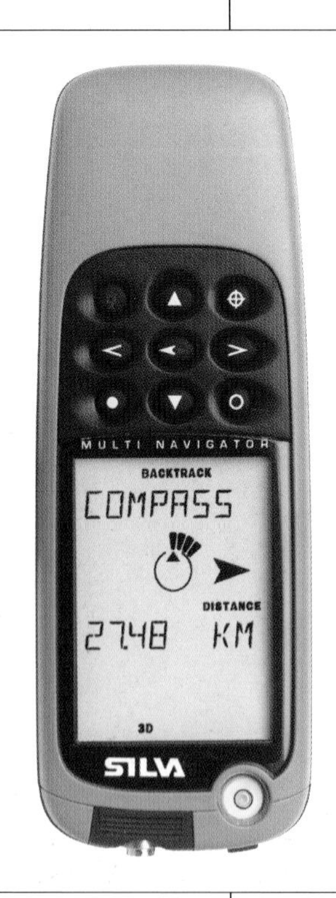

For exploring or learning any new area, buy the best possible maps. One of the best-known map-series is "NATMAP", and these cover almost all of Australia, in various scales. If you have a computer, NATMAP offers a two-CD set of all their maps, in three scales, plus an almost 3-D mosaic showing the surface of the country. You can print out your individual maps of specific areas if needed. Most maps are not expensive, and give good value.

Use a large-scale map to check out unplanned creek crossings and their entries/exits; that way you may be able to take an easier path if the contours show one, rather than get stuck from lack of planning. Look for gullies or valleys and allow for the possibility that these areas may be wet or boggy at some times of the year. In desert areas, check a map for lowest points, because if there has been rain, the interdunal corridors can stay boggy for weeks or months. From the symbols, you can find out where a bore or other permanent water supply is available. All it takes is a little bit of study, to find out just how valuable a printed map can be.

Going into unfamiliar country puts extra pressure on the driver. Good maps can help reduce this load by providing knowledge of what is ahead. The widest map source is probably the Government map shops found in most major cities. Their maps can usually be found in most good map shops. Used in conjunction with a GPS unit, the amount of land-based information available to you is simply amazing.

Using a compass

A compass can also be a valuable navigation aid. A compass inside a vehicle can be unreliable and a trap, unless it is one intended to be fitted and used inside a vehicle. Compass accuracy is affected by metal and the energy fields around radios. Unless you've bought a properly compensated compass and fitted it correctly, you might be better off with a cheaper hand-held compass. They are very reliable and simple to use. Because metal affects the needle in any compass, and can make it read incorrectly when you are taking bearings, you should keep a few metres away from a vehicle or other metallic objects when you are using one.

Global Positioning System (GPS)

Recent commercial developments with global positioning system satellites make navigation now fairly simple, and certainly easy. It would be very difficult to get lost with a GPS unit, either hand-held or fitted in your 4WD. Even so, you still need a reasonable-scale map to show your position relative to an overall location. GPS is a fascinating facility, and ought to be considered essential for any long and/or remote trips. Boating magazines are one good source of reference on GPS equipment. There are GPS units specifically made for use on boats, showing coastal information.

Many 4WD outback travel books now give precise locations of land based points of interest and camp sites for GPS use. These specific points are known as "waypoints". Most land-based GPS units are supplied with an inbuilt list of waypoints, usually towns and cities right across Australia. A basic GPS unit can indicate how far from where you are, in a direct line of sight, to a known waypoint. It can also record how far to travel to that same waypoint if you drive there along a road, or tell you which direction and how far to your nearest town. Some have many more functions than the few I've listed here.

On a small built-in visual display screen most hand-held GPS units can show the track you took to get from your start point to your present waypoint, and can also track you back to your start using the same track. If you are on foot it can also direct you back to the start in a straight line, always correcting itself for any deviations you might have to make.

You can enter any point of reference you choose onto your GPS unit as a waypoint for your use. Hand-held GPS units are usually about the size of a mobile phone, and huge improvements in technology now mean battery usage is minimal. Providing the GPS unit can see the sky through the front windscreen of your 4WD it will usually operate well, and many offer the ability to run off 12V from a power-point as well as AA-battery function. External antennae and vehicle-mounting cradles will make your GPS even more adaptable.

If you have a laptop computer, many more options to make use of GPS become available. Data can be downloaded and uploaded between laptop and GPS unit. Vehicle-mounted GPS units can provide data to computer-programs offering complete and detailed national roadmaps, and streetmaps of most towns and cities.

Specific programs also can provide quite detailed outback track, road and resource data. These programs may also allow you to edit, mark and save your own tracks for reference. Programs to help you find specific locations are easily available, all through a satellite-based Global Positioning System unit.

VEHICLE-MOUNTED GPS UNITS CAN PROVIDE DATA TO COMPUTER-PROGRAMS OFFERING COMPLETE AND DETAILED NATIONAL ROADMAPS, AND STREETMAPS OF MOST TOWNS AND CITIES.

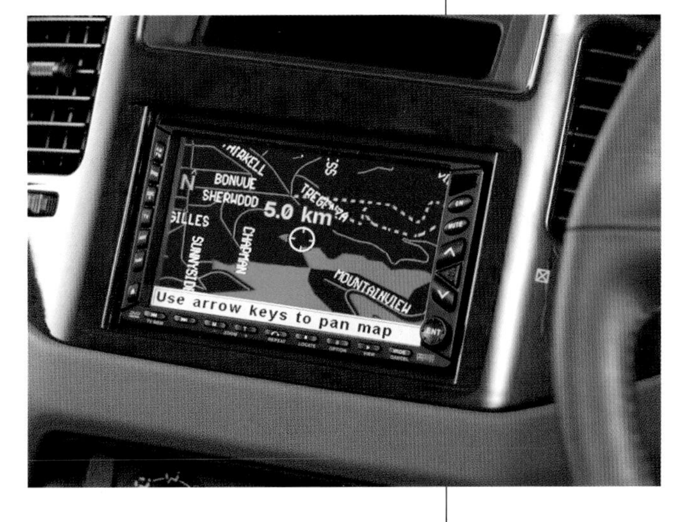

Trip Planning and Safety

Preparation for different trips

Planning for a six-month around-Australia trip can really be one of the most enjoyable parts of a trip. Preparation is just as important whether the trip is for one day or several months. It might grow into a year of decision making, many weekends of vehicle mechanical preparation and perhaps a few hours of "bank trauma".

Planning ahead for a basic weekend trip, with just a camp overnight on the Saturday, usually needs only a few pleasant hours thought and effort, if the 4WD has been maintained properly.

Keeping others informed

Whether you break down at the Erldunda turn-off 4,000 kilometres from home, or just ten minutes from your driveway heading out for the weekend trip, the result is the same – your plans have been altered. If a person is depending on your arrival at another planned destination, that arrangement will also be changed. "Let someone know before you go", as the catch-phrase says. Stick to the planned itinerary.

It is useless for a search to be conducted near Arkaroola, if you are at Broken Hill. If you are expected to be at Arkaroola, that's probably where the search will start. Notify the relevant people of any major change to your itinerary as soon as possible.

People to be notified might include family, local police or people at the original destination. If, for some reason, you are forced to abandon the vehicle and try to walk out for help, leave a clear message inside the vehicle advising possible searchers of your new plans. Leave written details of your departure time, route, destination, expected arrival time and personal or group details.

4X4 **Tip**

A VITAL PART OF DRIVER SAFETY IS KNOWING EVERYTHING YOU CAN ABOUT YOUR VEHICLE.

Safety

It is essential to allow for safety in planning and operation of any outback trip. With major changes and improvements in communication systems you may now be considered totally irresponsible if you venture into remote areas without proper means of communication. The 4WD High-Frequency [HF] Radio Network "737" has largely replaced the Royal Flying Doctor [RFDS] radio network for outback 4WD travellers. Several companies offer communication via virtually-immediate 24-hr world-coverage satellite telephone networks. This type of phone may be vehicle-mounted or hand-held. Some satellite-phone networks also supply a dual-use sat-phone combined with a normal-type CDMA mobile phone. Many hire services provide this type of equipment for 4WD trips at reasonable cost.

Whilst both these options are not cheap to buy, in a genuine life-threatening situation no price can be put on saving human life. The often-enormous cost of mounting a search using emergency-service personnel may not be necessary, or may be greatly minimised, if remote-area 4WD travellers have, and know how to use, proper resources for communication.

Satellites also provide a message-centre for small devices known as "EPIRBs". The letters stand for "Emergency Position-Indicating Radio Beacon". EPIRBs can be either ocean- or land-based, and are coded to indicate which type has been set off. These are mainly small personal transmitters using specific frequencies which transmit data to particular satellites. They are monitored by all overflying aircraft, and Search-and-Rescue centres world-wide, who relay the data to the relevant S&R centre. This data indicates your GPS location, and provides an identifying number registered specifically to you. I believe EPIRBs should be compulsory for all outback travellers, but there is a drawback in their very nature. If one is set off, the presumption is that a situation is critical, and rescue services remote from the problem are brought into action to search for the EPIRB location. Logically, it can be an offence to use an EPIRB in a situation which is not absolutely desperate and potentially life-threatening.

Walking out

Leaving your vehicle and attempting to walk for help is not usually a wise move. In deserts, walking out is strongly advised against, and historically this has proved correct. If you plan for emergencies, carry sensible survival material, and stay with your vehicle you will normally be found in short time. It is much easier to spot a vehicle than a person from the air. Circumstances can change with locations and local knowledge, and a considered decision can really only be made by you, the person in the situation. The danger here can be that many people really in trouble with a vehicle or injury don't have the state of mind to make that considered decision.

There is sadly another risk that needs to be remembered, if you do abandon your vehicle. That is the unfortunate potential for theft of, or from, your vehicle. There is no practical answer to this problem, apart from leaving someone with the vehicle or better still, avoiding vehicle breakdowns. It is also a very good reason for not driving solo if possible.

Local information

Local weather reports can be very important, and there is no better condition report than one from the person on the spot. If you are planning on crossing country on little-used tracks, contact the appropriate government department for local

Tip

THERE IS SOME CONSOLATION AFTER PAYING OUT FOR SPARES: IF YOU DON'T NEED THEM YOU WILL EASILY BE ABLE TO SELL THEM WITH THE VEHICLE, AND THEY WON'T DROP IN PRICE.

A SOUND KNOWLEDGE OF YOUR VEHICLE IS NOT A BONUS – IT IS ESSENTIAL.

knowledge and information about track closures/openings and conditions. Local landholders can be a goldmine of information. Local four-wheel drivers usually have knowledge of probable conditions in areas they use. In remote areas police may be able to advise of road and weather conditions.

Camping equipment

Choice of camping equipment and clothing depends largely on personal preference. Most campers you meet out in the bush are pleased to tell you about their choice in tent, sleeping bag, etc. They've used each item, so they know the good and bad points. The same goes for waterproof or cold weather gear, and useful clothing. If most people you see at a campsite are wearing the same brand of parka, or using the same model of camp-stove, it is reasonable to presume that item is worth buying. Accessory dealers and camping stores can also be a good source of information.

Insurance and roadworthiness

After a tough 4WD trip on a hot day, a cold beer can really go down well. The most important word in that sentence is "after". Insurance may be voided where alcohol is proved to be present or a contributing factor at a motor vehicle accident. Civil claims for compensation against alcohol-affected drivers are becoming common.

If you are towing a trailer, check to see how your insurance cover affects this situation, both from liability and theft/damage aspects. If you are involved in an accident which is not your fault, don't just assume your insurance company won't apportion blame to you because they may very well do so, to your detriment. You really do need to be aware of the limitations of your insurance policy.

Case Study

Lack of knowledge can be dangerous

About an hour's drive west of Wittenoom, Western Australia, there is no human habitation for 60 kilometres in any direction. The track there is about one and a half vehicles wide, and very sandy. In June a few years ago we came across six people in a fairly new twin-cab diesel. The driver had borrowed the vehicle to take his family for a drive inland, about 270 kilometres south-east from South Hedland. They had been stranded for about four hours, in more than 40°C temperatures with an empty fuel tank when we came across them. However, only the main fuel tank was empty – but we found the auxiliary tank was still fairly full. This particular driver had:

- No knowledge of the fuel system
- No manual for that vehicle to help him
- No familiarity with the mechanical aspects of the vehicle
- No apparent effective means of transferring fuel from one tank to another
- No real mechanical ability
- No drinking fluids
- No means of radio contact

After providing some drinking water, we used our experience of diesels to get the motor started. Priming the fuel pump took longer than normal because the driver had tried to bleed the system in several places, allowing air to enter the fuel line. Although it was not a common system, the fuel tank set-up was quite basic — we traced the wiring to a switch that that controlled a concealed electric pump. This was designed to transfer fuel from the accessory tank, behind the cab in the back of the ute, down to the main tank. The driver had run the main tank empty. All he should have done was wait for some fuel from the main tank to be used, then pump some from the accessory tank down to the main tank to replenish it. Those vital ingredients, knowledge and preparation, were both completely missing in this situation, which could have caused loss of life.

Keep your vehicle roadworthy and comprehensively insured. Part of most vehicle insurance is a requirement for a sound vehicle. If a vehicle is proven to be in an unroadworthy condition and is involved in an accident, perhaps resulting in a fatality or permanent serious injury, you may well not receive an insurance payout. Even worse, the prospect of being sued is very unpleasant to consider.

Maintenance and parts

No matter what kind of environment you are heading for, basic planning for vehicle maintenance should include the appropriate and recommended manufacturer's services. This is important if you are heading a long way from home. Needed for maintenance are all the fairly common replacement parts for the vehicle, and some of the less common ones should be carried as well. Petrol engines need ignition components, and for injected petrol motors perhaps a spare injector should be carried. Electronic ignition poses some difficulties, as most parts are expensive, and if they fail they are not commonly found in small outback towns, so keep this in mind.

Injectors and glow-plugs are often expensive to replace. A major diesel fuel-injection service is important before leaving on a long trip, and perhaps a spare injector or tips should be included. Buy a service and repair manual. Even if you can't fix the fault yourself, there is a fair chance you could find another person who may be able to, if you have the right parts, books and tools.

Ten major 4WD trips in outback Australia

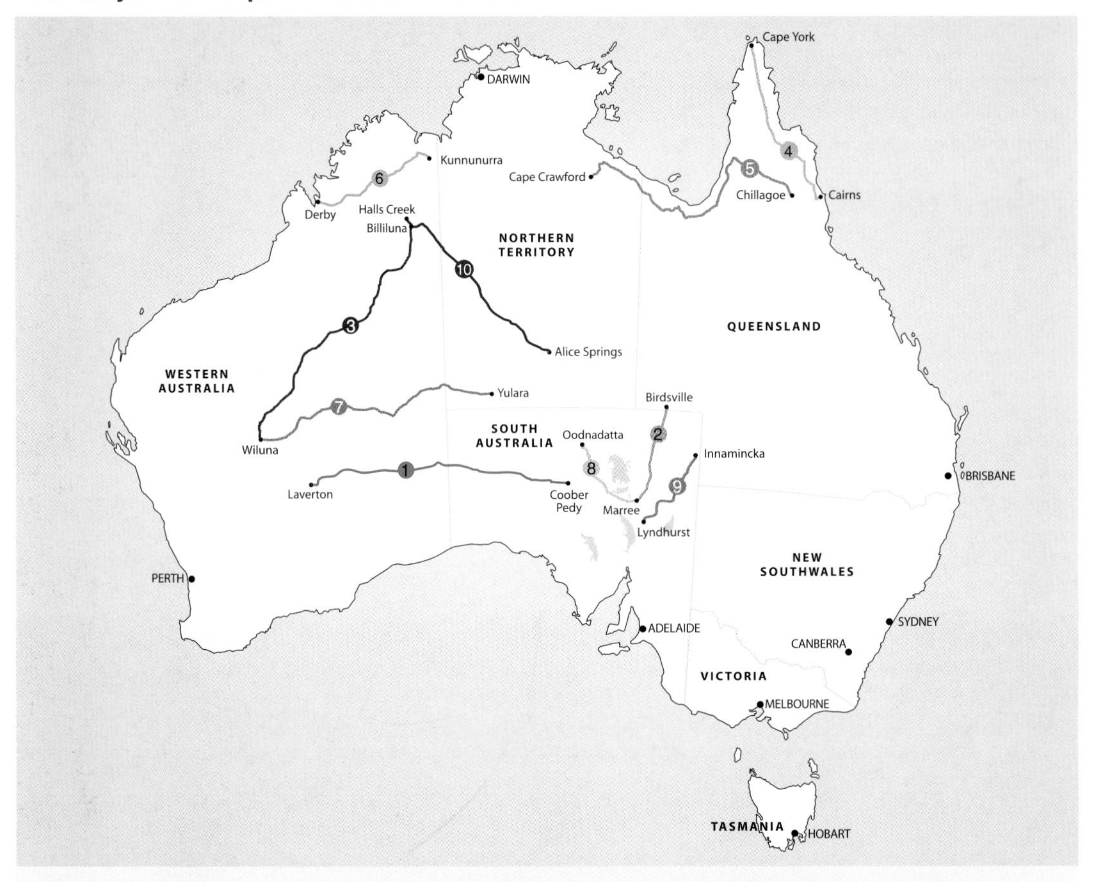

1 Anne Beadell Highway

Running mostly north of the east-west Indian-Pacific rail line, this Len-Beadell-surveyed road crosses the edge of the Nullarbor Plain. Running from Coober Pedy in South Australia to Laverton in Western Australia, the very remote trip passes atomic bomb test sites, nature reserves and salt lakes. Travel permits are required, and human habitation is uncommon. Scrub varies from stunted trees to bare spinifex plains. Bird and animal life is minimal. Sandy soil conditions are poor, often with slippery surfaces and erosion washaways.

2 Birdsville Track

If you want to see the horse racing in September at Birdsville in far south-western Queensland, head almost north from Marree on this track. It passes Sturt's Stony Desert, crosses the world's longest dog-fence, and its remoteness and heat has been responsible for the death of many travellers in early days. Now trafficable to most well-prepared vehicles in the dry season, this famous outback track begins in South Australia.

3 Canning Stock Route

Originally surveyed as an overland route to drove cattle from northern properties in W.A. to southern markets, this difficult track issues a real challenge for drivers of properly-prepared four-wheel-drive vehicles. It has big sand dunes, saltpans, great stony patches and washaways. Along its length are over 50 wells dug by hand to provide water for cattle. There are natural waterholes, some with good campsites. Aboriginal rock art, wildflowers in season and the Wolfe Creek meteorite crater are some of the points of interest. Fuel supplies for travelling vehicles must be arranged. The track runs from Wiluna, at the southern end, to Halls Creek at the top.

4 Cape York Peninsula Development Road

Probably the best-known Australian 4WD track, the “Cape” road begins in Cairns, Queensland. With some very difficult creek and river crossings [and now with a ferry alternative] this route is not trafficable in the wet season (Nov-Mar). In the tourist season the road is heavily travelled, and becomes very corrugated. Passing through grass plains, mountains, patches of tropical rainforest, and light scrub, this is perhaps one of the greatest wilderness areas on the continent. From the most northerly town, Bamaga, it is still over 50kms to the actual top of Australia.

5 Chillagoe–Cape Crawford Road

Starting at Chillagoe, about 200 kilometres west of Cairns, in Queensland, the route loops up into the edge of the gulf country and back down via Normanton. Across “savannah” grass country, it heads west through giant anthills, over river crossings and past thermal springs. Other famous places like Burketown, Hell’s Gate and Borroloola are on the way to the western end, at Cape Crawford in the Northern Territory. For much of the wet season this area can be impassable, and in the tourist season the western end can be noticeably populated.

6 Gibb River Road

Three different groups of mountain ranges make the Gibb River route spectacular viewing. Dependent on road management, severe corrugations in some parts can make vehicular travel difficult. It has a reputation for damaging equipment but is quite trafficable to most well-prepared vehicles moving at steady speeds. As some river crossings are wide, access in the wet season can be restricted. Starting near Derby in W.A., the road ends 590 kilometres later at Kununurra.

7 Gunbarrel Highway

One of the earliest roads constructed by surveyor Len Beadell and his “Gunbarrel Road Construction” crew, as part of the early British atomic trials at Woomera, “the Gunbarrel” begins practically where the bitumen ends, just west of Yulara near Ayer’s Rock [Uluru] in the N.T. About 120 kilometres into W.A. the track heads off north-east, and eventually ends at Wiluna, about 550kms north of Kalgoorlie, W.A. This can be a long, difficult and tiring drive, even in well-prepared 4WD vehicles. [The Gunbarrel Hwy should not be confused with the easier-travelling “Great Central Road” between Leonora and the N.T. border. Both roads pass through quite remote areas].

8 Oodnadatta Track

Running generally north-west from Marree in South Australia, this track passes the front door of the famous “William Creek” pub, to end at Oodnadatta. Several western turnoffs will lead out to the Stuart Highway. (Following the old “Ghan” railway line through Finke the track can go on to Alice Springs.) Some points of interest include unusual “mound springs” caused by artesian water, and a number of old building and railway ruins. Like any in this area, this track can be very slippery in any wet conditions.

9 Strzelecki Track

Beginning at Lyndhurst, 80 kilometres south of Marree, S.A., the Strzelecki Track runs almost parallel to, but east of, the Birdsville Track. 50 kilometres shorter, it ends at Innamincka on the bank of Cooper’s Creek, and almost on the S.A.-QLD border. The famous “DIG” tree, part of the story of the explorers Burke and Wills, is not far from there. A waterhole never known to run dry, abundant birdlife, the rebuilt “A.I.M” hospital and aboriginal rock art are some of the local attractions. The Moomba oil- and gas-field traffic has resulted in improved road surfaces.

10 Tanami Track

This track begins near Alice Springs, N.T., leads north-west through Yuendumu, and passes the well-known Rabbit Flat roadhouse. In W.A. it joins with the Canning Stock Route, ending close to Hall’s Creek. It crosses the Central Desert, and has a considerable number of sandy patches, which can make driving difficult in some places. Much of this track is in quite remote areas and help may not be readily available.

Checklist

Basic parts worth carrying on a long trip

- All drivebelts, (alternator, water pump, radiator fan, power steering, air-conditioner).
- All engine hoses (heater, radiator, bypass, power steering).
- Sufficient quantities of correct lubricants (differentials, gearbox and transfer case, engine sump, automatic transmission if fitted).
- Fluids (radiator coolant, power steering fluid (usually ATF), brake and clutch fluid, distilled water).
- One each of all filters (air, fuel, oil).
- Several of each type of light-globe on the vehicle.
- An efficient trouble-light.
- Full set of electrical fuses.

EVEN IF YOU DON'T HAVE THE NECESSARY SKILLS TO FIX IT YOURSELF, HAVING THE RIGHT SPARES CAN ENABLE SOMEONE ELSE TO FIX IT FOR YOU.

Parts to carry

Some 4WD clubs insist on a predetermined list of spare parts to be carried, graded according to the kind of trip to be undertaken. You should carefully note the parts nominated, as these lists have been drawn up from hard, often costly, experience. It is expensive to buy genuine replacement parts, and in some cases less expensive non-genuine components are satisfactory. In the case of heater hoses, for example, some vehicles simply must be fitted with the genuine part because no accessory company makes an alternative hose. Be sure the part you carry actually does fit, by buying genuine parts or trying the fit.

Replacement parts may also need clamps, funnels, containers and maybe Special Service or Dealer Tools to change them, so these should be carried as well. Basic personal survival and vehicle recovery equipment should always be carried, apart from these parts. Again, these will vary according to the kind of trip planned.

Other essential items

In hot weather, you will need plenty of water to drink, and enough for the radiator as well, if things go wrong. Food is always required. Warm clothing is vital. It might be 40°C in the outback during the day, but below freezing point at night. Breakdowns often happen in the dark, so sufficient lighting to work on the vehicle is needed. A small tarp or similar to lie on while underneath the vehicle is a very useful item, and the same tarp could also be used for shielding the motor during deep water crossings. Don't go out without an effective tow-rope; it can be used by you for someone else in distress, or vice versa. The extras list, which can be quite long, needs to be determined according to conditions where you are going.

Fuel

If you are planning to cover long stages with no guaranteed source of fuel, you should be well aware of the fuel consumption of the vehicle before you leave. This is quite easy to check. Fill the fuel tank(s) to the top, and drive it for a tankful in similar conditions and with a load similar to that you are planning to carry on the trip. Refill the tank properly at the end of the test, calculate the usage, and you'll have a fairly reliable basis for working out how much fuel will be needed to cover the long sections, and over a general distance. In really bad going, always allow for using half as much fuel again as you calculated in the first place.

Working out ways to carry enough fuel can be a source of concern. Jerrycans are good, but they should not be carried on vehicle roofracks. (There are specific jerrycan-racks that can be fitted on the rear bumper or spare tyre holder on some vehicles.) Carrying jerrycans inside the vehicle is dangerous; carrying fuel in a trailer is okay, but not everyone wants to tow a trailer. An alternative, and not a cheap one, is to have an auxiliary fuel tank fitted. Most 4WD shops can arrange this, or do-it-yourself kits are available.

A GOOD SUPPLY OF THE RIGHT TOOLS IS ESSENTIAL. MAKE SURE YOU KNOW HOW TO USE EACH ONE.

Preparation Checklist

Using a checklist for preparation can reduce risks and increase your trip capabilities. Add ideas to help rough out additional plans of your own before setting out. Although this looks like a serious list it isn't really, and it could help save you from a life-threatening situation. Some of these questions may not be relevant to the average 4WD trip, but for a major outback journey many of these points need careful consideration.

- Who should be notified before you go concerning your route, possible stops, likely camp spots, expected times and estimated return time?
- Are you experienced enough to safely do the trip you are planning?
- Are the other drivers, if any, capable of driving in the conditions you expect to find, and what happens if there is a sudden emergency?
- Is your vehicle (and accompanying vehicles) in a roadworthy and safe condition to do the trip?
- Do you have recovery gear, survival clothing, first-aid kit, adequate food and drink in the vehicle for the trip, and do you know how to use all of the equipment safely?
- Have you checked the telephone network coverage pattern to find whether mobile phones work where you are going?
- If you are going to a remote area, do you have a Royal Flying Doctor Service or 4WD HF "737" Network radio with decent antenna (and appropriate licence), do you know their RX/TX system, and can you use the radio effectively?
- Are you carrying any EPIRB, HF transceiver or two-way radio, mobile or satellite-phone capable of getting an emergency or communications signal out if necessary?
- If you can't make needed communication from your location, could you carry your radio/battery/antenna to a high point, reassemble it, and make it work up there?
- Have you prearranged radio schedules and frequencies or channels or other message method with someone reliable to advise of your progress, location, or to get help?
- Assume your vehicle is broken down, immobile and you are overdue on time — if you can make radio or other contact with someone unknown to you, who do you want the message delivered to – home, work, friends, 4WD club, police, doctor, etc.?
- What information will you include in the message?
- If the message is to someone at a private residence, will the person be there at the time to accept the message, and what backup do you have if the person is not home?
- What fail-safe have you built in to your trip timing – who should notify what necessary people if you or your group are overdue by what margin of time, and does your main contact know the names and phone numbers of all the people in the group?
- How long should your main contact or base wait before finally and officially notifying the relevant authorities, and what bodies should be notified?
- In the event of a mechanical breakdown, is there a back-up crew that could get in to assist you, or will police, rescue personnel or commercial vehicle recovery help be needed?

- If your trip comes to a stop from mechanical causes or minor injury or illness, could you or your crew solve the situation?
- If there are injuries, could you determine if they are really serious enough to require official and urgent help?
- If your vehicle is bogged, would you reasonably expect to extract it with the equipment you are carrying?
- Do you, or one of your group, have enough mechanical knowledge to diagnose mechanical problems and are you carrying the necessary service and repair manuals, tools and spares to attempt a basic repair on-site?
- In the case of a serious mechanical breakdown could you rig something up temporarily to get you back out of trouble?
- If the 4WD mechanical breakdown is terminal, would it be safe to walk out for help; and where is the nearest likely help?
- Do you have tools and recovery gear in your 4WD, or shared among the group, appropriate to do most mechanical repairs, and spares appropriate for most immobilising breakdowns that you could realistically fix?
- In a worst-case scenario, if running late in bad off-road conditions at night, do you and the rest of your group have the knowledge, skills and abilities to continue driving safely?
- If you are going into a wet area, have you allowed enough trip time in your plans to wait for the tracks to dry out so you can drive out when it is dry?
- Are you comfortable enough with map reading and/or your GPS unit to confidently establish your position or find your way on the map, and have you read the map properly and checked the routes and/or waypoints before leaving?
- Do you have the necessary permits, if your trip will go through restricted areas?
- If you have to detour during the trip, do you have enough local knowledge or good maps or a GPS unit to plan an alternative route out?
- Do you know basic "ground-to-air" signals in case something goes really wrong and an air search is begun?
- If the worst happened and medical evacuation was needed, does the recovery kit contain smoke flares or similar?

MAINTENANCE AND MODIFICATIONS

IN THIS SECTION

- Maintenance of 4WDs
- Mechanical Exercises
- Modifications and Clearances
- Steering, Tyres and Suspension
- Gearboxes and Gears
- 4WD Transfer Gearbox and Hubs
- Clutch, Brakes and Differentials
- Breakdowns, 'Fixits' and Services
- Emergency Vehicle Starting
- Accessories, Tools and Parts

Maintenance of 4WDs

Advice

RARELY IS THERE ANYTHING UNACCEPTABLE ABOUT ORIGINAL-EQUIPMENT STOCK-SIZE TYRES, AND FOR MOST DRIVING CONDITIONS AGGRESSIVE RUBBER PROBABLY ISN'T THE ANSWER.

Manuals

What price would you put on avoiding the combination of (a) being broken down in the desert, (b) with sufficient tools, (c) a good chance of being able to fix the problem, (d) another driver to help you, but (e) no specific information about the lift pump on a current 4WD diesel? Perhaps you have all the right spare parts and ample tools but you still can't get going. The odds of finding another driver who can help and one who knows enough about the particular trouble are fairly good. But without the necessary manual, your chances are a lot worse. Having a service and repair manual and knowing how to use it is a worthwhile investment.

Tools

An absolute must to include on any trip well away from home is a decent tool kit. If your vehicle is not "metric" (most Japanese vehicles are metric) be sure to buy the correct "imperial" tools. Common terms for imperial tools, including nuts, bolts and threads are: SAE, AF and Whitworth. Land Rover (British) and Jeep (American) are normally imperial. Imperial applies to nuts, bolts, threads and tools which are measured in inches, e.g. $^{9}/_{16}$-inch AF (short for "across flats", which means across the two parallel flats on a bolt head or nut) is a common size for the heads of 4WD nuts and bolts. Metric tools, bolts and threads (including a type known as ISO) are measured in millimetres or parts thereof. As a general rule, metric spanners will fit sufficiently well onto imperial nuts and bolts, but this happens less the other way around. Spanners known as "metrinch" will cope well with both metric and imperial items.

Tyres

Tyres on a 4WD are not that easy to fit on a concrete garage floor, much less on the side of a hill in the wet and dark. I have had good cause to really appreciate those five white-spoke split rims on one of my 4WDs, because the tyres fitted to them were not hard to remove or refit when a tube was punctured. The rims look good, unlike normal commercial type wheels, because the split is on the inside, not

Case Study

A tyre survey

I once pulled in to the famous William Creek pub near the top of South Australia about the same time of day as a crew from an oil exploration company. There were 15 assorted Toyota 4WD vehicles, a Nissan and a Holden ute. Just to satisfy my curiosity I looked at the tyre types and sizes. The two Hilux utes had stock 205SR16s all round, the Nissan on its standard grey steel split rims had 7.50x16 radials, and all the other 4WDs were factory-type 7.50x16s on original rims. Later on I asked one of the desert-based seismic exploration crew about his tyres, and his answer was pointed. He said, "If I needed better or bigger tyres or wheels, I'd have them fitted. I can get a spare 7.50x16 tyre almost anywhere, and with a standard split rim I can easily fix it if I have to. Why change?"

normally seen. See pages 125–133 for more information on wheels and tyres.

Aftermarket accessories and fittings are sometimes the best way to get a vehicle set up for a specific trip. But if a vehicle absolutely had to have twelve-inch-wide aggressive-tread steel-belted radial tyres, with the brand name highlighted in raised white letters on the sidewalls so that it would perform as the manufacturer intended, wouldn't the original vehicle manufacturer fit such tyres?

Brakes

4WD vehicles are usually heavy, a good reason for having first-class well-maintained brakes. Most current-model 4WDs now have disc brakes front and rear. Checking front disc pads for wear generally only takes a minute or two, as in most cases they are easy to see when the wheels are turned to full lock either way. If your 4WD has drum brakes at the rear you will have to remove the two back wheels and then the brake drums, to check the condition of the brake shoes. Good brakes are vital, and for driving on sloped ground the handbrake is also important.

Rear drums are used for a handbrake because they are usually more effective for this purpose than disc brakes. A handbrake operating on the transmission, i.e., a band or drum brake able to stop the rear tailshaft from turning, is a very effective type because it positively locks up the rear wheels. Most handbrakes work mechanically on the rear brakes in each wheel via a cable, with a ratchet in the handbrake lever to lock them on. The pressure or leverage available through the handbrake is nowhere

Tyre comparison

AFTERMARKET
33 x12.5R15
8" wide rim
(203 mm)

15" diameter rim
(381 mm)

33" O/D
(838 mm)

12.5" wide tyre
(317 mm)

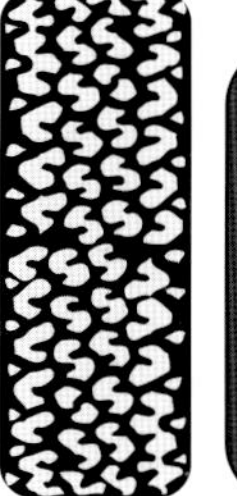

ORIGINAL
10R15
8" wide rim
(203 mm)

15" diameter rim
(381 mm)

30.8" O/D
(771 mm)

10.9" wide tyre
(274 mm)

GOOD BRAKES ARE VITAL ON A 4WD AND MAINTENANCE, ESPECIALLY ON DRUM BRAKES, MUST BE REGULAR.

near as powerful as with the normal, hydraulically operated footbrakes. Check your service manual for specific adjustment procedures with any brakes, or get them done professionally. For more information on maintenance and operation of brakes see page 147.

Rust and corrosion

4WDs are subject to rust and corrosion. Look at any vehicle regularly used on beaches, e.g. those on Fraser Island, and you'll find a 4WD with a body life-span generally of only a few years. Whether steel or alloy bodied, vehicles normally get eaten away by the various acids, alkalis and other destructive elements in which a 4WD can travel. Rust or electrolysis — the end result is the same: coal mines, cow yards, alkaline bore water or beach salt water all damage 4WDs.

When parking at the beach after launching the boat, even if your rear wheels didn't get far into the water, your vehicle has driven over salty sand and also probably has airborne salt spray on the paintwork. Look after it by washing it properly. After a great Sunday 4WD trip, taking an extra quarter-of-an-hour to clean the underneath and outside your 4WD is worth it to keep the vehicle living longer.

As a means of minimising rust in hot water service tank walls, sacrificial anodes are common. In a parallel way, similar technologies and other electronic rust prevention systems now provide rust minimisation for 4WDs. This concept is already well accepted on ships and buildings

Squeaks and rattles

Squeaks and rattles in 4WDs are fairly common without careful maintenance, and they tend to happen with the passage of time anyway. Plastic mouldings and panels are a typical source of annoying noises. Rattling towbar goosenecks, squeaks from dry springs or other suspension parts, grinding sounds from body panels as the body flexes, rattles in internal mechanisms inside the door — and so the list goes on. There is also vibration throughout the body, particularly with diesels. 4WDs ride harder or stiffer than normal cars to cope better with rougher roads, although with good seats the ride can be quite smooth. Most 4WDs feel the larger bumps and if the passengers feel a bump it was probably a decent pothole.

This toughness in 4WD suspension can lead to trouble when towing unless you make some allowances. Many drivers sitting up in the relatively isolated and reasonably comfortable cabin have no idea just how hard the poor old trailer or caravan is doing it,

Case Study

Bad vibrations

One example of vibration damage discovered during routine observation and maintenance involved a diesel-engine 4WD fitted with an aftermarket, in-line water-trap fuel filter on a specially made support bracket. The job looked first-class. When the filter element was routinely changed at 5,000 kilometres, the owner thought the glass sight-bowl below the filter canister felt loose. Careful checking revealed the main support bracket for the filter housing was faulty, although at first view it just appeared that the bolts mounting it to the engine block were loose. Tightening them made no difference to the movement. The unit was removed, and a virtually invisible fatigue fracture was found in the main weld.

hanging behind the vehicle in the dust or mud and bumps.

Vibrations

Travelling the length of the Gunbarrel Highway is a very rough trip. After this kind of trip it is not uncommon to find fatigue cracking in various metals. It is worth a careful examination. My bullbar suffered badly. It is alloy, but before steel disciples pay out and say, "That wouldn't happen with a steel bullbar", manufacturer or material would have made no difference on the seemingly never-ending corrugations along some sections of that six-days-travel "highway". Vibration can be a destroyer, so here are some valuable tips I found out the hard way.

Make sure all mounting brackets attached to the front crossbar to take driving lights or radio antennas are properly welded on both the top and the underside. If it is a bracket for a heavy antenna, gusset the underside as well.

All six brackets welded to my bar cracked from vibration fatigue. Cibie Oscars are solid driving lights, and a big RFDS radio antenna is also heavy. A 60-inch CB antenna is not very heavy, but the brackets carrying the antennae fatigued, drooped, and eventually broke. As a result of that experience these brackets are now gusseted as well as welded on both sides. The support mounts to the chassis on one steel bullbar also broke, leaving it dangling. Other light and radio antenna brackets

CAREFUL PREPARATION AND APPROPRIATE USE OF SPEED HELP REDUCE VIBRATION DAMAGE.

Welding to avoid vibration damage

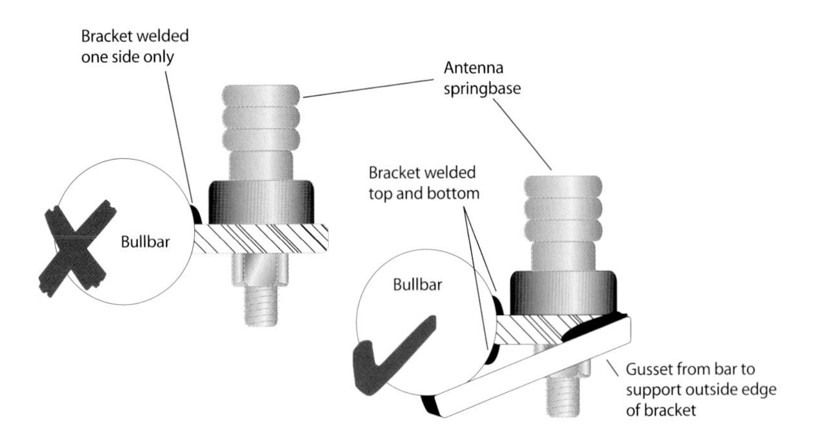

on steel bars were also damaged. On some vehicles radiator support frames cracked, and soldered top tanks on radiators had seams opened. Later examination of several 4WDs during the trip revealed damaged plates in batteries due to vibration, despite carpet and rubber matting under each battery. Helped by heavy loads, 4WD ride characteristics and those corrugations, damage occurred to mufflers, engine pipes, roofracks, mudflaps, trailer suspension and filaments in all kinds of lights. There doesn't seem to be a solution to this problem apart from careful preparation, and perhaps driving at a different speed.

Fans

Many vehicles have liquid-filled thermo-type fans which don't spin much until the central boss and the radiator get hot. Drivers of vehicles with this kind of fan don't need to worry too much on creek crossings. Vehicles with electric thermatic fans also have no real trouble driving in water, because these battery-driven fans can usually be switched off. But 4WDs with belt-driven radiator fans need a little extra time to prepare for crossing deep water. The blades on these fans are permanently spinning while the motor is running, and in deepish water they spray water around the engine bay. If in doubt, disconnect the fanbelt.

The sprayed water sometimes causes a failure of the electrical system, if it is a petrol engine, and often this results in a breakdown. In some cases water back-pressure can cause the fan blades to be pushed or sucked into the rear of the radiator cooling fins, causing damage to the radiator. The safest precaution is to loosen the fanbelt sufficiently or remove it so that it won't drive the fan, then tighten or replace it after the crossing. Many motors driving two or three belts are fitted with idler pulleys for each belt, so adjusting belt tension is relatively quick and easy (see diagram on page 159).

Fuel tanks

Working out fuel usage, I use "kilometres per litre", despite the efforts of some to convert me. I know my vehicle gets about 450 kilometres to a tankful in hard-going conditions. On the blacktop (bitumen) in easier driving, from the same tank I can get about 600 kilometres. When the gauge shows quarter full, that's about 20 useable litres left, so at 6 km/L I expect to be able to do around 120 kilometres. Notice the reference to useable litres. An empty, run-dry 90-litre tank might only take 75 litres on a refill. In this case

Advice

MAINTENANCE TIME DOESN'T COST – IT PAYS.

15 litres in the tank cannot be used. Check your vehicle and be sure just how much fuel you can really put into the tank, because capacities of individual vehicle tanks vary.

You'll get most distance on flat ground; sand dunes and mountain slopes sometimes slosh or drain the fuel away from the fuel inlet or pick-up point inside the tank.

Most fuel pick-ups or inlets are towards the front of the tank. In an uphill situation, remember that with not much fuel left in a tank, the fuel may be at the rear and air might get into the fuel line. This often causes engine stoppage. In most cases, restarting becomes merely a brief nuisance in a petrol-engine vehicle, but it can be time-consuming and annoying for some diesels.

Carrying and storage of fuel can be a nuisance. Many four-wheel drivers carry spare fuel in jerrycans, often up on the roofrack. Full jerrycans up there change the vehicle's centre of gravity and affect the way it handles. To help reduce body lean or sway the containers can be laid flat, which is a good way to carry them. However, the lid seals might leak unless they are in good condition. If the cans are too full expansion from the sun's heat can make them weep or bulge and split. Full fuel cans are heavy and place a lot of strain on the roofrack and its mounting points. Never carry them inside a vehicle as fumes can be very dangerous. Specially made carry-racks for jerrycans of fuel on rear bumpers is one effective way to carry them. Do not carry them at the front due to risk of them splitting and causing a fire in the event of a collision. LPG containers should not be carried inside a vehicle either. Regulations vary from state to state on carrying explosive fuel in a vehicle. Check with an authorised gas fitter to be sure.

The best option is dual (auxiliary or accessory) fuel tanks. There are several fuel-tank systems. In one type fuel is electrically pumped from the auxiliary tank to the original tank; in another an on–off tap controls gravity feed of fuel from the high-mounted auxiliary tank down into the original one.

Advice

BE SURE THAT YOU KNOW ALL POSSIBLE COSTS WHEN FITTING AN AFTERMARKET FUEL TANK. EXTRAS SUCH AS MOVING OR MAKING A NEW EXHAUST SYSTEM MAY BE REQUIRED.

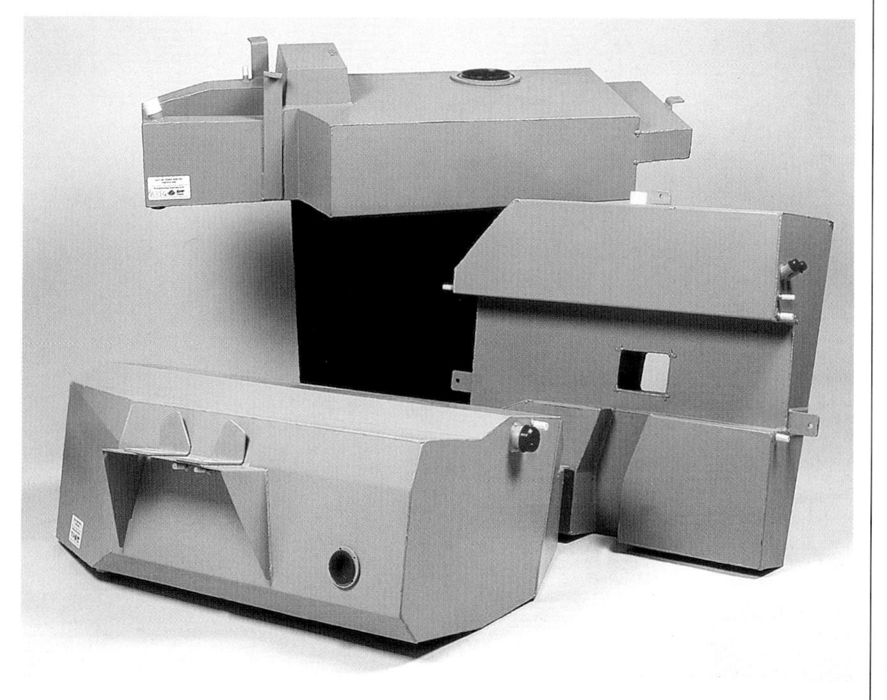

LONG-RANGE FUEL TANKS ARE GREAT FOR LONG TRIPS BECAUSE THEY AVOID THE NEED TO CARRY EXTRA FUEL ON THE ROOF-RACK OR INSIDE THE VEHICLE.

Caution

GO TO A REPUTABLE REGISTERED COMPANY TO HAVE INSTALLATION OR SERVICE DONE ON YOUR GAS SYSTEM.

Some vehicle manufacturers offer a larger replacement tank, which can be supplied in place of the standard one. A second factory-fitted tank is also available for some makes of 4WD. An extra tank can be made or bought aftermarket, specifically made to fit in any remaining space under the floor. Accessory fuel tanks, mounted underbody like the original, are very effective providing they are well engineered, properly fitted, solidly mounted and protected.

The switching for fuel feed between tanks, and fuel gauges to show content of each tank may be as simple as flicking a switch. Fuel is supplied from tanks to the motor in several ways. Most often it is held in both the original tank and the auxiliary tank, each of them with a fuel line connected to a double control valve or tap of some sort.

From a common point for the two inlets, a single fuel line usually runs forward to the engine. Mechanical twist taps with two inlets (from the tanks) and one outlet (to the engine) are cheap and effective. Another tank-switching method is an electrically powered solenoid-operated valve. A switch is operated by the driver to activate the valve and select the tank from which the fuel is taken.

Many current 4WDs have an auxiliary or sub-tank fitted from new. Both tanks usually have their own fuel gauge. In most cases engine access to the extra fuel storage uses the simplest system of all where the fuel is simply pumped from the sub-tank into the main one. It is pumped through a fuel filter on the transfer, and from there it is used normally.

Petrol–gas dual-fuel conversions are quite common, and gas is available on most well-travelled roads. It is used as a "commuter fuel" in petrol-hungry 4WDs and can be a very valuable conversion, but the set-up costs can be quite expensive. Most automobile clubs have articles in their magazines on this topic, a good place to start your research. In some 4WDs the space needed to fit a gas cylinder (or tank) means that the original fuel tank has to be moved, usually from behind the rear axle. In turn, another tank may be required to replace the original one in size and new position, all of which is added into the conversion cost.

Running on gas (LPG or LNG) is noticeably cheaper than petrol, balanced on cost per litre per kilometre. Because there are many different types of gas conversion, you should only go to a reputable registered company to have installation or service done on your gas system. Regulations on gas installations are strict and vary from state to state. If you have purchased a second-hand 4WD it is wise to have the gas system thoroughly checked by a licensed fitter, for safety and efficiency. Using gas as a fuel is easy, as is filling the tank. For safety reasons it is best to learn about your system from a person qualified to explain it to you. There can be traps in some systems when changing on the go from one fuel to another, and it may be necessary to follow special procedures.

Checklist

Regular checks

- Tyres with cuts in the sidewalls.
- Rusty stains anywhere on the radiator.
- Weeps or stains which could indicate a fluid or oil leak on the sump or sump guard, around filler or drain plugs or gaskets on the gearbox, transfer case or differentials, on brake backing plates, or around carburettors and fuel pumps.
- Exhaust pipes hanging down or with broken hangers or brackets.

Five-minute P•E•T•R•O•L check

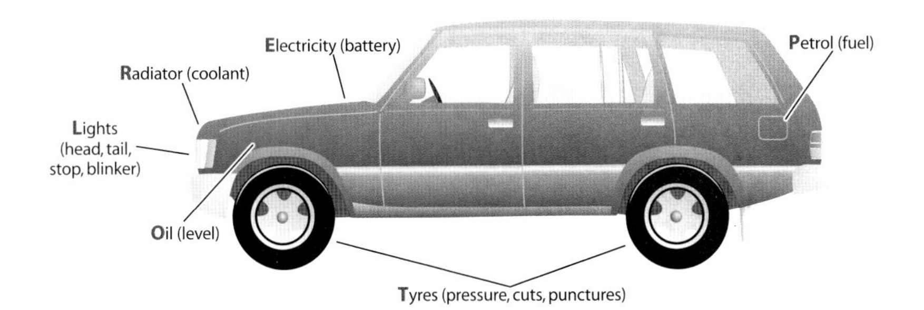

Some aftermarket fuel fillers can be a source of annoyance. Completely separate filler necks or different fillers for each tank are free from this particular nuisance. A Y-shape filler only has one fuel cap, where two tanks can be filled from the neck of the same inlet pipe. One filler pipe branches down to the original tank while the other goes to the auxiliary tank. The positioning of the fuel pump nozzle in the filler neck determines which tank gets fuel.

Regardless of which tank the fuel is being drawn from, excess fuel pumped up to the motor but not used is returned to a tank, usually the original one. Whether the fuel has sloshed into another tank or has been returned via the excess fuel line, fuel usage calculations may sometimes seem wrong. Checking content on a tank which was used well down, but which the gauge now shows to have more fuel in it than before, can be confusing. It is worth asking for an explanation of how the fuel system works from the accessory tank supplier before purchase.

Maintenance routine

Without sensible care a 4WD can be a major liability, rapidly taking the fun out of driving. Believing you'll get through a bad situation in a poorly maintained vehicle when you are way off the beaten track could cost you more than just dollars. The longer you leave maintenance, the more it is likely to cost. A badly maintained vehicle is more likely to break down, perhaps at the worst moment. Experience has shown that changing engine oil regularly at 5,000 kilometres can easily extend an engine's effective life by several years. A few oil changes is a small cost for that difference.

Keep a record of service and parts so that it is easy to check when a particular job was done or when a doubtful part was last serviced. Record the odometer reading, replacement item and cost and keep service receipts to help sell your vehicle when the time comes.

There's a simple acronym to help remember a basic maintenance routine each time you refuel: P.E.T.R.O.L. The check only takes a couple of minutes. The letters stand for:

Petrol (or whatever fuel your vehicle needs)
Electricity (the correct electrolyte level in the essential batteries)
Tyres (air pressures and obvious tread or sidewall cuts or bubbles)
Radiator (coolant level, via the overflow bottle if fitted)
Oil (sump content via the dipstick)
Lights (stop, tail, head, blinkers and numberplate)

Listen to the motor when it is warm for unusual noises which might indicate a need for proper checking. As a general rule, cold motors make horrible noises and most of them go away when the motor has warmed up. If in doubt, reassurance from a good mechanic also having a careful listen to noises in your motor usually costs nothing.

Most four-wheel drivers are optimists. They expect that nothing will go wrong during the short trip just up into the local mountains or across into the local sand dunes. Most times nothing does. The best plan is to take into account the worst-case scenario, and allow for that. Full recovery gear shouldn't be necessary if three well-prepared and properly maintained 4WDs are just going up into the local hills in bright sunshine at 9.00 am, half-an-hour from home.

But if you are several hours from home, alone and without communication, it is beginning to rain, the country is steep, it is almost dark and then you puncture a tyre, things can get a bit miserable. Then when you find the spare tyre has only 10 pounds per square inch (psi) of air pressure, it gets very miserable very quickly.

Proper and regular maintenance is one of the most important aspects of owning a 4WD. Most owners feel that because the vehicle is tough it doesn't matter if it gets a bit of a hard time. A 4WD is designed to take much more abuse than a normal car, but on the other hand it needs proportionally more maintenance. Use only top-quality greases and oils for reliability and value. Read the vehicle handbook or a service and repair manual to check on all the parts which need servicing. Note and remember the total number and location of grease nipples, oil filler plugs and other details needed during routine interval servicing. (Check that you have the necessary tools if you are planning to do your own servicing.)

On one of my vehicles there were eight grease nipples — three on the tailshaft, three on the propshaft and one on each end of the steering tie-rod. These were all I had to grease on each 5,000 kilometre service. I also made a quick oil-level check of five filler or seal plugs — sump, gearbox and transfer, front and rear diffs. By the time I had a look over the vehicle for things obviously wrong, it had taken only about half an hour to do all of this.

Unfortunately the ignorance of many 4WD owners [and in some cases I'm sure it is deliberate] makes them victims. Certainly it has lead to rip-offs by some dealers and mechanical service outlets. Perhaps the ignorance is wilful and deliberate on the part of the mechanic, or the workshop supervisor, or the service manager, but there is no doubt at all that it exists. Pleading "pressure of work" is not an excuse. Many unknowing 4WD owners, amongst others of course, are the losers.

For just one example, I was recently told by a 4WD owner about an oil filter. He bought the vehicle second-hand from a chap whom he believed assured him honestly that the vehicle had been faithfully serviced by a well-known Sydney 4WD dealer's workshop. The service book did show the vehicle had been well-serviced five times, with new oil and filter each time as the original owner had directed. It was due for a 30,000km service, and from curiosity the new owner checked the oil filter.

He found that without any doubt at all the filter was the original one fitted to the vehicle when new. The original paint was obviously still in place, but there were signs that someone had attempted to forcibly but unsuccessfully remove the filter. The second owner put the vehicle in for service at the same dealer, without mentioning the oil filter matter. He was not surprised when he checked again after the service, to find the original filter still there, but the service invoice showed the oil and filter had been changed. Mechanical ignorance is not bliss!

With a large investment of money in your 4WD it makes sense to stick

4X4 **Tip**

KEEPING YOUR VEHICLE CLEAN INSIDE THE CABIN, IN THE ENGINE BAY, OUTSIDE AND UNDERNEATH IS JUST PART OF GOOD MAINTENANCE.

Under the bonnet

Some quick and basic checks include:

- Are the fluids for automatic transmission, brakes, clutch, power steering, radiator and/or overflow, batteries, and front and back screen washers, all at their correct level?
- Are the clamps for all hoses tight and in their correct positions?
- Are the drivebelts tight?
- Is the bracket holding the horns loose?

Pushing on a battery to see if there is any movement in the hold-down clamps, pulling on an exhaust pipe to see or hear if a support bracket or hanger is loose or broken, looking at a brake drum or backing-plate to see if there is a visible weep of fluid — these things take hardly any time at all to do and are all simple, sound maintenance practices.

Checklist

to the recommended schedules for maintenance. As well as regular commonsense checks, the recommended 5,000 and 10,000 kilometre checks and services improve the mechanical safety of your vehicle, and preserve its value. Because 4WDs are made for tough conditions, owners sometimes relax their maintenance schedule and don't worry too much if a grease and oil-change or new filter is well overdue. Doing this consistently could be very expensive. Regular checks of the vehicle should become a habit and the few minutes it takes may well save work-hours and parts-dollars later on in the vehicle's life. If you routinely open the bonnet, as well as climb under and walk around your 4WD, carefully looking at all the different parts, you tend to become familiar with how they look. It becomes easy then to notice if something seems to be different from the last time you looked.

Keeping your vehicle clean inside the cabin, in the engine bay, outside and underneath is just part of good maintenance. It is much harder to see if something is amiss if your vehicle is dirty, simply because dirt can hide a multitude of faults. When you wash the engine bay, check each part as you clean it as a part of sensible preventative maintenance.

There are some easy checks listed above that only take a few minutes to do while the bonnet is open and the vehicle is on flat ground.

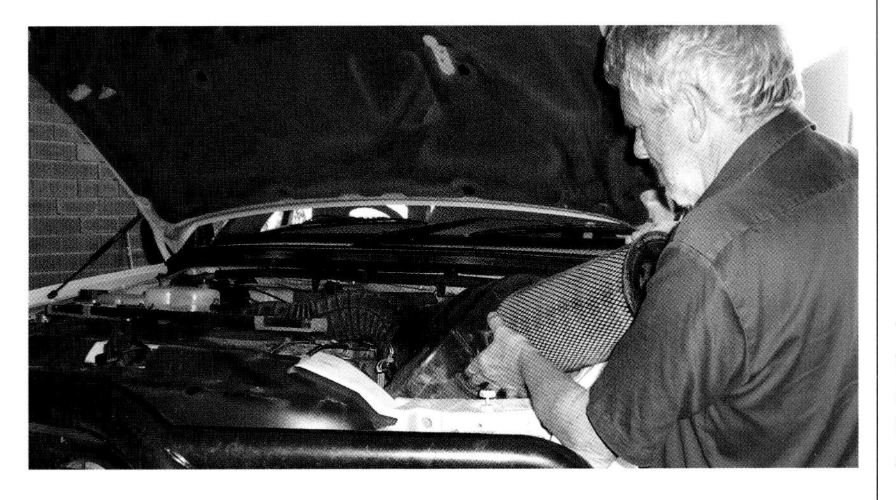

TO ENJOY GETTING WHERE YOUR 4WD CAN TAKE YOU, MAINTENANCE IS A MUST.

Mechanical Exercises

Dry runs

If you are not mechanically familiar with your vehicle there is no better place to experiment and learn than in your own backyard. Little harm can come to a 4WD parked in the driveway. Besides, if you flatten the battery it is easy to get help from a battery charger, or someone with another vehicle and a pair of jumper leads. With help from a service and repair manual most jobs tackled by owners are straightforward. Other drivers with similar vehicles can also be a valuable source of information, and this is another good reason to join a 4WD club.

There is no better way to find out about your vehicle's mechanicals than to work on it yourself. It is far easier when there is no pressure on you, and is clearly more dangerous to have to learn when you are in a bad position. As well as learning about your vehicle in a static environment, don't forget to practice various tasks while you are up in the hills or out in the desert — it is all a learning process.

Advice

PRACTICE TIME TAKEN DOESN'T COST —IT PAYS.

Starting

Vehicles with auto gearboxes will normally only start with the gear selector lever in either "P" [Park] or "N" [Neutral]. Starting the engine itself is exactly the same as for any other vehicle. If your vehicle runs on Liquefied Petroleum Gas [LPG] or Liquefied Natural Gas [LNG], providing there is gas it will normally start when the key is turned. In general, there is no need to touch the accelerator pedal till the engine actually starts. There is no choke on a gas converter, which does the same job as a carburettor on a petrol engine. Some models of LPG/LNG engine may have a primer pump, where a button is pushed for a second or two to allow gas to enter the cylinders to aid starting, but this is not a common function.

Experiment with starting your vehicle. But first, make sure you are sitting properly in the driver's seat. Before starting the engine you must have control of the vehicle, so that it does not move during the operation. If you have a vehicle with manual transmission, push the clutch in before turning the ignition key. If you have not checked that the gearbox is in neutral, the depressed clutch will prevent the vehicle lurching. Most drivers know how to start a petrol motor when cold. Unless it has an automatic choke it is usually just a matter of pulling the choke knob full out, and turning the ignition key to start the motor, generally using no (or very little) accelerator. Then again, some petrol-engine 4WDs just don't want to start first up without full choke and full throttle. By trying out combinations it is surprising what you learn.

In a petrol engine the choke has the effect of making the fuel-to-air mixture richer and easier to burn. The word "choke" is appropriate it cuts the air supply, and this has the effect of increasing the fuel-to-air ratio. After the motor is running the choke can be pushed in and more accelerator can be used to keep the engine running. In most current petrol-engined vehicles this gradual adjustment is a function of the automatic choke assembly.

Some carburettors enrich fuel-to-air mixture by increasing the amount of fuel for starting. If this richer start mixture is reduced too early the motor might stall, simply due to lack of rich fuel to keep it going until it has warmed up. Petrol is a thin, easily vapourised, very volatile liquid, usually mixed as an engine fuel at about 15 parts of air to 1 part of petrol [15:1]. When it is drawn inside the motor, this mixture is ignited by a strong electric spark. The spark occurs when the piston inside the cylinder has compressed the explosive air/fuel mixture into a tiny space at the top of the cylinder. When the mixture ignites and explodes, the expanding gas pushes the piston back down the cylinder, which in turn causes the crankshaft to rotate, and power to drive the vehicle is generated.

Diesel fuel is not like petrol; it is more like sewing-machine oil and not as explosive as petrol. The piston compresses only air within the cylinder, but under very much higher pressure than that of a petrol cylinder. Instead of an electric spark igniting a compressed fuel/air mix at the top of the cylinder as in a petrol motor, diesels create intense heat due to the very-highly compressed air. Fuel is then squirted as a vapour spray under very high pressure into the cylinder through a tiny hole in the injector when the piston comes up to the top of the cylinder.

At this point the high-temperature air ignites the mist of fuel. The expanding gases then do their job of pushing the piston back down the cylinder, generating power. The very high compression in a diesel is a major reason for the weight difference between the two motors. The diesel engine is heavier and stronger due to thicker metal in the engine-block castings needed to withstand the higher cylinder pressures.

Over time, you'll probably notice a difference in fuel between summer and winter starts. Most suppliers provide a "winter mix", in diesel and petrol fuel, for easier cold-weather starting. Starting diesel motors in most common 4WDs is straight-forward. Diesels don't have chokes to make the fuel starting mixture richer. They are usually fitted with "glow-plugs", which in most cases need to be used only first-up in the morning, or in unusually cold conditions.

Glow-plugs are just like a little electric radiator element, one per

Checklist

Tyre-changing practice

Just changing a 7.50x16 tyre on dry, level, warm concrete, you'll learn several things:

- The spare wheel is heavy.
- The big hydraulic jack from your garage is easy to use.
- You'll never ever let the person at the tyre place do up your wheel nuts with an air-powered rattle-gun ever again.
- Changing a tyre on a 4WD is really easier than you thought it might be.

Then to really learn, find some sloped local ground, perhaps the local football ground. Drive there and fit another wheel on your vehicle using only the manufacturer's tyre-changing equipment, and/or tools carried in your vehicle. What do you do when the vehicle starts to roll away down the slope? How would the same job be if it was raining and the surface was bad uphill rocks or slick clay or mud, not bitumen or firm gravel?

cylinder. They heat up the space at the top of each cylinder inside the head near the fuel injector tips. Glow-plugs have the effect of making the highly compressed air even hotter for the first few seconds as the motor is cranked over, helping to ignite the fuel more easily. Average glow-plug time on a cold motor varies from perhaps five to fifteen seconds for the initial starting heat-up, but after that the key can normally be turned straight to start, as with a petrol motor. Most diesels have glow-plugs for starting. Glow-plugs use quite a bit of battery current to operate — one reason why diesels need strong batteries.

When the key is turned on to the "ignition" position, the glow-plugs operate. There is usually a warning light to show when they are on prior to starting. Heating-up time is normally controlled by a timer solenoid. Turning the key to the "start" position then operates the starter-motor, generally while the glow-plugs are still operating. Some diesels have this function automatically operated, offering virtually instant starting at any time.

Learning about your vehicle

How well do you know your vehicle? Can you find the radiator drain cock in the dark (does it have one?), or change a headlight globe quickly? Do the grease nipples on the front propshaft universal joint and the sliding spline line up,

Checklist

Begin with something simple

Try these straightforward jobs:

- Changing a fanbelt
- Replacing a headlight globe
- Replacing the ignition points, if your vehicle has them
- Priming a diesel engine fuel supply
- Putting in another fuel pump diaphragm on a petrol motor
- Jacking up the vehicle several different ways

You will probably find some little part of a procedure that's not so easy. When you get back to your own garage you will be able to make the modification or add another tool to the kit to help make the job easier.

making them easy to find and grease? To be safer on a long desert crossing, how many litres of oil, and what type, should you carry to cover emergencies with components which run in oil? Reference to a service and repair manual will give you this information — but have you got the right one? Make sure that you read the owner's manual too.

Practising in different conditions

While you are experimenting with your 4WD, find some dirt somewhere safe to play around, and experiment by using the four-wheel-drive low range gears. (See page 135 for an explanation of gear ratios.) Notice the difference in engine revs on the tachometer, and available power. Range selection is usually via the transfer gearbox lever. To engage many transfer gearboxes, so that the front wheels can provide drive, a small lever similar to the usual gearbox lever has to be moved. In some vehicles the same thing is achieved simply by pushing a button. Read your driver's handbook carefully, as some transfers can be engaged into 4WH at any practical speed, while others must be below 40kph.

These different gearbox ranges are intended for quite different purposes. Speeds in 2WH (two-wheel, high range, normally just the two rear wheels driving) and 4WH (all four wheels driving) are the same. In low range, the speed is somewhere about half that of the same gear in high range. That is, L2 (low range, second gear) goes about as fast as H1 (high range, first gear), L4 is similar to H2 and so on. A major benefit is that while the speed may be halved, the engine power is effectively doubled. 2WH is the normal position for

Petrol 4-stroke cycle

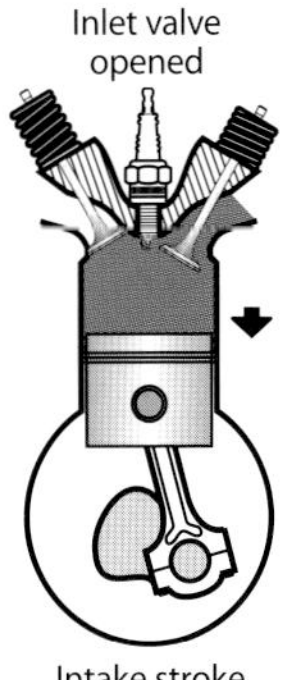

Intake stroke

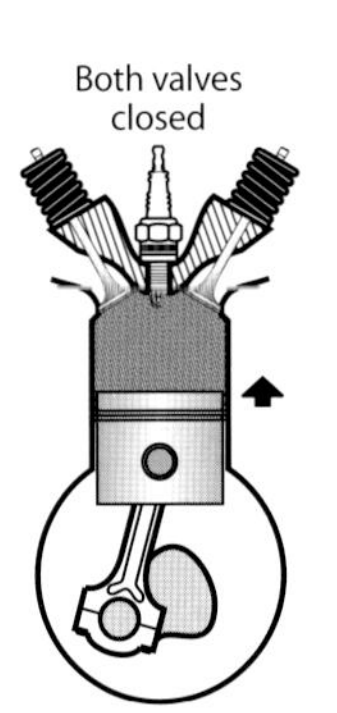

Compression stroke

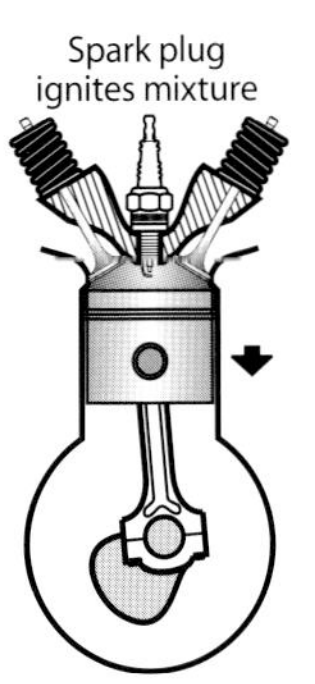

Power stroke

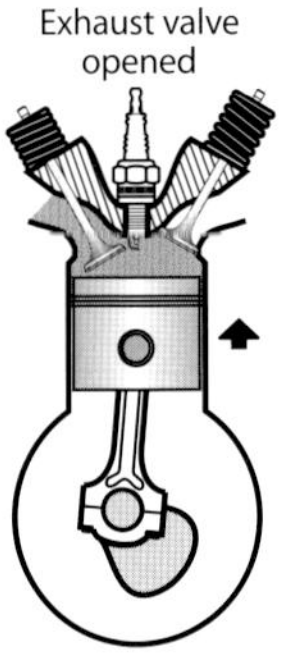

Exhaust stroke

Diesel 4-stroke cycle

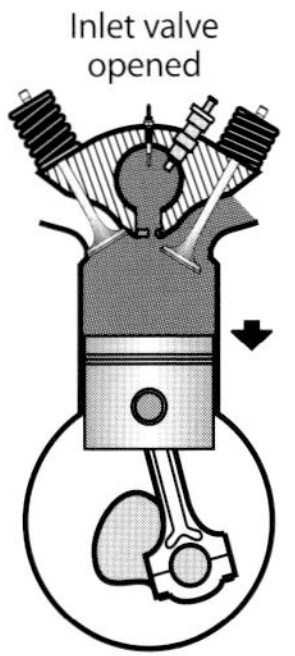

Intake stroke

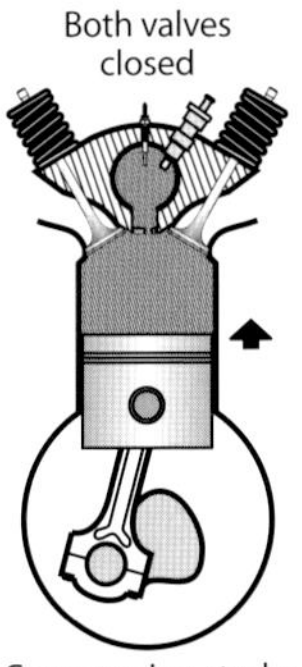

Compression stroke

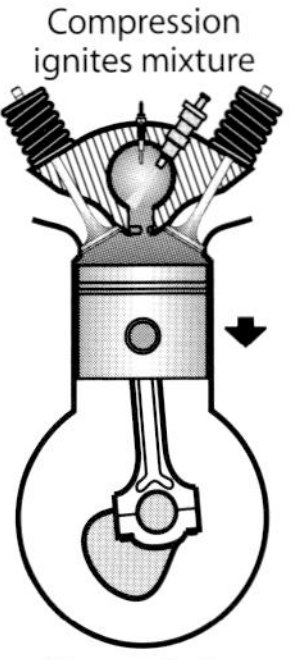

Power stroke

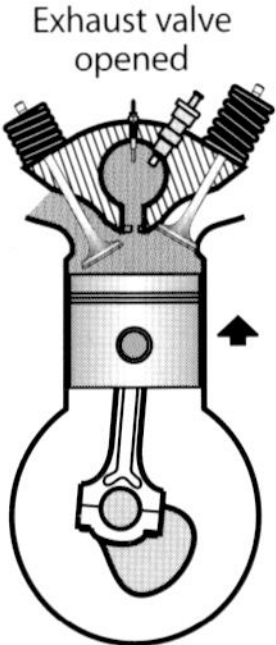

Exhaust stroke

GRAVEL IS A TYPICAL ROAD SURFACE TO FEEL THE ADDED STABILITY OF 4WH.

everyday driving. Some vehicles have manufacturer's limits recommended for maximum speeds in 4WH. Assuming your vehicle is not the type which is or can run full-time four-wheel drive, 4WH should not be used on any dry bitumen or hard-surfaced roadway. It is intended for slippery or soft going, and the same applies to 4WL (4WD, low range).

There is a neutral position in the transfer gearbox. Neutral is used only when a function such as Power-Take-Off [PTO] winching, the most common use, is required. This disengages the drive to the vehicle's wheels but allows the PTO shaft to be driven, via the transfer gearbox, by the vehicle's motor. Operation of PTO winches can be confusing at first, as one type is controlled via the normal gearbox and another is driven by the vehicle's clutch. If your vehicle has a PTO winch refer to the winch manufacturer's instructions. The PTO and hydraulic types use the engine for power. Most recreational 4WDs have electrically driven winches, powered by the vehicle's batteries. Winching can be dangerous, and you must be familiar with the proper operating procedure for your particular winch. For more information on winching, see page 73.

Typical gearbox and transfer box patterns

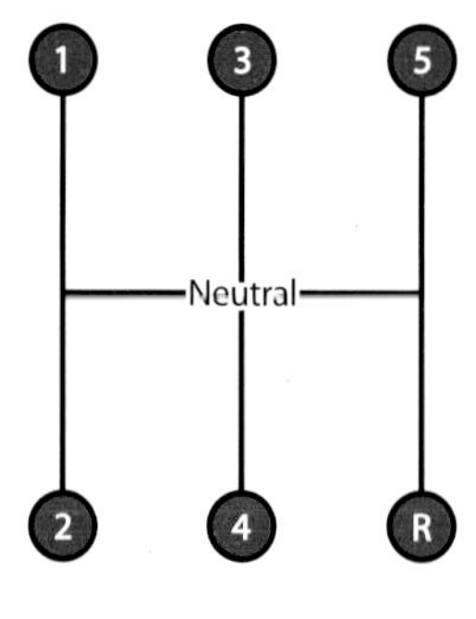

Gearbox – operates normally, regardless of transfer operation

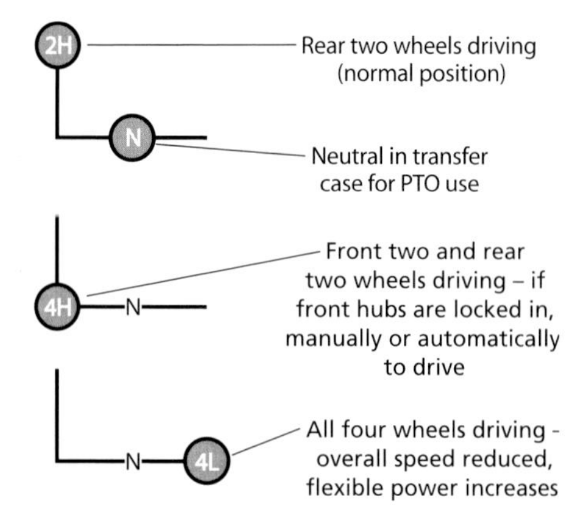

Modifications and Clearances

Spring sagging

Suspension is vital to a 4WD which gets worked hard, so the subject of suspension in various forms is discussed in several different sections of this book when it is relevant. This section looks at what happens when suspension doesn't do what it really should. It is not uncommon for original leaf springs to lose their curve and drop, causing the vehicle to have less ground clearance. Sagging can also happen with coil springs.

Spring sagging can be caused by age and use, incorrect manufacturing standards, or carrying heavy loads. Towing a large caravan can also cause springs to sag. If you have to carry heavy loads, avoiding trouble may only be a matter of having an additional leaf fitted in each of your springs to stiffen them, and reduce their softness. To do this in a coil-sprung vehicle may require spacers or replacement springs of a heavier rating. Spring manufacturers can recurve or rewind and retemper original springs. Aftermarket springs can also help cure this problem.

For any vehicle that spends a lot of time off-road there is no doubt that increased wheel travel and more flexible suspension is a major benefit. When you jack up the body, the wheels have more space to move. Spring and shock-absorber replacement kits usually produce a noticeable improvement in the vehicle's ability to handle rough off-road going through increased body clearance and greater available wheel movement. The cost of aftermarket springs is often much less than replacing with original ones, unless it is done under a warranty claim.

Even though not common now with advanced metal technology, a problem which sometimes occurs due

Advice

IF YOUR VEHICLE HAS A PTO WINCH REFER TO THE WINCH MANUFACTURER'S INSTRUCTIONS. WINCHING CAN BE DANGEROUS.

A SUSPENSION KIT CAN BE ADAPTED TO SUIT THE REQUIREMENTS OF THE OWNER.

to extreme cold in the desert is broken springs. First up after a freezing night, sudden bumps can cause cracks or breaks in springs.

Spring kits

Spring kits which increase ride height also increase body roll due to greater leverage of the 4WD body pivoting around the spring and its mounting points. Some poorly designed attempts to increase body height consist of longer, multi-position side-plates to replace original leaf-spring shackles; these are basically spacers to move the body up and away from the springs.

In most vehicles there are movement limiters called bump-stop rubbers fitted on the underside of the chassis rail, usually close to the spring mount. When the spring reaches its travel limit and the vehicle body has moved downwards in parallel, the spring mount axle tube or suspension arm contacts the solid-rubber bump-stop and "bottoms out", preventing metal-to-metal contact. There is normally a polished mark showing this point of contact. If this bottoming-out occurs continually, get the springs and shockers checked by a 4WD suspension specialist.

Problems with safe clearances and relationship to original parts can occur if aftermarket spring kits are fitted. Be sure to check the length of the flexible hoses which connect the chassis-mounted hydraulic brake lines to the brake calipers or backing plates at each wheel. These brake hoses are made a particular length. If an axle or wheel can now move more than originally intended by the maker, the hose may well be too short or stretched more than originally intended, past its safety limits. In such cases these brake line hoses should definitely be replaced with correct longer hoses.

Modifications and braking

Some vehicles have a device known as a load sensing and brake proportioning valve (LS&BPV) incorporated in the braking system. If you fit a high-lift spring kit, check whether your 4WD has such a device, and inquire as to whether the modification could affect your braking. The LS&BPV is usually mechanically operated using a metal rod or linkage to connect the rear axle to the chassis rail where the valve is mounted. When the back of a vehicle is loaded it drops and the linkage position changes, altering the LS&BPV setting. In effect this measures the amount of load carried in the back of the vehicle and the valve allocates more brake percentage to the rear wheels if needed. If the body height is altered with a high-lift kit the linkage must be altered proportionately. This adjustment is not easily made by 4WD owners; it needs a dealer service, with special tools and measuring equipment.

Reduced braking efficiency is possible if a vehicle is fitted with wheels and tyres of a much larger diameter and width than originally fitted. For example, think of the difference in mass between an original 16-inch wheel with a 7-inch wide tyre, and an aftermarket 16-inch wheel fitted with a 12.5-inch wide tyre. The overall mass and leverage of a much bigger tyre and wheel rotating around the original braking mechanism can impose additional, possibly unsafe loads on some components, because they may not still be within original design limits. The original parts are designed to cope with stresses that the original tyres and wheels might develop. Significantly increasing the rotating weight and diameter of the wheel and tyre, then expecting the original brake mechanism to efficiently and reliably stop that wheel, is not mechanically sensible. You could be asking for trouble unless engineered modifications are made to compensate

Advice

REDUCED BRAKING EFFICIENCY IS POSSIBLE IF A VEHICLE IS FITTED WITH WHEELS AND TYRES OF A MUCH LARGER DIAMETER AND WIDTH THAN ORIGINALLY FITTED.

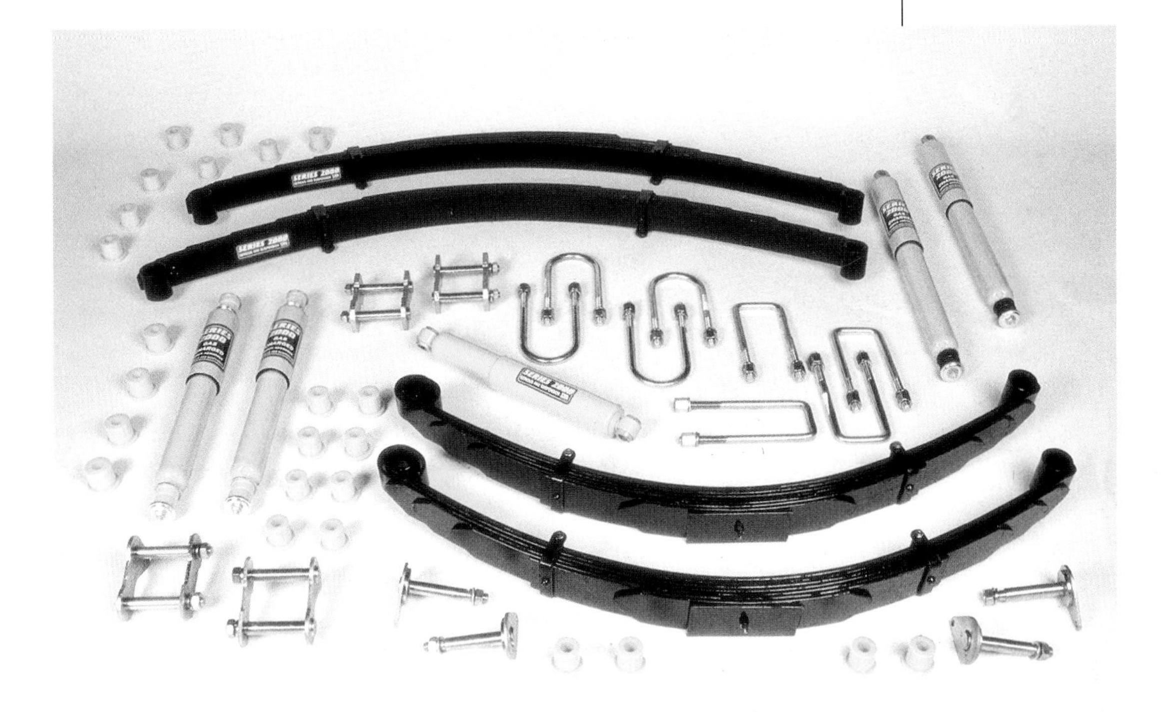

A FULL SUSPENSION KIT FOR A LEAF SPRING VEHICLE INCLUDES A LOT MORE THAN JUST THE SPRINGS.

IF YOU FIT A HIGH-LIFT SPRING KIT, CHECK WHETHER YOUR 4WD HAS A LOAD SENSING AND BRAKE PROPORTIONING VALVE (LS & BPV) INCORPORATED IN THE BRAKING SYSTEM AND INQUIRE AS TO WHETHER THE MODIFICATION COULD AFFECT YOUR BRAKING.

for the changes. There may be reduced physical clearances around brake and steering components, increased strain on wheel bearings, altered clearances between tyres and wheel arches and so on, with larger wheels and tyres.

In some cases owner-modified vehicles don't handle or stop as well as the factory original. Engine swaps often produce a large increase in the power-to-weight ratio, which can make vehicles less stable, not as effective in braking, and far less able to put the power to the ground properly. I know of one Toyota utility which had a Chev V8 engine installed, and which was then

AFTERMARKET WHEEL CARRIERS CAN INCREASE CLEARANCE ON VEHICLES WHERE THE SPARE WAS ORIGINALLY LOW MOUNTED.

often unable to gain or retain traction on most off-road hills due to savage wheelspin from engine torque. It destroyed tracks, and the environment. On wet bitumen roads it was unstable and unsafe.

Shock absorbers

Top-class aftermarket shock absorbers can control or reduce body movement, but at a cost. This is not a cheap modification, but if you are after better off-road performance it is one of the most important changes to make. If your vehicle will be mostly commuter and five percent off-road, get a ride or drive in a suspension specialist's demo vehicle before parting with money. Be sure any spring/shocker change is really what you want.

If you do decide to buy aftermarket shock absorbers and/or springs, you will have to trust the specialist. Ask around before buying. Perhaps the only safe way is to get the generally recommended best brands. Test shock absorbers regularly for damping and rebound condition, check them for large dents and oil leaks; or remove them and take them to a suspension specialist for testing. Shock absorbers are a forgotten item on many vehicles, but they can make a considerable difference to vehicle stability and handling, particularly if they are in poor condition. Shock absorbers are generally a throw-away or replacement item, but some oil-damped, adjustable models can be reconditioned. For information ask around among users, and go to reputable dealers.

Clearances

Changing the size of tyres and wheels on your vehicle from the manufacturer's standard can affect handling, speedometer accuracy, and even manufacturer warranty or insurance cover. Changing to a wider tyre usually increases the diameter, lifting vehicle height. It can be a risk to buy aftermarket wheels without good advice. Correct brake component clearances on the inside of the rim are vital; correct rim offsets and body-panel clearances are essential for safety, tyre life and handling, apart from being a legal requirement.

Changes may contravene the mechanical requirements for vehicle registration, so check carefully. From the purely mechanical aspect, for example, a rim with incorrect offset which relocates the tyre tread further

SOME AFTERMARKET SPRING KITS ALLOW VASTLY INCREASED SUSPENSION TRAVEL.

Case Study

Trackwidth trouble

One example of trackwidth variation occurred in the Simpson Desert quite a few years back near a place called Purni Bore. The soil was very boggy, and unfortunately at that time there was no other practical way around the sticky section so we had to cross through it following some existing tyre tracks. One of the vehicles involved was a 1986 model Suzuki. It was an excellent vehicle in the desert but this time had a bit of hassle, with not very much distance between the inside of those tyres on each axle. Another vehicle on the trip was a Ford Bronco, with twelve-inch wide tyres and the biggest of all 4WD trackwidths. The Ford and a number of Toyotas had left two big deep wheel-track imprints as they moved forward through the bog. Following in the tracks the Suzuki finally became hung up, with all four tyres unable to touch the bottom of the grooves, its skid-plate sitting firmly on the top of the hump. The mud left in the centre, between the wheels of the other vehicles, was too wide to clear beneath the Suzuki and the tyre grooves got too deep for its wheels to drive. It eventually came to a stop without steering or traction and had to be snatched out. There was a fairly simple solution to stop the Suzuki hanging up in the Ford's wheel grooves — we should have sent the smaller vehicle across first, and kept the biggest 4WD with the widest tyres until last.

out from the original and manufacturer-intended tread centre can place enormous strain and weight loading on the wheel bearings through incorrect leverage. Stick with reputable 4WD tyre and wheel specialists, and avoid problems.

Clearance is important when off-road driving. Some vehicles carry their spare wheel below floor level, centrally behind the rear axle. This can greatly limit ground clearance and risk damage to the wheel. If you intend to drive off-road frequently and your vehicle has the spare underneath the floor, it is wise to buy an aftermarket wheel-carrier that holds the spare up on the back bumper bar or rear door.

The type of terrain in which you are travelling is a simple guide to likely damage. Any 4WD with a low-hanging exhaust system is asking to have it dented or ripped off by a rock or the centre-hump in between wheel tracks. Large mirrors are often damaged by scrub, particularly those bolted tight or not spring-loaded and designed or allowed to swing away on impact. Radio antennas can easily be bent or broken and roof-racks are often an invitation to damage in thick bush. In some commercial carparks in metropolitan areas, generally designed with roof-height clearance for cars, 4WD radio antennas, roof-racks and even the vehicle rain gutter mounting-points are frequently damaged.

Other parts that can cause clearance bother include towbar goosenecks left sticking out in place on tow hitches, bullbars with cow-catcher extensions below the bar itself, and some aftermarket sidesteps. If you spend your time on gravel or sand tracks these items probably won't cause any real trouble, but if you venture into rougher country, they often suffer damage or cause hold-ups.

Approach and departure angles

Approach (or departure) angle is a confusing term for some four-wheel drivers. As an example, a large sedan with a heavy load in the boot sometimes drags the towbar or rear bumper bar on the ground as it drives over a dip in the road. In this case, the "departure angle" is very poor. Compare this with a Mini with its rear end close to the wheels; it doesn't even remotely drag

4X4 TIp

'APPROACH ANGLE' IS THE ANGLE FROM THE FRONT OF THE TYRE AT GROUND LEVEL TO THE LOWEST POINT OF THE VEHICLE BODY AT THE FRONT.

Approach and departure angles

the rear bumper bar because it has no overhang behind the wheels. Its departure angle is perfect.

"Approach angle" is the angle from the front of the tyre at ground level to the lowest point of the vehicle body at the front. The steeper this angle is, the less the vehicle tends to get caught or hung up. This clearance angle can be very important indeed, particularly when crossing creeks, washouts and gullies, or driving over rocks or fallen trees.

Trackwidths

Other underbody dimensions important to 4WDs are tyre size and wheel-width or tyre-track. Most of the 4WD vehicles working in outback Australia still seem to be running stock rims, and original 7.50x16 tyres. Most trackwidths, and their bone-shaking corrugations, are Toyota-sized. Over time, in the deserts and in the bush these will change, because many newer vehicles have followed the trend towards lighter magnesium wheels and fatter-profile tyres. Some mid-sized vehicles, with their generally narrower trackwidths, are becoming more common in 4WD-only areas.

Variation in trackwidths and tyre grooves is a part of four-wheel driving, and just has to be allowed for or put up with. I've seen a few hold-ups for bigger 4WDs in the bush where fallen

Vehicle dimensions from the driver's seat

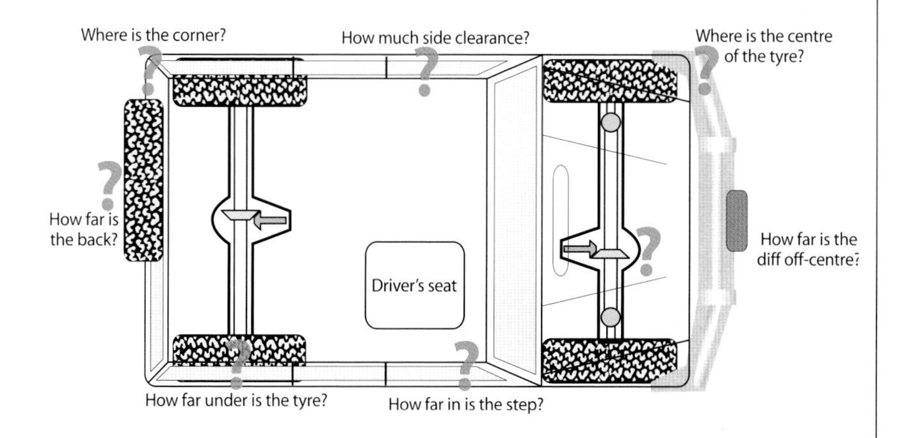

trees may completely block a track. The usual way to clear a path is to use an axe or chainsaw on the log, cutting sufficient space for the vehicle to pass through. In some instances the gap may be ample for a Suzuki and barely wide enough for a Toyota, but a Ford driver would have to widen the gap to get the vehicle through. The logical and sensible method is to clear the entire trackwidth if you have to cut a path for vehicle clearance; sometimes I wonder if the narrow gap is a Suzuki driver scoring a little of his own back.

Differing trackwidths can really cause trouble in some circumstances, and a prime example is off-road trailers. It is surprising how many drivers buy or pull a trailer that has a different trackwidth to that of their tow vehicle. The trailer tyre, having to make its own track, is deflected by anything in or on the track that has more resistance than the unpowered tyre, so the trailer drifts or is flicked from side to side as it is pulled forward. Some trailers can become very difficult to manage, quite apart from excessive wear on the trailer tyres, increased tow vehicle fuel consumption, greater chance of tread and sidewall damage and rough travelling for both. The trailer contents obviously suffer as well.

Body dimensions

Although they are bigger and taller than conventional cars, it is usually easy to adjust to driving a 4WD. Getting used to clearances for width, length and wheel location however can be difficult for some drivers. Practising in a quiet area will result in a lot less scratches or dents than in hard-going off-road situations. One placement many drivers have difficulty visualising is the location of the differential housings on the axles. For example, looking from the front my vehicle's front diff housing is well off-centre, towards the right. If you have to negotiate a way over a big rock in the track it can be very expensive if by mistake you think the front diff housing is to the left of centre and steer so the rock passes clearly inside the right front wheel. Check your vehicle, and learn the dimension clearances and locations.

Part of safe and proper four-wheel driving is knowing your vehicle. Included in the purely mechanical part of this is "knowing the parts of your vehicle". It is important to have a mental picture of where the wheels and mudguards are. For some people, this seems to be difficult because it is not quite what it seems. Just because the driver can see the rear quarter pillars doesn't mean that the wheels are right there. Without

Effects of body lean on turning vehicle

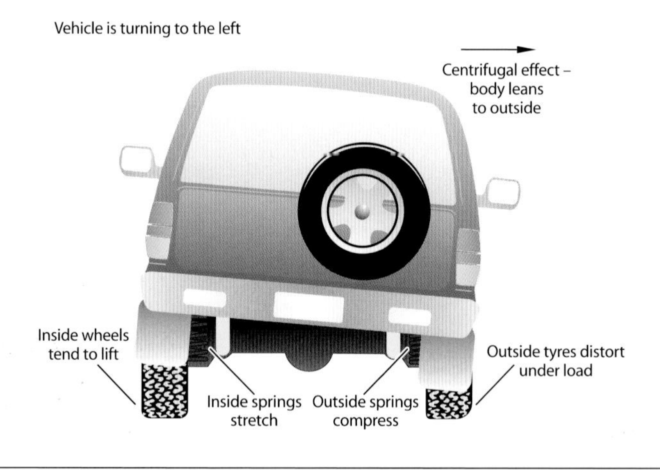

having a good feel for wheel placement, the chances of damage in off-road conditions are far greater.

Probably the simplest and quickest way to get to know wheel location is to find a spare bit of road gutter and do a number of parallel parks, left- and right-handed.

Using a log or a bit of gutter for reference, driving or reversing towards it will soon show how far under each end of the vehicle the wheels actually are. Sitting in the vehicle driver's seat, mentally picture where the wheels are, how close to the obstacle. Imagine where the mudguards and tail-lights are, how much clearance remains between the obstacle and the bullbar or bumpers. Then get out and physically check these obstacle-clearances each time. Compare it with your mental picture. When you get into a sticky situation this will pay good dividends.

This practice will also show you the steering limits, because the constant-velocity joints in the front axle physically limit how sharp your 4WD can turn. If you have to backtrack for some reason and need to make a multi-point turn on a narrow off-road track, not knowing these limits and dimensions is inviting almost certain vehicle damage .

As a common example, most supermarket car-park spaces are simply not made big enough for the larger 4WDs. In almost all cases the turning radius available in roadways is nowhere near enough for easy access into a parking space. Knowing your vehicle's dimensions is essential in this environment to prevent panel and wheel damage.

LAND ROVER VEHICLES FAVOUR THE USE OF ALLOY PANELS.

Body lean

When you begin to drive a 4WD it generally feels different to a car. Like any tall and heavy vehicle, some allowance

Steel versus alloy

Checklist

- Steel rusts, alloy doesn't.
- Alloy is affected by electrolysis, steel usually is not.
- Aluminium weighs much less than steel, but steel is usually easier for an owner to fix than alloy.
- Steel will dent but can be welded by anyone with relatively simple equipment and a little knowledge of welding. Alloy tends to spring back and is hard to dent, but then again, welding aluminium requires considerable skill and machines suitable for welding it are not found in many home workshops.

is needed when cornering, braking and parking. Cars, being much closer to the ground, have less body lean than 4WDs. Range Rover 4WD suspension often surprises new passengers or drivers, being so flexible in a big vehicle. As it is usually coil-sprung all-round it does initially have a disconcerting "body lean" in corners.

A roofrack makes a vehicle even taller, and if it is loaded with any great degree of weight it will aggravate the lean angle noticeably. Roofracks should really be used for carrying lighter items that are difficult to fit inside because of bulk, such as a tent or chairs.

Body lean happens because centrifugal force pushes the bulk of the taller, heavier body towards the outside of the corner. This compresses both the front and rear outside springs, causing increased load to be placed on the outside two wheels, and less load on the inner two wheels. In some cases, this lightened load on the front inside steering tyre has the effect of also reducing steering efficiency, requiring more driver input to remedy. Vehicle reactions vary according to mixtures of speed, load, road surface, tyres and steering, combining to make driving more tiring than expected.

Body construction

Compared with cars, most 4WDs are simply made to be tough, to fill a particular role. While this may not help with good fuel economy, it is a major reason why many last so long and can absorb hard knocks. A strong steel chassis or subframe is the base, with body and mechanical parts helping to form a solid box. Body panelling is made from heavier gauge steel, although the Range Rover family has mostly aluminium bodies. The benefits of steel versus the advantages of alloy have been chewed over between four-wheel drivers for years. Arguing the points for each one can be a great way to kill a few hours sitting around a camp fire. Choice of aluminium alloy or steel bullbars is a typical argument. There are valid points on both sides.

COMPARED WITH CARS, MOST 4WDS ARE SIMPLY MADE TO BE TOUGH, TO FILL A PARTICULAR ROLE. WHILE THIS MAY NOT HELP WITH GOOD FUEL ECONOMY, IT IS A MAJOR REASON WHY MANY LAST SO LONG AND CAN ABSORB HARD KNOCKS.

Steering, Tyres and Suspension

Steering

If your vehicle is fitted with power steering, remember that the pump for it is engine-powered. It may also be the power source for driving a hydraulic winch as well. Stall the vehicle, and you've lost the benefits. "Armstrong" steering might be all right for Arnold Schwarzenegger. However, if your vehicle is fitted with wide tyres and suddenly has no power-assist for steering, you'll probably wish you were Arny, because turning the wheel takes a whole lot of effort.

To begin with, the centrifugal effect of a 4WD going around a corner increases load on the outside tyres; the unpowered one, usually the front, tends to dig in and scuff or drag. When this happens, there are three practical choices:

- reduce speed with the same steering and allow the vehicle to drop back tighter into the corner;
- increase the steering to make it come around more; or
- accept the wider turn.

Speed and the resulting lean from centrifugal effect is one way to lose some steering efficiency, but it can be made even worse. Hard braking to quickly reduce the speed around the corner can actually add to the loss by further increasing the load on the outside front tyre through weight transference.

Riding a bicycle gives a simple example of the interplay between steering and suspension. Travelling forwards, if the bike's front-wheel brake is applied strongly, the rider's weight is moved rapidly forward onto the arms. If the front wheel isn't straight ahead when the brake is applied the usual result is a crash because the turning moment is quite severe. In a car weight is similarly transferred forward under braking. (The same effect also happens in reverse.) When the wheels are braked the front springs are compressed but the body still wants to keep on going forward. Body weight tries to compress the springs even more, so the forward shift in the vehicle's body results in

Caution

IF YOUR VEHICLE IS FITTED WITH POWER STEERING, REMEMBER THAT ITS PUMP IS ENGINE-POWERED. STALL THE VEHICLE, AND YOU HAVE LOST THE BENEFITS.

Forward and reverse steering

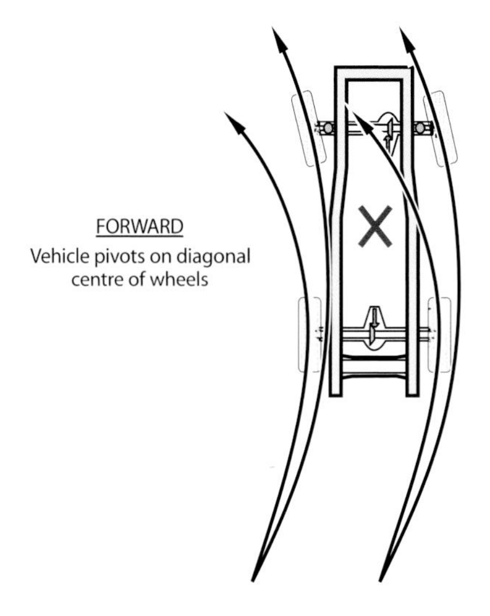

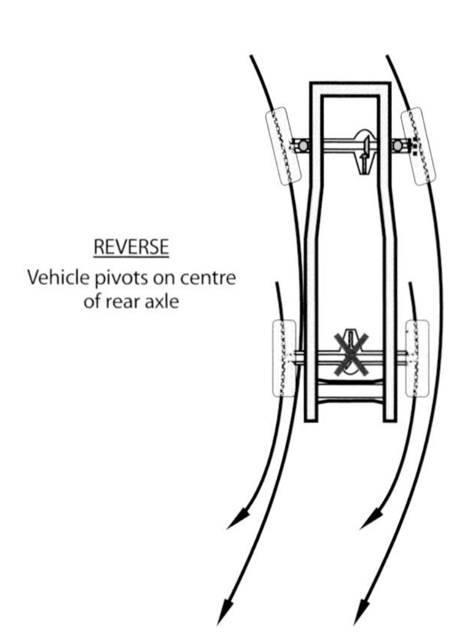

OVERSTEER CAN BECOME DANGEROUS IN MUDDY OR SLIPPERY CONDITIONS.

more weight loaded onto the front tyres and less on the rear. The harder the braking, the sharper and more pronounced is the weight transference.

Now let's add braking to centrifugal effect. As the vehicle goes around the corner, by applying brakes an increased percentage of this shifted weight moves forward over onto the outside tyre. This tends to scuff its way around the corner even more. The front outside wheel would have the most weight, then the outside rear, and the two inside wheels would have the least percentage of weight. In effect, the whole vehicle would be unbalanced. It is easy to create a situation where braking wouldn't give the normal or expected response, because the wheels would not have normal weight on them.

If the front of the vehicle has more weight on it as a result of the hard braking, then plainly the back must have less. When the front end drops, the back end lifts, so rear tyre adhesion is reduced. With sufficient speed, this can turn into a nasty situation because without much friction between tyres and road a vehicle is more easily affected by other forces. In this case the same centrifugal force that tends to tip the top of the 4WD towards the outside of the corner can cause the whole back end of the vehicle to swing towards the outside. When the rear does not follow the front despite the driver steering, but swings out to one side a bit like a pendulum, the action is known as "oversteer".

Steering in reverse

Steering effect in ordinary cars is simple; they're relatively light, and often have power-assisted steering. Driving forward, a front-wheel-steered car pivots around a point aligned with the rear axle. Driving in reverse, due to the pivot point still being at the rear axle, it reacts very quickly. In effect, it is steering with what has become the rear wheels, like a forklift truck.

In a 4WD, although the pivot point in reverse is still the back axle, there is a somewhat different reaction when the front hubs are locked in and 4WD is engaged. The kindest way to describe it is that it usually scrubs or drags. It can feel heavy to turn, even with power steering. The constant-velocity [CV] joints on the axles just inside the front wheels limit the degree the wheels can be turned. Considerable twisting stress is placed on the CV joints and repeated forced tight and loaded turns can do them damage. Always go easy applying power when the front wheels are near or on full lock, the vehicle is in 4WD and in rough country.

Steering traction

With a lot of power on, wheelspin can easily occur. Burnouts at the drag strip are a great example of this rather wasteful habit. The tyre scuffing or spinning doesn't provide any effective power to help propel or steer the vehicle until it grips the surface and drives. Wheelspin happens often when one wheel has good traction and the other wheel, on the same axle, has reduced or no grip at all. By adding a soft, hard and slippery or loose surface (or too much speed) to this combination it is easy to imagine the possibilities.

Losing traction with front or steering wheels in a 4WD is fairly common on slippery clay tracks, even at slow speeds, despite the wheels being turned in the required direction. Steering effect can be totally lost when neither of the front wheels has sufficient grip on the road to do what the driver wants. When the front of the vehicle doesn't go around the corner, or on the line the driver intended by steering, the effect is known as "understeer".

In slippery conditions, if the vehicle has too much momentum or speed (or

IN SLIPPERY CONDITIONS, IF THE VEHICLE HAS TOO MUCH MOMENTUM OR SPEED, STEERING CONTROL CAN BE LOST.

just more than the friction of the small contact patch between tyres and ground can manage) it tends to keep going in the same direction that it was before the wheels were turned. Tyre tread pattern, wear or incorrect tyre pressures don't help here either. Gravity pulls things downwards. If the slippery track slopes both downhill and off to one side, then without positive traction that's where the vehicle will try to slide. These reactions are natural and can happen relatively easily in 2WD when only the rear wheels are driven. If the vehicle is in 4WD the effects are often noticeably reduced because the vehicle has better and more positive ground contact when all wheels are driving.

Suspension and weight transfers

4WDs have tough suspension components designed to cope with bad or unexpected road conditions, but they certainly are breakable. One of the most common abuses of vehicle suspension is the head-on wheel crunch, which happens on hitting either a step-up (railway crossing, gutter, hump, blade-cut, etc.) or a drop-off (washout, pothole, etc.).

The impact is often caused by plain driver error. There is a simple way to minimise this undesirable, potentially damaging crunch in normal driving, and the same technique works equally well at slow 4WD speeds in off-road conditions. Effectively, you are trying to make your vehicle lift the front end under acceleration for a moment, thus making it lighter in the front as weight is transferred towards the rear. Given that you do see the obstacle ahead in time, all it takes is sharp acceleration, but in the right place.

On braking, the front of the 4WD dips, and the harder you brake, the lower the front drops. If your vehicle has a low bullbar or similar, and you leave the brakes hard on as you approach the obstacle, there's a good chance that the lowest front point on the bar might hit it, even before the tyres contact it. Instead of compressing the suspension by braking, it would probably be better to do nothing. That way, you would let the unloaded suspension cope with the impact to its designed limits rather than hit the obstacle with compressed suspension and weight transference. If the obstacle is bigger or deeper than you judged, the already-loaded suspension, which can't compress much more, may very well be unnecessarily damaged on impact with the obstacle, caused mainly by your untimely braking.

The sequence is relatively simple but takes practice to master. If you see the situation ahead early enough, simply decelerate. Give the suspension a chance to level out before the object arrives. Tap the brakes sharply to quickly drop the speed before hitting it, and get off the brakes before you hit it. Get back on the accelerator pedal as soon as possible after braking and just a fraction before hitting the object tap it sharply for an instant. (You'll have to make allowances for how quickly your motor responds and lifts the front, and only practice will show you this; the timing is critical.) Acceleration results in lifting the front end, in effect making the front end go light or weigh less. As soon as you've accelerated hard, get off the accelerator again and let the suspension settle to take the crunch.

The front end will tend to ride over the object much more easily. The front lifts under acceleration and the back drops a little at the same time. When you get off the pedal the back comes up a bit so it has a chance to ride over, rather than slam into, the obstacle. At slow speeds it is quite possible to brake before an object, blip the accelerator to lift the front end, brake again to slow the vehicle before the back wheels hit, and minimise tyre, wheel and suspension damage potential quite considerably.

There are other intermixed reactions that occur in this "front-end suspension compression" stage to keep in mind. Harsh braking on any form of road surface, whether dry, wet or greasy, can cause difficult handling. Repeated gentle and quick on/off braking to slow the vehicle rather than constant braking is useful here. As the front end becomes much heavier and the rear end becomes proportionately lighter from transferred weight, the front tyre contact patch with the ground becomes slightly larger due to tyre distortion. In this case the point loading can actually increase in pressure. (More weight is imposed on the contact patch than the normal weight percentage resting on the tyre.) However, it will not necessarily grip better just because it has more weight on it.

If a vehicle is already going too fast for the circumstances (otherwise you would not have put the brakes hard on), then the chances of a skid due to insufficient friction between tyre and ground are increased. This is when understeer happens; the result is that either the vehicle front wheels don't steer, or they steer but not as much or where you want them to. Combine this with the lightened rear end and its reduced braking effectiveness, and you may well have an interesting few seconds. With the back end having much less than normal contact patch or tyre friction, if your reactive steering is not spot-on, then the vehicle's rear end may well slide out to the side, usually opposite to the way you are steering.

Spring and axle set-up

There are quite a few configurations of axle/suspension fitted to 4WDs. Spring combinations are complex, and many newer 4WDs have coil springs for each wheel, or even torsion bars, as their suspension method, with the wheels kept in place by locating arms. These carefully engineered arms allow the flexible travel ability yet maintain the position of each wheel and axle. Although the most common may be still the live-axle set-up with leaf-springs, coil springs have found a place with virtually all manufacturers. Some models are available with a choice of either type.

A live axle has both the front and rear axle housings as one piece from wheel to wheel across the vehicle. The bulge for the differential is somewhere near the centre of the housing. These axles are commonly mounted with coil

Tip

UNDERSTANDING WEIGHT TRANSFERENCE, WHICH APPLIES TO ALL VEHICLES, CAN HELP MINIMISE FRONT-END AND SUSPENSION DAMAGE.

Weight transference under braking

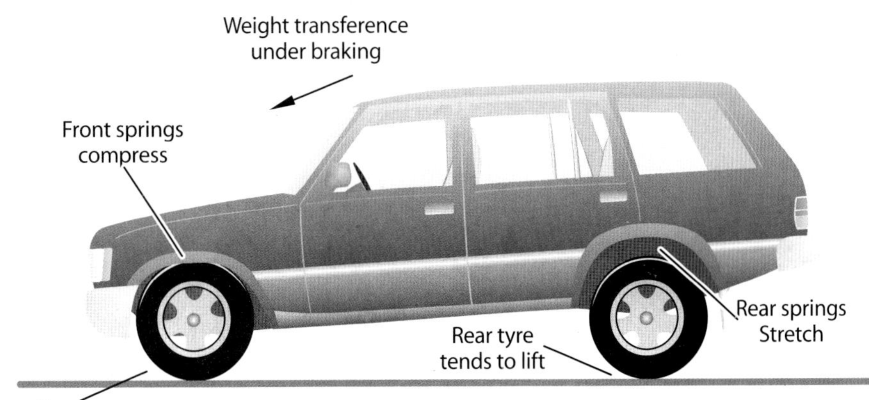

4WD WITH SUSPENSION AT FULL TRAVEL.

or multi-leaf springs, one inboard of each wheel, two per axle.

Perhaps the best example of independent suspension is the Range Rover, with great suspension flexibility but also great body lean angles. (They won't actually tip over going around a corner at safe speed, but it can be difficult to convince yourself of this when riding in one for the first time.) Independent suspension with half-shafts has a major advantage over the more conventional leaf-spring live-axle set-up, apart from the generally softer ride. Unless the terrain is very rough, all-independent wheels tend to stay firmly on the ground for best traction and there is usually much less deflection or shock effect from potholes compared with that of normal coil or leaf-spring suspension.

Some newer vehicles have fully independent suspension, with the differential bolted direct to the chassis and exposed half-shafts (like small tailshafts) running out to each wheel (similar to current front-wheel-drive cars).

The amount of curve in the leaf spring, or the number of coils and the thickness of each, helps determine the amount of wheel travel. In some cases a chain or strap "travel limiter" is fitted between chassis and axle to limit excessive movement. Some traction loss can occur on severe body lean angles from the effect of the chassis lifting the spring which in turn can lift the axle and wheel.

4X4 Caution

HARSH BRAKING ON ANY FORM OF ROAD SURFACE, WHETHER DRY, WET OR GREASY, CAN CAUSE DIFFICULT HANDLING.

Sway bars (Stabiliser bars)

Some short-wheelbase 4WDs suffer from "rock 'n' roll" due to their short wheelbase length, and some early-model 4WDs with fairly agricultural suspension design can become a bit unstable, even with good replacement units. Sway bars are designed to help reduce twitchiness in vehicle suspension, and improve body stability. They come in quite a selection of different sizes. Torsional twist stiffness in the bar limits or damps the amount of movement between axles and chassis without restricting suspension travel to any great extent; they can reduce body lean angles. It is a very complex field. There are suspension specialists who can minimise or remedy 4WD handling troubles if yours has them, but unless you are prepared to spend a considerable sum of money on modifications, some instability will probably be just something to live with and adapt to. Many late-model 4WD vehicles come with stabiliser bars as standard equipment and they can be fitted to the front or rear suspension or both.

Wheels and rims

Wheels, rims and tyres seem to be a very personal thing, with alloy wheels much in vogue. It is common to see a brand-new vehicle already fitted with aftermarket "mag" wheels and big, wide aggressive tyres. Likewise, early-model 4WDs are often fitted with "widies", as part of the "dress-up" game. Whether they actually do anything better than the stock wheels apart from some traction improvement in some off-road situations is doubtful.

Steel rims, especially when being used in the bush or away from civilisation, have one clear point in their favour. If you dent a rim at least there's a chance you can beat it back into some useable shape. If you have tubeless tyres, forget it, because a dented rim flange won't seal properly against the tubeless tyre bead. A tubed tyre can cope with quite a noticeable rim deformation and still not deflate. Magnesium alloy wheels are usually good-looking, and take a lot to break. When they do, welding is usually the way to repair them. So if you happen to crunch one on a rock and crack it, it can't be repaired in the field. Both mag and standard steel wheels are dished, made in one piece with fixed rim flanges. Getting tyres on and off them can be a real nightmare, particularly if you have to do it on your own out in the bush.

The compromise for relatively simple tyre changes is a split rim. These are steel and made in two parts, with one rim flange made to be removable. Like

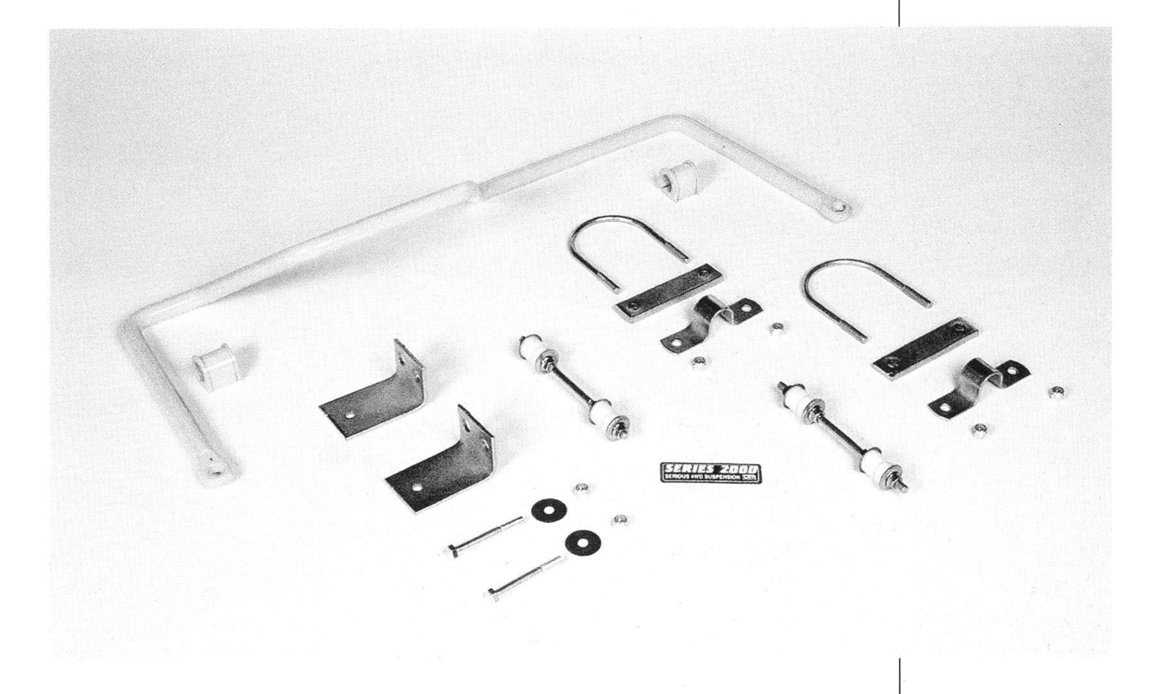

STABILISER BARS ARE FITTED TO MANY LATE MODEL 4WDS TO REDUCE BODY ROLL. A KIT SUCH AS THIS ONE CAN BE FITTED TO EARLY MODEL VEHICLES TO IMPROVE HANDLING AND REDUCE SWAY.

all tyre changes, split-rim wheels can be difficult, but much less so than one-piece wheels. Instead of having to force the tyre bead over the rim flange with tyre levers, with a split rim the tyre can slide off the wheel centre when the rim flange is removed. Most "commercial level" vehicles are fitted with split-rim wheels as original equipment. There can be a risk with split rims — physical injury can happen if the rim flange is not properly refitted back into its groove. Fortunately this is very rare but it does happen.

Take a lot of care to reseat the split-rim flange correctly. If not, when the tyre is being inflated, air pressure from the expanding tyre could fire the flange up into your face. In some states tyre workshops are required by law to have a strong steel safety-cage to put split-rim wheels in when inflating their tyres, just in case. Out in the scrub a quick substitute for a cage while inflating a tyre on a split rim wheel is to slide the wheel well in under your vehicle or alternatively turn the wheel so the split rim is underneath. Clip the compressor air-hose nozzle onto the valve stem and keep your hands and face well out of the way. Tyres are one of the most critical areas of any 4WD and when they go wrong it is rarely in good weather conditions in your own driveway. A wise move is to do your homework, check your vehicle handbook and learn about your wheels and tyres, practising in safe and easy conditions first.

Wheel nuts

4WDs aren't the only vehicles to suffer from a really annoying wheel nuisance. I call it "rattle-gun" syndrome. It happens when the tyre service person puts on a wheel, saving time by using an air-driven tool with a socket that fits the wheel nuts. This tool has an effect a bit like a hammer, with repeated strikes to tighten or loosen the nut as required. The resulting noise sounds a bit like a very loud rattle, thus the commonly used name of rattle-gun. Removing the wheel is no worry to them, but when this person puts the wheel back on using the same air-driven tool, that certainly can cause a problem for you.

The effort needed to later undo those same wheel nuts with an ordinary wheelbrace from the 4WD toolkit can be considerable. What's worse, trying

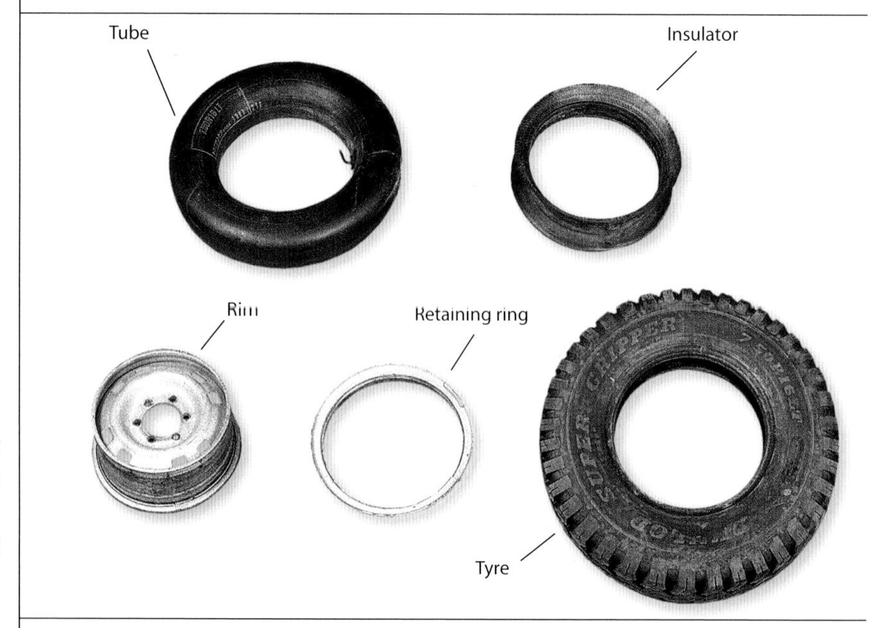

SPLIT RIMS ARE VERY POPULAR IN THE BUSH BECAUSE TYRE CHANGING IS SO MUCH EASIER.

to undo them in unpleasant or unsafe conditions can be downright dangerous. Make sure that your wheel nuts are only hand-tightened — remember, you are probably the person who will have to undo them.

Wheel nuts are one of the forgotten parts of a 4WD. They don't normally get looked at unless a tyre needs attention. Rust can make them very difficult to get off but this can be minimised.

On 4WDs there are significant differences between the nuts for steel wheels and those of mag wheels. To be safe you should be aware of them, and make note of the correct type on your vehicle. The same wheelbrace fits both kinds of nuts.

Whilst there may be exceptions in individual cases, in general those nuts for 4WD steel wheels have a 30degree tapered face angle. This taper wedges into the matching angle machined into the steel wheel face.

Mag wheel nuts usually have a squared-off end, and are made to fit down into a recess in the face of the 4WD wheel. These two types are not interchangeable. If you have a steel rim on your spare wheel, then be certain to carry a full set of correct wheel-nuts for it, if your four normal wheels are mags.

Mag wheels can be very expensive and some owners opt to fit lock-nuts to prevent theft. There are normally four in a set, and usually one nut is replaced on each wheel. The lock-nut requires a specific key to remove it, and although it may be a nuisance to the owner, it is a much bigger nuisance to a potential thief.

There is a third kind of wheel-nut available, specifically for mag wheels on caravans. It combines features of both these steel and mag nuts. For safety it should not be used on any 4WD wheels.

Spare wheels and changing tyres

Repairing a tube on a steep track with dark and rain to compound things is no joke. It is simply hard work. Carrying a complete spare wheel is much easier. In fact, if you are going right outback and remote, two complete spares is even better. That way you can hopefully do your tube repairs back at the campsite or when travelling is done for the day, thus losing less driving time.

To learn how to do a safe, quick and efficient 4WD wheel change if you are a beginner, most clubs have mechanical or practice days, and they generally have good tips and clues. There are some items for tyre/wheel changing that make the difference between quick, and back-breaking. If your vehicle has split-rims, be sure to buy good quality tyre-levers, but they should be designed for split rims. The end taper and shape is different from conventional levers. While normal tyre levers, or perhaps big strong screwdrivers, might do the job

Tip

SMEAR A BIT OF VASELINE OR MOLYBDENUM GREASE ON THE WHEELSTUD THREADS BEFORE DOING THE NUTS UP; OR WITH CAPPED OR MAG-WHEEL NUTS PUT A FEW DROPS OF OIL INSIDE THE HOLLOW NUT BEFORE DOING IT UP.

Wheel nuts

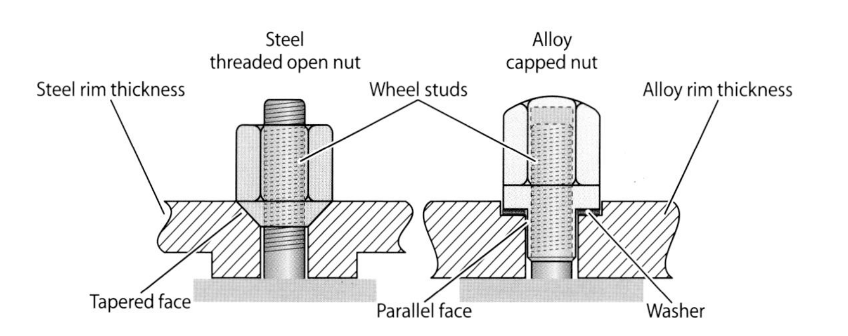

WHEEL NUTS ARE NOT INTERCHANGEABLE. IF YOU CARRY BOTH ALLOY AND STEEL WHEELS, ENSURE THAT THE CORRECT WHEEL NUTS ARE PACKED IN THE VEHICLE.

on a split-rim, the proper ones make it relatively simple and easy.

If you have normal rolled one-piece rims, you'll need top-quality levers, and a decent-sized rubber mallet. A small bottle of detergent, to make the rim and tyre bead slippery on replacement, is handy. For the rotten job of breaking the bead, that is if the tyre hasn't already ripped itself apart and spun around the rim, a tool called a "tyre-plier" or similar is very handy. Another way to break the tyre bead away from the wheel rim is to drive another vehicle over the tyre, as close to the rim as you can; you usually have to do this at a few places around the tyre. A highlift jack can also be handy for separating the tyre bead and wheel rim. Put the tyre on the ground under the bullbar and jack the vehicle up from there, so that the jack presses down on the tyre, to break the bead away from the rim.

If you are carrying only one spare wheel on a long, remote trip, for safety sake take at least one additional good-quality tube, and a spare tyre casing. Don't get caught in the common scenario of a flat tyre — the vehicle has four mag wheels, and the spare is also good, but on a steel rim. No problem? It can be, if you haven't included a full set of ordinary wheel nuts for the steel rim, because mag wheel nuts generally won't safely fit steel rims. Another situation I have seen is a vehicle with four 10R15 wide tyres on mag wheels, no spare tube, and the only spare tyre a standard steel-rim 7.50x16. That would be an interesting combination, especially if one of those 10R15s blew out somewhere deep in the middle of rough 4WD-only hills. This is an easy trap to fall into.

A tube-patch kit with all the necessary components, including a tyre innersleeve, needs to be included in the vehicle survival kit. There are points for and against each kind of tyre, but the lesser of two evils is probably tubed tyres if you are going into remote areas. With tubeless tyres, there is a kit that allows a rubber plug to be glued into the puncture hole if it is in the tread. This works with steel-belted radials as long as the wire belt is not really

SOMETIMES A HEAVY-DUTY TIE-DOWN STRAP WILL ASSIST IN THE INITIAL INFLATION OF A TUBELESS TYRE. A LENGTH OF ROPE AND A TYRE LEVER CAN BE USED AS A SUBSTITUTE IF A TIE-DOWN STRAP IS UNAVAILABLE.

TYRE PLIERS ARE A FAST WAY TO BREAK THE BEAD.

chewed up. It does work, but there is one difficulty with tubeless tyres in off-road situations. In order to reseat them if they have become unattached at the rim bead by running flat, it can take a large volume of compressed air at good pressure to blow them out sharply so they press against the well in the rim and seal enough to inflate properly. The old idea of running a belt around the centre of the tyre tread, then pulling it up very tight to make the sidewalls press out hard and seal against the wheel rim, is very difficult to do with a big strong 4WD tyre, but in an emergency it is worth a try.

Tyre pressure

Underinflated tyres can make steering heavy on your arms and shoulders. Tyre pressures are more important than many people imagine. Apart from the cost of replacing tyres, incorrect pressure causes premature (and unnecessary) wear, so you may be up for replacement cost long before you really have to. Low tyre pressure causes heavy steering, needing increased effort by either you or the power-steering unit. In the long term it creates undesirable heat build-up in the tyre; softness makes it much more likely to be damaged by rocks or other sharp objects, and the sidewalls bag out more than they normally should. When you fit new tyres the new rubber will be relatively soft and the tyres will flex quite a bit more than the older, stiffer tyre casings and age-hardened rubber you removed. To get rid of this flexy feeling try pumping them up a little higher than normal (say 2 psi) for a few weeks, then put them back down to the preferred pressure.

You might even find the slightly harder tyre pressure makes your 4WD handle better. Equally, you simply may not like a harder ride, and decide to run your tyres a little lower than average — it's all subjective.

The tyres on a 4WD or trailer are rated to carry a certain load, and should be pumped up to the recommended pressure. If you are carrying a heavy

4X4

Advice

AS A GENERAL RULE, TYRES INCREASE IN PRESSURE, OFTEN 4-PSI OR MORE ABOVE CORRECT COLD READINGS, AFTER ABOUT AN HOUR'S DRIVING, OR SAY 60 KILOMETRES. THIS INCREASE IS NATURAL, AND SHOULD NOT BE ALTERED. THE PRESSURE WILL REDUCE TO NORMAL WHEN THE TYRES COOL DOWN.

Tyres with lowered air pressure

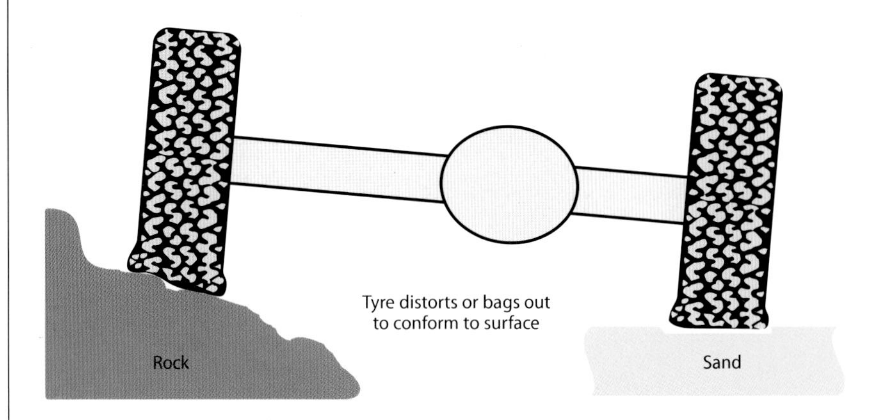

load be sure that the tyres have adequate load capacity for the job. Check with a reputable tyre specialist, as well as your vehicle handbook, for information on what the correct pressure should be, because it alters depending on what you want to do. It's not uncommon to increase the pressure of rear load-carrying tyres by 6psi or more when fully loaded, for example, from the everyday commuting 32psi to 38psi for a long and heavily loaded road journey.

Pressure changes can quite drastically alter 4WD handling characteristics. Under-inflation often results in understeering or scuffing and poor cornering; over-inflation can reduce tread-contact patch and increase chances of skids or slides. Either way, tyre life is lost.

In cornering, tyres scuff their way around. Properly inflated, they roll best and scuff least. If tyres are over-inflated several things can happen. First, the centre of the tread usually wears down more than the outsides; next, the high air pressure in the tyre may not let it move or deform as intended, so that it presents the best, correct footprint and resists undesired slippage. Under-inflated, tyres can overheat very quickly; the tread edges usually wear more than the centre, and the vehicle commonly has slow or sloppy handling.

A tyre can be forced or distorted considerably sideways on a wheel rim by centrifugal pressure exerted when a vehicle drifts or is forced to the outside of a corner. Higher air pressure tends to minimise this, and lower pressure tends to allow it more. If tyre pressure is too low from any cause, scuffing or drag can be worsened, even to the extent, at speed, of the tyre actually being rolled off the rim.

In a tough 4WD situation, letting tyres down from normal pressures so that they deliberately bag out and make a bigger footprint is accepted practice. In soft sand or bad mud sometimes this is the only way to get traction, but it is important to remember to pump them back up to normal pressure as soon as possible. Tyre pressure increases with heat, and can be several psi higher when re-measured after an hour of driving. Don't adjust air pressure in hot tyres; do it when they are cold.

As examples of pressure variation, with tubeless LT265/75R16 tyres on mag rims fitted to my current 4WD I've found that for everyday bitumen driving 34psi all round suits me, measured when the tyres are cold. Fitted with Polyairs the suspension is a bit firm, but that's my preference. However, for long-distance and loaded faster bitumen travelling, I put front and rear tyres both up to 40psi. For heavily loaded and relatively slow

Tip

KEEP A RECORD OF THE TYRE PRESSURE CHANGES, SO YOU CAN GO BACK TO THE ONE YOU FEEL IS BEST.

desert trips, I've found 36psi rear and 32psi front works best on my vehicle. Towing a big caravan at a regular 85-90kph on good roads, 38psi in the 4WD tyres and 40psi in the four van tyres gives the best results.

In sloppy mud, sometimes I've dropped the pressures as low as 20psi all round, but the risk with this is hitting a hidden rock in the boghole and fracturing the tyre wall. In soft sand pressures down to 18psi have helped get the vehicle over very fine or soft, loose sandhills, and pressures lower than 15psi are risky. Deflation devices which can be set to a preferred pressure, and which screw onto the tyre valve, are available. If they're noticeably under-inflated, tubeless tyres can move on rims during cornering, separating the seal between tyre bead and rim, thus deflating quickly.

With very low pressures, the tyre bead can also creep around on the rim well as the vehicle is driven. One way of noting tyre-to-rim creep is to use a crayon or similar, to mark the rim and tyre at a common point, perhaps in line with the valve stem or wheel weight. Any change in the line position or distance will show if the tyre has crept while running low pressures.

On tubed tyres, in most cases the valve stem pokes out through a formed hole in the wheel rim; the tube is virtually held located by this hole. If the tyre creeps enough, it will drag the tube around as well, due to friction between the inside of the tyre and outside of the tube. This is enough to cause the valve stem to eventually be ripped out of the tube. Not only will you then have a flat tyre but the tube will be unusable.

Experiment, but keep a record of what you do so that you can repeat the pressures when you want. It is all subjective, and what suits your vehicle might simply not work on mine at all. Try it for a week or two at a time so you can become used to the settings.

Tip

MONEY SPENT ON QUALITY TYRES IS MONEY SPENT ON SAFETY.

IN SANDY CONDITIONS LOWERING TYRE PRESSURE IS THE NORM.

4X4 **Tip**

EXPERIMENT, BUT KEEP A RECORD OF WHAT YOU DO SO THAT YOU CAN REPEAT THE PRESSURES WHEN YOU WANT. IT IS ALL SUBJECTIVE, AND WHAT SUITS YOUR VEHICLE MIGHT SIMPLY NOT WORK ON ANOTHER VEHICLE.

Use your vehicle handbook — learn the recommended tyre pressures, and generally stick to them. Good tyre dealers can advise on proper tyre inflation pressures.

Tyre sizes

Take your pick of tyres — with new vehicles being produced rapidly the tyre options grow every month. However, consider whether it will be easy to get a matching tyre if one is wrecked, because there are many different sizes and makes and types. For replacement, buy five matching wheels and tyres, so that the spare tyre and rim are consistent, and make sure the wheel nuts fit all of the wheels. 7.50x16 is very common on commercial and split-rim wheels; 205SR16s are like hen's teeth if you are kilometres off the main road, and 31.10R16s not much better. It doesn't matter at all if the tread pattern is different, and even though it is not good, if it is for survival you could run a steel-belt and a nylon radial of the same size, or even a cross-ply, on the one axle. (Tyre size, type, measurement and numbering is complex; for information on this ask at a reputable tyre service.)

Many rims are interchangeable, fitting the very common six-stud 4WD hubs, but be careful if you have to use a spare wheel that someone lends you to get out of bother. Stud patterns, rim offsets, and steering and brake-component clearances may be different. Remember that steel-rim and mag-wheel nuts are not the same. What you should not do is run two tyres with differing overall diameters on the one drive axle, for example, a 7.50x16 and a 205SR15. Handling problems will occur and damage to the differentials is quite likely. If there is one thing easy to justify spending money on, it is tyres.

Point loading

Point loading refers to the way vehicle weight is distributed; examples are:

- Consider a waterbed, which is quite heavy. It won't actually collapse the floor, because the weight is shared over a large area. Actual pressure for a column of water over a particular small area of floor is relatively small.
- Compare the difference between tracks going across a boggy paddock left by a Caterpillar bulldozer (two flattened strips) with those of a normal wheeled tractor (two deepish grooves).
- Dragsters, motorcycles and other competition vehicles run no-tread slicks for maximum surface contact in dry weather, and change to grooved tyres for wet tracks.

We can compare two different sizes of tyre on a vehicle weighing about 3.5 tonnes, to show the difference in weight placed on a square inch. The basic figures are only rough equivalents, and indicate the changes in point loadings.

The tyre footprint can be calculated as follows: tread width multiplied by length of ground contact, then multiplied by four wheels for the total contact patch. The vehicle weight is divided by the total contact patch to give the loading on a specified point.

Point-loading comparison

As an example, a 7.50x16 tyre running 35psi is about 7" wide, and on the ground about 8" of the tyre tread makes contact at any one time. So — seven multiplied by eight equals 56 square inches of rubber in each tyre has to carry the vehicle weight.

If we have four tyres, each with about 56 square inches of contact patch, the total is 224 square inches. Assuming the vehicle weighs 3.5 tonnes, each square inch of rubber carries about 35 lb of weight, or put another way, the "point loading" is 35 pounds per square inch (psi).

On the other hand, using the same method of calculation, a 31.10R15 tyre has somewhere around 80 square inches contact (10" x 8"), so these four tyres total about 320 square inches. The same three and a half tonnes carried on 320 square inches equals about 25lb/psi point loading. That is, it puts less weight on a square inch of ground than the 7.50x16 example above. In some cases this can be a benefit. There is a noticeable reduction in point loading (weight) with the wider 31.10R15 tyres. Perhaps this seems to be a lot, but in real terms the vehicle weight is actually spread across quite an area.

How does this work in the real world? On the one hand, the wider track spreads the weight over a bigger area and tends to sink in less, and on the other, the narrower tyre presses down harder and cuts in more. Every bit of rubber that is missing in chunky or aggressive-pattern tyres is reducing actual and available contact surface on hard slippery surfaces. Off-road, they can bite into the ground, but how much of your driving time is actually off-road? It could equally be argued that, while the tyre/road contact is reduced by the amount of rubber missing due to grooves in the tread, the remaining rubber actually has a higher loading and should therefore bite in more. Tyre technology, tread patterns, widths and air pressures can suddenly have a new meaning looked at in this way.

A logical alternative could be to keep two sets of wheels and tyres, one for everyday use and one for off-road trips. Your safety depends on your tyres. Quite a bit of experimenting can be needed to determine what tyre suits your terrain preference and driving style.

BEACH SAND IS ONE PLACE WHERE LOWERED TYRE PRESSURE IS EFFECTIVE.

Gearboxes and Gears

Advice

USING FIFTH GEAR TO TOW WITH IS NOT ADVISABLE. USE FOURTH GEAR INSTEAD OF FORCING YOUR ENGINE TO LABOUR AT LOWER SPEEDS IN FIFTH GEAR. USING FOURTH GEAR LETS YOUR ENGINE DEVELOP GOOD POWER FOR STEADY TRAVELLING. SAVE FIFTH GEAR FOR NO-LOAD EASY DRIVING.

Gearboxes

Depending on the age of the 4WD, there are gearboxes with different numbers of gears. Almost all of them have a single reverse gear. Here, we are thinking only about an ordinary 4WD gearbox, used in the every-day two-wheel drive, high-range position. Older Land Rovers usually have four forward speeds. Early Nissans have three forwards; early-1980s models have four, and after 1984 Nissan and Toyota and most other 4WD vehicles generally have five forward gears. It is uncommon now to find a 4WD vehicle with only three forward gears. In most cases the fifth gear is actually an overdrive, with the fourth gear as the common 1:1 ratio top gear.

Automatic gearboxes

Because many 4WDs are never driven off-road, and shifting a heavy gearbox in traffic can be a chore when the 4WD is being primarily used as a commuter vehicle, automatic transmission is becoming more popular. Progress in automatic transmission functions and toughness has meant that many 4WDs used in off-road areas now have auto gearboxes. Major advances in electronic technology and the introduction of on-board computers on current vehicles has made major changes to vehicle driveability in some off-road conditions.

An automatic transmission uses a fluid-filled torque converter instead of a clutch and has a set of hydraulically actuated gears which are controlled by valves. A special oil is used and this is pumped around inside by a pump driven by the engine. Some of the latest automatics are electronically controlled and may have power and economy modes or the ability to start off in second gear for slippery conditions.

Used in off-road situations, current 4WD automatic transmissions usually perform very well. In some cases, for example starting off on a difficult uphill, automatics take a lot of the pressure and effort off a driver. Pressing one accelerator pedal down is far easier than juggling a clutch, the engine revs, a gearbox and a handbrake. On hills, most current automatic gearboxes can be manually shifted to a low gear, where they act virtually the same as a manual gearbox. For knowledge of how to operate an automatic gearbox in your particular 4WD, the best and most specific information is in the vehicle handbook and correct service or repair manual. 4WD clubs can also provide useful information.

Gear ratios

Understanding manual gearboxes and their effective use is important in off-road driving, but it seems to be a mystery to many drivers. Most people have ridden a bicycle, so we can use a bike with ten-speed gears for an example. Connected to the pedals on a bike, there are two chain-ring gears, one noticeably bigger than the other. A chain connects these to the rear wheel sprocket which has five different-size toothed gears on it much smaller than the two at the front. When the chain is put on the biggest front chain-ring and the biggest rear sprocket at the same time, pedalling is easy, but the bike doesn't go very fast in the lower gear ratio. By changing the gears in steps from biggest rear size to smallest pedalling gets more difficult but the bike goes faster in the higher gear ratios. The bike can be ridden all the time using the biggest chain ring for driving the five rear gears, and that's exactly the same principle as a normal "high range only" gearbox in a normal car. The newer "on-demand" and "all-wheel-drive" Sports Utility Vehicles [SUVs] usually have only a single-range gearbox, despite having other traction benefits.

However, when the pedalling gets difficult on a ten-speed bike you can change the ratios again by swapping to the smaller chain-ring gear at the front. The five rear gears remain the same but the overall effect is to make them all proportionately easier for you to pedal by driving them with a smaller front gear. Doing this is virtually the same as changing to low range in a 4WD gearbox; this selectable function gearbox (high range and low range) is the main operational difference between car and 4WD gearboxes. The more-powerful "go-anywhere" 4WDs all have dual-range gearboxes.

Refer to the diagram below for a comparison of car and 4WD gearbox ratios. Each vehicle is shown with five forward gears. While they both have similar top speed in fifth gear, the other gears provide quite different speeds. In a manual gearbox car designed for roads for normal vehicles, the spread of forward gears might be as simple and evenly spaced as shown. That is, each gear more-or-less does an even amount of work. (If you are wondering what happened to reverse gear, in most cases it is the same as first gear, but just made to run backwards.) In direct comparison, the similar-purpose five forward gears in a 4WD, designed for

Advice

UNDERSTANDING GEARBOXES AND THEIR EFFECTIVE USE IS IMPORTANT IN OFF-ROAD DRIVING.

Comparison of gearbox ratios

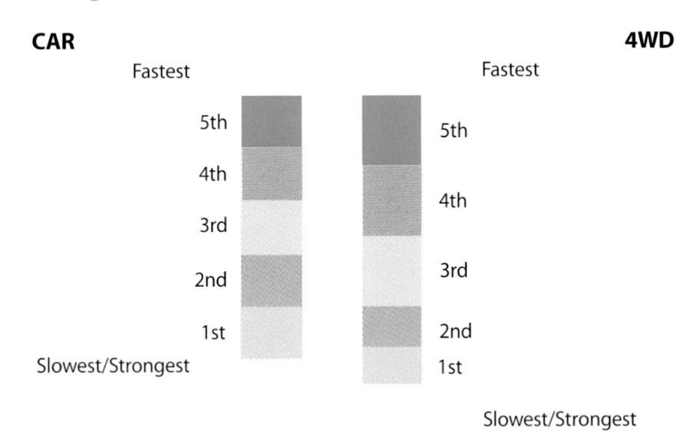

Overdrive gear system

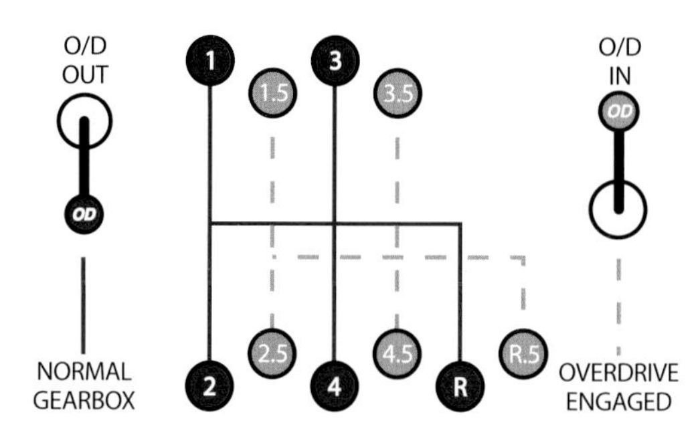

When overdrive is engaged, it creates a gear about half way between the normal gearbox ratios, in this case giving eight forward gears

use in potentially very bad off-road conditions, may well be like those in the diagram. This example 4WD gear ratio spread would be designed to keep the engine driving the vehicle at the best rev range, with ample reserve power in the lower gears, yet still give the ability to travel reasonably quickly on good roads.

The main difference is in the power available to drive the wheels, due to the ratios of gears within the gearbox (similar to the two chain-ring gears on the ten-speed bike).

The trade-off with these different ratios is that the 4WD is slower than the car getting up to the speed limit. However, a 4WD wouldn't go very well over rough ground, or be able to tow heavy loads well unless it had that very low first gear to use. Because the car doesn't need to slog uphill or through bog, its first gear ratio, which is much higher than the 4WD first gear, is ample for starting it off.

While the job of brakes is to temporarily slow and/or brake the vehicle, the gears are used for permanent mechanical speed control through varying the engine revs for the particular circumstance. High range gears are fast for normal everyday driving; low range gears are slower for off-road or heavy-duty driving. Use the gear you need because of the speed. It is quite possible to change directly from fourth down to first gear, provided that the vehicle has been slowed down to a level that is suitable for driving in first gear. Likewise, it is quite possible to change up from first to fourth, if the vehicle speed is right. As the driver, you simply select the gear you want to use, based on the circumstances.

Adding a low range to a 4WD gearbox (regardless of whether the four- wheel-drive facility is used or not, because the 4WD system has no effect on the gearbox ratios) doubles the number of gears available for a 4WD vehicle. That is, a five-speed gearbox with one reverse gear will now have effectively ten forward speeds and two reverses. However, it is difficult to use them all at the one time in a big long string, like one-to-ten, for example. Changing from 2H to 4H is easily done at any time and at most speeds by pulling a lever or pressing a button. Changing into four-wheel-drive low range (4L) usually needs very low speed or a stopped vehicle, and changing out of low range while moving sometimes takes a couple of tries. It is possible to split-shift change from L3 to H2 by moving the transfer gearbox lever out of low range back into high range and the main gear lever from third back to second gear. Getting these split changes right each time under pressure can be quite a challenge. For simple and easiest result, gears are best used in the same range, all low or all high.

You could mix-and-match or split-shift the gears to obtain a precise speed for a desired rev range if you had to, but this takes quite a bit of practice and experimentation. As an example, at a constant engine rpm you can travel about the same speed in high-range first gear as you can in low-range second gear. While you may have the same road speed, what you won't have in high-range first gear is the same great flexibility or instant power, when compared with virtually immediate acceleration anywhere in low-range second gear.

Overdrive

One of the best investments I ever made was an overdrive for my 4WD. They are now available for many different manual 4WDs, and what this accessory does in effect is to create a "half-gear" in between the other normal gears. By adding a couple of extra gears into an existing gearbox, usually by fitting a housing enlarged for these extra gears (or a sort of additional mini-gearbox bolted onto the standard one) it is relatively simple to change the normal ratios. They are expensive, but mine was really worth every dollar I spent on it, and unbeatable in any situation.

To operate it you only have to move another gear lever in a straight line to put it either "in" or "out" of operation. In my 4WD first and second gears are ratioed relatively close to each other; then there's quite a spread in ratio to third, and about the same gap again to fourth. (See diagram on page 135 comparing gearbox ratios.)

In practice, this second-to-third gap often means that when towing a load or climbing a steep hill, to change from second gear to third in the normal gearbox a lot of power has to be developed in second gear. Without considerable acceleration, there may not be sufficient vehicle momentum built up to carry the vehicle long enough to change up into third gear and still

4WD GEAR RATIOS ALLOW THEM TO GET TO PLACES NORMAL 2WDS CANNOT GO.

Advice

DOUBLE CLUTCHING IS A WAY TO MAKE A FAST GEAR-SHIFT, BUT TO DO IT QUICKLY AND CONSISTENTLY TAKES PRACTICE.

be able to pull away cleanly. In this situation, by engaging the overdrive, there is effectively a gear half-way between second and third, right where it is needed. Because it works on any gear regardless of the range, overdrive can be used anywhere, in normal road conditions or in bad off-road 4WD driving. That virtually eliminates the need for the hard revs and makes managing vehicle speeds and loads a lot easier. The only drawback is that sometimes you need to be able to juggle two gear levers.

Occasionally, due to bad corrugations or steep track or a heavy load, you simply can't get enough speed up in a 4WD to change to the next gear. Without a gear right for the situation, there's only one other option — be prepared to travel at whatever speed is relevant to sensible engine revs in that gear until conditions alter and allow a change up to the next gear. This doesn't happen with overdrive, and I've found that it is the total answer to just about any needed gear, on or off-road. For towing a van or boat, there's nothing to equal it. Even in city traffic, it makes life a lot more bearable with a manual 4WD vehicle because it gives a useful revs-to-speed range, to keep smoothly on speed limits with minimal drive-train shudder or engine strain.

Gear selection

Selection and use of gears in a 4WD can be critical in off-road driving. It also shows up differences in driver ability and experience. With a low and powerful gear a sharp increase in engine acceleration produces wheelspin. In slippery going, use as high a gear as practical, with minimum engine revs, just sufficient to maintain headway. The higher gear gives slower vehicle response to the throttle, thus less chance of the wheels and ground breaking traction contact.

Compared with level ground at constant revs, there will always be some loss of forward speed and engine revs in bad traction, steep uphill driving. The steeper and longer the hill, the more drop in engine revs will be noticed, even sometimes despite acceleration to overcome the loss. Changing to a lower gear to increase the available engine power may be the answer. This is when practice to know your gear ratios pays big dividends. By knowing the speed and power available from each gear at the best engine revs, it becomes much easier to pick an appropriate gear/speed for any situation.

Wrong gears

Trying to slowly climb up a large sand dune in third gear in high range at normal engine revs and without 4WD is futile. Momentum is essential in some four-wheel driving. Maintaining it can make the difference between getting over or through an obstacle at the first try and spending much time and effort in repeated attempts. Climbing the same dune in 4WD low-range second gear with plenty of engine revs and a good deal of momentum to help carry you over the soft crest will produce quite a different result.

Think about which gear you are likely to need before you get to the hazard, instead of trying to change in the middle of hard going. No matter how good a driver you are, momentum is lost during a gear change. This might be just enough to stop you making it up the climb in one go. You may not need a long run-up to get sufficient momentum for a sand dune. Often just a few vehicle lengths will be enough, providing you use plenty of acceleration and maintain it. If this doesn't work, then sometimes the only way is to back off the obstacle for perhaps 100 metres for a run-up. Accelerate hard enough to allow changing up a couple of gears, charge the climb and let kinetic energy help you up and over. (Before you do this it is wise to walk the climb, if practical, to be sure you are not heading blindly into disaster.)

Double-clutching

In strongly built manual 4WD gearboxes sometimes a gear change can be comparatively slow due to the heaviness and relative inertia of components. The synchromesh mechanisms (look them up in your service and repair manual) can drag slightly, making a normal shift just too slow for your needs. One way to overcome this is to "double-clutch" during the gearshift. The gears are "speeded-up" by the action, and the gear change is actually faster. This is not difficult, but getting the repetitive actions fast and fluid takes some practice.

As an example, consider a straight-line-pattern change from fourth to third gear. Drag or slowness of change can occur during the movement of the lever from fourth up to third. The normal three-step sequence is:

1 Clutch in and foot off the accelerator at the same time.
2 Move the lever from fourth across neutral to third while the clutch is still in.
3 Clutch out and power on again at the same time.

"Dumping" the clutch during a gear change at low or medium revs and speeds (just taking your foot straight off it without attempt to let it out smoothly) usually results in a solid clunk through the drive-train; this happens quite often as the speed of the gears catches up with the engine revs. Synchromesh is supposed to keep the gears spinning internally at compatible engagement speed, but this is not always the case, making double-clutching necessary. Double-clutching is not much different in sequence from a normal gearshift movement, and while it is actually one more physical clutch movement, it can be a lot faster in effect. The four steps of this sequence are:

1 Clutch in and lever out of fourth into neutral at the same time.
2 Clutch out and rev the motor sharply at the same time.
3 Clutch in and lever into third at the same time.
4 Clutch out and power on at the same time.

Dumping the clutch out with the lever in neutral and applying engine revs causes gears to whizz around in the gearbox much faster than normal. When the gears are selected by the next movement of the lever from neutral into third, they enmesh much faster. Because the engine revs and gear rotation are already fairly high, letting the clutch out sharply again doesn't usually cause a clunk, and with practice

THE RIGHT GEAR AND FLEXIBLE REV RANGE MAKES TERRAIN LIKE THIS FAR EASIER TO DRIVE.

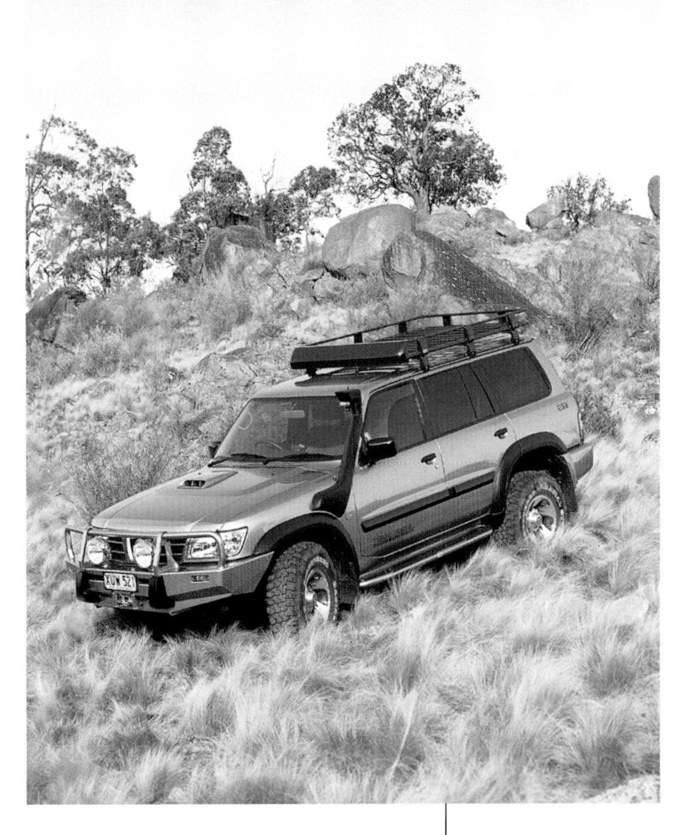

the change is made faster than normal. The secret is to make all the actions fast and positive, use plenty of revs and accelerate again quickly.

Drive-train

The "drive-train" is made up of the parts of the vehicle that transmit the power developed by the motor to the ground, to make the vehicle move. First the clutch does its job of connecting the engine to the gearbox. Behind the clutch are the various-sized gears inside the gearbox, which you move with the gear lever, selecting whatever combination of internal gears you need for the conditions you are in. As the engine crankshaft rotates, if the gearbox is in gear and your foot is off the clutch so that the two are connected, power is transmitted through the gears in the gearbox to the main output shaft. In turn, this shaft rotates and so does all the rest of the drive-train.

The main output shaft which comes out through an oil seal at the rear of the gearbox usually has a universal joint at its rear end. This joins the output shaft to the front of the tailshaft which is located along the centre of the vehicle below the floor in a normal rear-wheel-drive 4WD vehicle. The universal joint is designed to allow flexibility and keep correct alignment of the tailshaft. The tailshaft is a strong tubular shaft with a splined section to allow for changes in length with suspension movement. The tailshaft transfers the rotating drive from the gearbox to the differential on the back axle. There is another universal joint at its rear end to connect it to the differential. (This set-up is virtually duplicated for the front drive-train, ahead of the transfer gearbox.)

The rear universal joint connects with the input shaft for the rear differential; it allows alignment and movement while smoothly and continuously powering the vehicle. A differential turns the drive from along to across the vehicle. It uses a system of bevelled gears at right-angles from the tailshaft (along the vehicle), to rotate two axle shafts within the axle housing (across the vehicle, one each to left and right). The outer ends of these are firmly anchored to the centres of the left and right hubs, and the wheels are bolted onto the hubs. The tyres are fitted onto the rims and when they make contact with the ground the drive-train is completed from clutch to ground. Your vehicle's service and repair manual will give the exact description for each component, but in essence they are all very similar.

Lubrication of gears

Gears must have a film of lubrication between the loaded teeth faces, or they wear out quickly. Gear teeth are designed to have load or effort applied to them, and while this happens, either under forward load (driving effort) or backward load (over-run on trailing throttle), the oil is designed to adhere and slide over the faces. When it does its job it minimises wear. However, gears can get into an "unloaded" position where, because the engine effort to keep the vehicle in motion is virtually balanced against the load, the minute spaces between the faces of the gear teeth are put into a pressure-on/pressure-off condition. The strong engine-firing pulses of powerful engines also contribute to the on/off load condition of gears, and possibly to the same condition in other vehicle components.

Apparently what then can happen is that the on/off load pressure forces or squeezes most of the lubricating oil off the faces and out of the way. The unlubricated faces can then hammer against themselves at their constant contact points, and the repetition causes wear. This can eventually cause hard-faced gear teeth faces to pit, flaking or spalling the hardfacing off tooth surfaces. Top-grade gearbox oil minimises the chances of this. Correct lubrication is critical in any vehicle and cheap oils and greases should never be used on a hard-working 4WD.

Practice

There is only one way to learn the gear and range differences, and available speeds and power of a 4WD gearbox — get out somewhere on flat ground and try them all. Pick a suitable and steady engine speed, stick to it for fair comparison, then note their effective maximums and compare their acceleration rates. As an example, you'll find that sometimes off-road the vehicle's speed is right for the circumstances, but you just can't get the engine flexibility where you want it in, say, H2. Usually a change down into low range and up a few gears (say, into L4), will allow the same speed but produce the right spread of engine power you need. Finding out these different effects and combinations is something you really have to experiment with on your own vehicle before you get into the hard stuff. Learning it takes practice but the satisfaction of being able to get it right every time is hard to beat.

Trying to "mix-and-match" gears in hard going without practice beforehand can be difficult. In many vehicles it is simple to change between 2WD and 4WD in high range at almost any sensible speed, and on the run. Some current models offer this ratio-changing function as a push-button option. On most 4WDs you can't change down into low range from high range without bringing the vehicle to a stop, which can sometimes be a nuisance. It shouldn't be a worry if you plan ahead as you drive, but double-clutching (see page 139) can be one way to overcome it if needed urgently. (You can sometimes change up, out of low into high, on the move.)

Occasionally, even when stopped, when you try to change from low range back up into high range, the high–low range gear lever on the transfer gearbox simply won't move. This is usually due to some "winding-up" in the meshed teeth of the gears in the box. To get them apart here's a simple clue. Change into reverse gear and back up a body length, then try to move the lever again. A few tries at this, switching between forwards and backwards, will usually work to free up the tightly meshed gears and allow you to change back into high range. Sometimes as the gears become free there is a horrible-sounding but apparently harmless "clunk" as the drive-train equalises and the gear lever moves sharply back into the neutral position.

4WD drive-train (manual transmission)

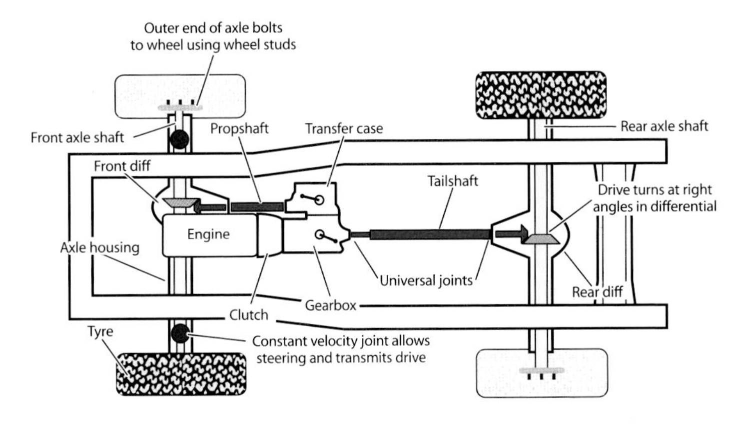

4WD Transfer Gearbox and Hubs

Options

If your vehicle is not full-time 4WD, as many current 4WDs are, when you select 4WD a relatively simple mechanical process occurs. All you really do is bring another drive system, via another built-in gearbox (called a transfer gearbox), into mesh with the normally used one. The number of wheels propelling the vehicle can then change from two to four. (Remember, in many vehicles the front hubs have to be manually locked in before they can actually transmit the driving power now available.) Gear drive, or a strong toothed chain in some cases, connects power from the gearbox in the permanent drive system across to the transfer gearbox, adding the switchable additional system gearbox at your choice.

When this happens, gears in this transfer gearbox then drive another shaft, exactly as for the rear one, but going to the front axle. The difference is really in name only — the front shaft does the same job as the rear tailshaft but is known as the "propshaft" to distinguish it from the rear one. It drives what is simply a front drive-train, the same as the normal rear one, except that the front wheels steer.

Full-time 4WD

There are 4WDs that have all four wheels driving permanently as a normal function, so drivers don't have to worry about operating 4WD mechanisms at all. In this case, safety and handling is generally improved all round. Range Rover, Discovery, most current Landcruisers and many other vehicles have or offer full-time 4WD. Pajero and Jeep, amongst others, have a sophisticated optional system allowing full-time or part-time 4WD. Some more road-oriented single-range gearbox full-time four-wheel-drive vehicles, such as Subaru, give the best possible road-holding, and still give good fuel economy. In big and heavy dual-range 4WDs, many of which are never used off-road, there can be a penalty for having a full-time 4WD feature. Apart from unwanted wear on some parts, higher fuel consumption is common. (Many petrol-engine 4WDs are converted to LPG when new to offset this high fuel cost.) For vehicles with manually

Caution

DON'T FORGET TO UNLOCK MANUAL HUBS BACK INTO THE 'FREE' POSITION WHEN GOING ONTO BITUMEN ROADS.

FULL-TIME 4WDS ARE BECOMING MORE COMMON.

operated front-wheel hubs the cost of somewhat less drive-train wear and fuel cost, compared with full-time 4WD, is that the driver has to get out of the vehicle to switch in or engage both hubs.

Engagement

Going into 4WD does not allow driving power to get to the front wheels unless the hubs are locked in. Locking in the manual front hubs is simple. They are well marked, and usually take a quarter- or half-turn by hand to engage or disengage. This has the effect of locking the hub to the axle, generally by a sliding cam turning inside the hub. Axle splines mesh, the two parts become interlocked and the wheel can then be driven by the axle instead of free-rolling. If the hubs are locked in when you activate 4WD with the lever or button from inside the vehicle the complete system works immediately. Manual hubs are locked out into the "free" position for normal on-road driving, and rotated into the "lock" position for harder going. (Never

Engaging 4WD

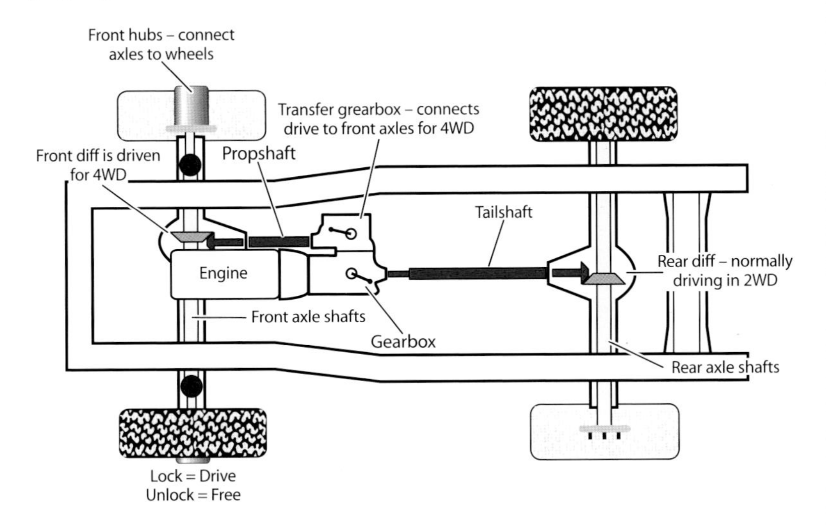

forget to unlock them properly back to the free position when you finally come back onto the bitumen.)

Power to the front wheels can be disconnected in two ways. The first way (although 4WD may be engaged via the transfer box, with driving power going forward along the front drive-train right out to the ends of the axles) is by not actually having those axles locked to the front hubs; the wheels can't be driven by the engine. The second way is not to have 4WD engaged even though the hubs are locked in. In this case, driving the vehicle forward makes the wheels turn just by rolling on road contact. This turns the locked axles and thus powers the drive-train all the way back to the transfer box. All of this does nothing, apart from perhaps causing wear on parts from their unnecessary turning.

Hubs

IF YOUR VEHICLE HAS MANUAL HUBS MAKE SURE THAT BOTH FRONT HUBS ARE EITHER ENGAGED OR DISENGAGED.

The front hubs of some vehicles are automatically engaged when the transfer lever is moved into four-wheel drive. But manual front hubs have to be deliberately locked in at each of the front wheels — you have to get out of the vehicle to do it. Providing the front drive hubs are not engaged, not much harm will occur if you do inadvertently move the lever into 4WH and drive for a short distance on bitumen, but it is not desirable; it can be harmful to cruise at 100 km/h in this condition. The opposite, driving on bitumen with the manual front hubs locked in (but 4WD definitely not engaged) doesn't seem to do harm; in fact, some manufacturers recommend it once a month to ensure the front drive-train mechanisms are kept lubricated.

Engaging the front hubs on a conventional 4WD gives the same result whether automatically or manually done — it allows the front wheels to be driven. With front hubs that can be engaged or disengaged at the driver's choice, a mistake in locking in only one of the front axles could be very expensive. With only one hub locked in when working, the axle load is unevenly shared and the loaded single front axle shaft may break under much less apparent load than normal. This can happen even with automatic front hubs.

Unless physically twisted to unlock (to the free position at the front hub), manual hubs should not unlock while the vehicle is being driven in either forward or reverse direction. It is uncommon for a hub to get unlocked from being hit by scrub or sticks in the bush. From the locked position, to get one axle unlocked requires forgetfulness or confusion on someone's part.

Warming up

There are reasons for driving along with locked front hubs, but not actually activating 4WD until needed. Coming off the dirt onto bitumen for a short time, and then going back onto the dirt or slippery section where 4WD will be needed again is one reason. If travelling only a few kilometres it is probably not worth getting out of the vehicle to unlock or free the hubs. Another good reason for driving for a short time with hubs locked in is to properly lubricate the complete drive-train. It is sensible to have the front drive system warmed up before getting into the hard going, so you could stop a few kilometres before going off the bitumen to lock the hubs in, then engage 4WD when you leave the bitumen.

Wear factors

Only 4WDs with a full-time 4WD feature, or with a special differential allowing difference between the tailshaft and propshaft drives are safe to drive on hard dry surfaces in 4WD. Unless your vehicle is designed this way carefully avoid travelling on normal bitumen in 4WD with the front hubs locked in. In a relatively short time, considerable tyre wear can result, and mechanical damage as well.

Here's why. In normal 2WD each of the two wheels on the rear axle can travel at the particular rate they need, automatically adjusted as needed when cornering, via the differential. (The inner wheel travels slower and covers less distance than the outer wheel on a corner). When all four wheels are being driven in standard high-range 4WD the gearbox drives the rear wheels and the transfer box drives the front wheels at exactly the same rate. Mechanical connection between all four driven tyres is direct and unbroken. On gravel road or other soft surface there is ample loose surface to let each tyre wheelspin a little as needed. But on dry bitumen the grip between tyre and road is strong and tyres can't slip very easily. Any mechanical load or wind-up has to be taken by the whole drive-train, and not through slippage of the tyres.

Slow travel

Making sure the front hubs are not engaged and then using low range to very slowly back a caravan down a narrow lane is common practice among 4WD owners. Some with steep driveways back up to their houses using two-wheel drive, but in low range. A large amount of torque is generated when in low range and it is easy to get wheelspin with too much acceleration. Speed of a 4WD in low-range reverse is about half that of normal two-wheel high range reverse for the same engine revs, helping to make backing at idle revs much easier. The best way to find out whether your particular vehicle can be used in low range two-wheel drive would be to ask experienced people with the same vehicle or ask around. For example, early model Land Rovers are renowned for snapping back axles under load when trying to use low-range with the front hubs unlocked unless the driver is very careful.

THIS AUTOMATIC HUB IS UNIQUE IN THAT IT CAN BE LOCKED MANUALLY USING A SPANNER.

Torque

In some current 4WD vehicles the rear axles have larger shaft diameter than the front ones because they're used a lot more. However, it is still possible to break them under strong acceleration or with a heavy load up a steep climb. Off-road, there is no valid reason to attempt steep climbs or any section of hard going in 2WD. If possible when off-road, avoid placing the vehicle load only on the two shafts of just one axle, not shared between four.

Clutch, Brakes and Differentials

Clutch

Refer to a service and repair manual for the exact explanation of how the clutch on your vehicle works. Clutches on early 4WDs were all mechanically operated simply by the driver's leg-power pushing against springs; power-assisted clutches are becoming much more common. 4WD clutches are usually much bigger than those for a car, and designed for very heavy duty. Although they are able to take a bit of abuse if occasionally needed, consistent slipping or riding the clutch to start off through being in too high a gear will quickly cause damage. Choosing the appropriate gear to cope with the situation, use the clutch cleanly and keep your foot completely off the clutch unless it is really necessary.

Clutches don't go wrong very often. Most vehicles have hydraulically activated clutches, making their physical use relatively easy. Be sure to keep an eye on the fluid level in the clutch master cylinder; because they don't often play up, it is easy to overlook such a basic check. The slave cylinder, which actually pushes the clutch operating-arm and is usually located somewhere down on the bell-housing between engine and gearbox, can leak hydraulic fluid. Unless you check for visible leaks each time you service the vehicle you could one day find yourself with a clutch that won't work properly. With mechanically operated clutches, unless the actuating cable or rod breaks, the clutch will usually work. After years of use some clutches shudder a fair bit when letting them out. If this happens, try using a few hundred more revs each time you move off. Sometimes this helps, but if not, get the clutch checked by a mechanic.

4WD clutch-plates are designed to work dry, depending on controlled slippage and positive friction to connect the engine to the gearbox. Even if you drive through wheel-deep water, it

4X4 Advice

CHOOSING THE APPROPRIATE GEAR TO COPE WITH THE SITUATION, USE THE CLUTCH CLEANLY AND KEEP YOUR FOOT COMPLETELY OFF THE CLUTCH UNLESS IT IS REALLY NECESSARY.

is unlikely to get into the clutch while you are moving because the pressure needed to keep the faces together and driving is enough to repel water, and it is spinning at whatever your engine revs are. Keep the water out; plan your gears and speed before any water crossing and avoid changing gears in the middle if at all possible.

Brakes

Braking systems are hydraulic and there is the same need to check for correct hydraulic fluid levels as with the clutch, plus a greater need to look for any leaks. Many 4WDs have vacuum power-assisted brakes, making the driver's pedal effort very much easier. To operate them, petrol vehicles can draw their power-braking vacuum from the engine inlet manifold which is relatively simple. Diesels haven't got the same degree of vacuum in their manifolds, so in most cases a vacuum pump has to be specially provided to give the boost needed for braking assistance.

On most diesel 4WDs the vacuum pump is fitted on the rear of the alternator, and there can be two potential drawbacks with this. Firstly, the pump is driven by the same shaft that turns the alternator armature. If the alternator doesn't work and has to be removed for servicing or replacement, the vacuum source for the power-assisted brakes has to go also. The second drawback is the expense of repairs. Check your service and repair manual to find out how your power-braking system works.

Many 4WDs have disc front brakes and drum rear brakes, although four-wheel disc brakes are now almost the standard set-up. Most rear drum brakes are fitted with a built-in self-adjusting mechanism but they can be manually set, through a slot in the brake backing-plate if needed. Disc brakes are self adjusting. The purely mechanical handbrake usually works on the rear wheels by expanding the shoes inside the brake drums at each wheel. A noticeable build-up of very fine powdered brake-shoe material collects inside a brake drum. Whenever you do a brake check and adjustment, this powder should be carefully removed. A wire brush and a hacksaw-blade scraper are quite efficient. 4WD vehicles with disc brakes on all four wheels often have a special drum brake fitted on the tailshaft for a handbrake, a very effective arrangement for locking up the back wheels, and one that holds positively just about anywhere.

Brake fluid

4WD brakes often get abused and worked very hard. Keeping an eye on brake fluid level in a 4WD is important because 4WDs can get into sticky situations and brakes may be essential to help get out of it. Water and brake fluid mixing is to be avoided. Brake fluid is hygroscopic (attracts moisture), so make sure any rubber seal on the top of the master-cylinder reservoir is kept clean and properly fitted. Check the service and repair manual for the correct interval to completely drain and replace the brake fluid, and stick to it as cheap insurance. Make sure that brake fluid is graded at least as DOT-3 or better, as this has a higher boiling point and is suitable for use in disc brakes.

Caution

POWDER FROM BRAKES MAY CONTAIN ASBESTOS, AND SHOULD NOT BE BREATHED IN. USE A VACUUM CLEANER RATHER THAN BLOWING IT OUT WITH COMPRESSED AIR, AND USE A MASK FOR EXTRA PROTECTION.

REGULAR CHECKING OF THE BRAKES DOES NOT TAKE LONG AND SHOULD BE PART OF YOUR MAINTENANCE.

CHECK THE BRAKE MASTER CYLINDER AT REGULAR INTERVALS AND TOP UP IF NECESSARY. IF CONTINUAL TOPPING UP IS REQUIRED EXAMINE THE COMPLETE BRAKE SYSTEM FOR LEAKS.

In some circumstances, usually when you've been doing a lot of hard braking, the brake fluid gets very hot and can cause the brake pedal travel to drop. Slightly pumping the pedal might be needed to get sufficient braking. After the fluid cools down the pedal should return to the normal position.

Oils for differentials, gearbox and transfer box

When putting oils in diffs, gearbox and transfer box, it is pointless overfilling them. Take the time and dip them a few times to check you aren't putting in too much. The alternative is to undo the drain plugs and leave them for a good while to properly drain, then refill with a measured amount of best-quality and correct-grade oil. (The service and repair manual has all the necessary information.) Make sure the parts are hot before you start the job, otherwise all the old oil won't run out. Overfilling can create pressure inside the housings, causing seal leakage through excess internal pressure. High internal air pressure will aggravate any seal-leak condition. A common, relatively minor trouble that occurs with some models of gearbox is that the oil seal between the gearbox and the transfer box leaks.

Typical grease and oil points

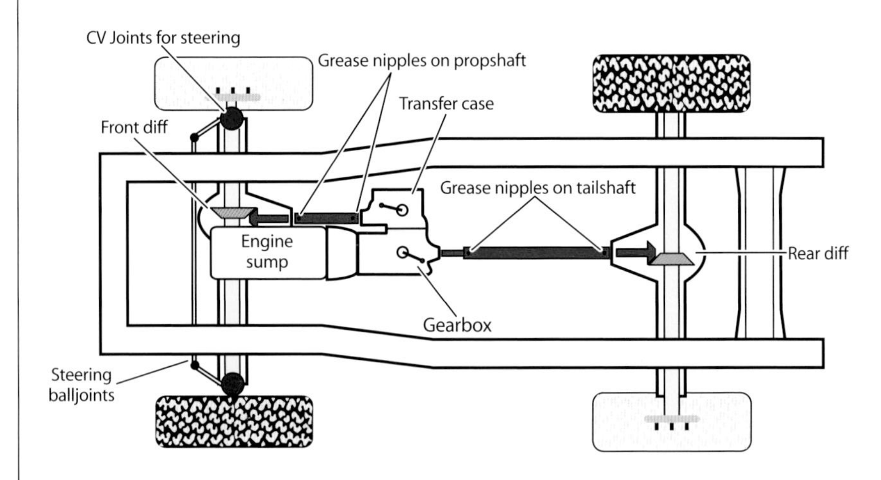

As a result, the oil level lowers in one and rises in the other. One quick fix for this is simply a tube running externally between the two allowing built-up oil to transfer back to its right place.

Oil frothing can occur if there is too much oil. Froth won't circulate or provide the proper lubrication and coverage of the gear teeth. For heavy towing or off-road usage if you have an automatic transmission it pays to fit an additional oil-cooler radiator for the gearbox. Most automatic gearboxes now come with this feature as standard.

Oil leaks from the underside of a 4WD can be a fire risk. I recall seeing an elderly 4WD begin to burn out near Lake Mungo in New South Wales. On a hot day, the driver had been tracking across a few paddocks with high and very dry grass. Some of this got caught under the vehicle and bunched up, apparently igniting where it contacted the exhaust pipe. The driver said there were a few oil leaks from the sump, diffs and gearbox. Although the grass looked like it was only caught in the door steps, the underside burnt well, with black smoke issuing everywhere.

Even though it isn't what the manual advised, in one of my previous manual 4WDs I ran the same oil in front and rear 4WD differentials, and in the gearbox and transfer box. By choice, I fitted an air-locker rear diff, so I had to run the appropriate oil. It was the best quality hypoid oil I could buy, and my enquiries from oil manufacturers showed that it was also correctly graded for the other components. It was a bit more expensive than regular diff or gearbox oils, but it had one major advantage — I only had to carry one type of oil on trips, and for me this was an important space saving. To be safe, before doing this check with your oil supplier to make sure this is okay, but after 266,000 kilometres it proved to be right in mine.

Running good-quality oil is vital, especially in locking or limited-slip diffs. Oil deteriorates with heat and it is very annoying to get bad stutter in a rear diff on the way home after a long, hot trip. Some diff oils can turn to thick goo when badly overheated. Most limited-slip diffs have friction devices to allow a set percentage of differential action slippage to occur. When they have to run in thick goo the cones or ramps sometimes don't release quickly enough. If they stick, when they should be providing a differential effect as in going around a corner, this can cause axle shudder.

The rear limited-slip diff in my manual vehicle had metal take-up ramps, and when it was fairly new I noticed a shudder, particularly on tight cornering. Talking with a few diff specialists, it turned out to be the type of oil in the diff. A change of grade and brand fixed the clunks. It recurred about 30,000 kilometres later, and another check showed the oil had lost much of its lubricating properties. A drain and refill cured the shudder, so now I change all the oils in diffs and manual gearboxes at 20,000 kilometre intervals.

Manufacturers make different oils for specific purposes, but all deteriorate and lose their properties if they get too hot. They then don't protect and lubricate properly.

Emulsification (resulting from oil and water being mixed or beaten up together) shows usually as white or greyish froth when you check the oil. If you do find this drain it promptly. If you find it in your engine sump, and you haven't been driving in water, then you probably have a serious problem. Like brake fluid, water in any of these oils is a bad thing, but it can be largely prevented. If your vehicle is doing a lot of off-road work, fit extended and water-sealed breather tubes for the diffs, gearbox and transfer box, running the venting ends of the new tubes up over mudguard height. They are simple to make using braided or reinforced fuel line.

Caution

CHANGE THE CLUTCH FLUID AT THE SAME TIME AS YOU CHANGE THE BRAKE FLUID. IT HAS BEEN WORKING HARD TOO.

Extended differential breather hose

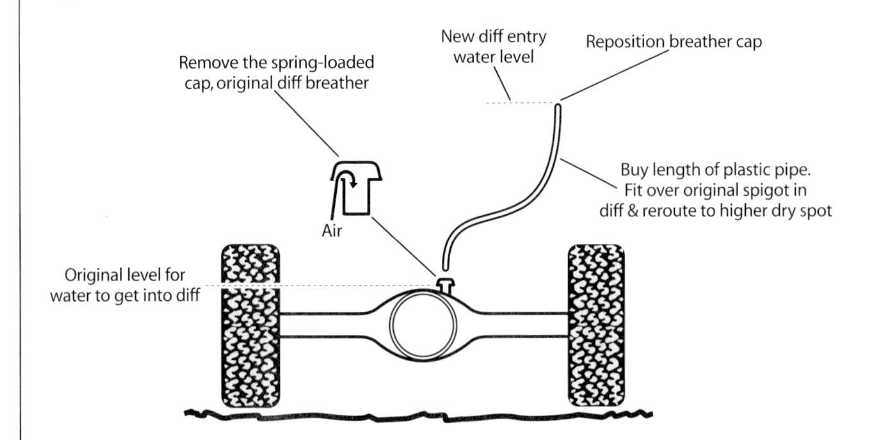

Water and oils don't mix

Water can get into many places in which it is not welcome through oil seals. As oil is meant to be inside housings and other components, seals are designed to keep it there. The lips on seals generally face inwards. This way, internal oil pressure tends to keep the thin seal edge down tight on the shaft or whatever runs through the seal to avoid oil getting out. Because these seals face inwards, it is comparatively easy for water to seep in from outside, the opposite to the way most seals are designed to work.

COMPONENTS OF AN AIR-OPERATED DIFF LOCK KIT.

This seeping effect can be aggravated by a natural condition. When a hot diff is suddenly chilled by immersion in a wheel-deep creek the internal air pressure drops somewhat. When this is combined with water pressure, due to the depth and distance to travel in the water, the inward-facing seals can allow water in. A typical place for ingress is wheel-bearing outer seals which permit water to trickle through into the axle housing from where it could seep into the diff centre.

One theory is that stopping for a few minutes before entering deep water will let the diffs cool and the pressures equalise a bit. If the water is deep, cautious drivers stop to check out the crossing path, and/or to tie a tarp across the radiator to act as a water dam for engine and fan protection. This could be enough time to let some cooling occur.

Locked differentials

A locked differential is the same as a solid axle or no differential. That is, both wheels on an axle turn at the same rate regardless of whether the vehicle is going around a corner or in a straight line. Locked diffs, or "diff locks" as they are commonly called, give a vehicle greatly improved traction abilities. Generally speaking, having a diff lock on the rear axle, which can be switched in and out at will by the driver pressing a button in the cabin, is a great benefit. Diff locks don't change vehicle mechanical safety or driveability on-road; off-road they can make a well-driven 4WD almost unstoppable in just about any terrain. Locked differentials can be ordered with many new vehicles or fitted as an aftermarket accessory, but they are quite expensive. On bitumen roads they are switched out and not used, but in off-road situations sometimes they provide traction when no other vehicle can get anywhere. Fitting to the rear axle only is adequate for most drivers.

Diff locks can in some circumstances provide a false sense of security and this should be kept in mind if you get into really bad conditions. One dangerous situation, with front and rear diff locks active, is when travelling more or less square across a hill on a side-slope. Diff locks will usually keep the vehicle driving, despite its natural tendency to turn down the hill, or side-slip downhill with the front wheels. They can sometimes give a false sense of security, and there have been occasions where vehicles have reached a sideways over-balance point because the driver has lost or not heeded the normal warning signs of front-end side-slip, indicating the need to quickly steer downhill to restore vehicle stability.

Another problem when the front diff is locked is some loss of steering. This usually happens on downhills where a drop in steering effectiveness can occur. The front wants to keep going, but generally in a straight line, causing some loss of control. Understeer is the usual result.

Caution

WHEN USING DIFF LOCKS IN BAD CONDITIONS, BE CAUTIOUS AND MAKE SURE THAT YOUR VEHICLE'S CAPABILITIES DO NOT EXCEED YOUR DRIVING SKILLS.

DIFF LOCKS ARE OF GREAT BENEFIT IN ROUGH CONDITIONS, GIVING TRACTION ADVANTAGE.

Breakdowns, 'Fixits' and Services

Maintenance and preparation

Unless you have the necessary skills and knowledge, major servicing is best left to specialists. But simple service jobs such as oil changes, tightening rattly exhausts, greasing steering components (if needed — check your service manual), cleaning air filters, topping up batteries and brake fluid, can easily be done by an interested owner. You will save money as well as getting to know more about your vehicle, which could help solve problems on your next trip.

Doing your own basic maintenance and vehicle preparation can be a very enjoyable part of four-wheel driving. A couple of hours of maintenance and preparation in your driveway or garage is almost nothing, compared with breakdown repair hours spent in unpleasant conditions out in the scrub. Quite a few of the 4WD breakdowns I've come across have been due solely to vehicle neglect by the owner prior to the trip, not necessarily lack of maintenance knowledge.

Hoping your almost-worn-out tyres will make it through a long-distance trip involving rough going and a lot of rock is inviting trouble. Breakdown chances are much increased, especially if you've not covered yourself by taking more than one spare wheel plus a tube and a tube repair kit. Fuel filters past their replacement time, paper air filters due for replacement or oil-foam filters in need of a thorough cleaning are other simple sources of trouble or breakdown.

4X4 Tip

BREAKDOWNS ARE PROBABLY CAUSED MORE BY LACK OF MAINTENANCE AND OWNER INTEREST THAN BY LACK OF OWNER ABILITY.

Water filters

On many diesels the primary in-line water filter is remotely mounted. Some 4WD owners have no idea that there is such a fitting on their vehicle. On some vehicles this filter is down on a chassis rail near the fuel tank — not easy to get at or clean, so it usually gets neglected. Most petrol-engine 4WDs have a plastic throw-away filter in line between the fuel tank and fuel pump, usually easy to see and replace. Few 4WDs come originally equipped with an easily accessible and visible permanent sight-bowl water filter in the engine bay, quickly cleaned and with easy filter-cartridge replacement. Because water in fuel is always a troublemaker, whether the engine is

SNORKELS ARE WORTHWHILE, ESPECIALLY IF YOU MAY BE TRAVELLING THROUGH WATER CROSSINGS, OR IN DUSTY ENVIRONMENTS.

petrol or diesel, it is cheap insurance to get an additional filter fitted.

Air intakes

Snorkels for air intakes may look a bit ugly or strange, but properly installed and waterproofed, as insurance against the worst of all possible situations they are a good investment. Water getting into the air intake and thus into an engine can be terminal. It is not compressible and if sufficient quantity of water gets above a piston the result can be very expensive. Raised air intake levels (by snorkel), or shielded air-cleaner intakes (by tarp or plastic sheet) are essential for deep-water driving.

Snorkels are also useful in dusty conditions, as often their inlet is higher than the normal road dust. On some models a basic precleaner filter can be added at the top of the snorkel for even better filtration. In bad conditions a basic paper air filter doesn't last long and is not reusable; better-quality paper air-filters can be air-blown or carefully washed clean and re-used. Oilbath filters are re-usable and have benefits, and wash/reuse oiled-foam filters are good value.

Water splash

Water can splash into the most remote of places in a 4WD, and many breakdowns can be traced to water short-circuiting a vital wiring connection. A good spray with WD40 or similar before driving into water pays dividends. Water in outback regions or muddy creek water is more likely to cause electrical shorts due to impurities or heavy mineralisation. The water-borne substances act as a connector, with water as the carrier agent. Sometimes the volume of water alone is enough to cause the stop, by virtually drowning the electrical system and causing a short circuit.

With mineralised or dirty water, engine heat will help dry off the water but the mineralised deposit often remains inside the wiring loom connector. Usually it gets baked on. It can be slightly corrosive and enough to cause intermittent short-circuiting of a component. Any water-dispersal fluid like CRC or WD40 will dry out a wiring connector in an already-wet wire, but the electrical fault can remain even after you have wiped the terminals clean. Spray is often not enough. It may take a good scrape with a file or wire brush to properly clean the terminal contact faces and remove the cause of the fault.

A DUAL BATTERY SYSTEM IS A COMMON ACCESSORY FITTED TO MANY 4WDS BUT MUST BE MAINTAINED PROPERLY TO FUNCTION CORRECTLY.

Wiring

Parts that work loose or are damaged by vibration are common causes of 4WD stoppage. Vibrations can cause the main high-tension coil lead to work loose at one end, disconnect cable-joins, or cause wires to break. In some cases there is no obvious wire break, but there is no traceable connection either. Cables can break strands inside the plastic sheath with no visible damage. A test probe or small multimeter kept in the glovebox is useful to test for faults like this.

Careful routing and tying with plastic wire-ties reduces the chances of wiring breaks. Loose wire terminals, poorly crimped lug connectors, dry-joints (where the solder hasn't made a proper metal-to-metal connection) in soldered connections, wire vibration fatigue and breaks from work-hardening in wires adjoining a soldered joint are all potential causes of vehicle breakdown. They are not difficult to fix. For many drivers the difficult part seems to be logically following stages or tracing the wires back to find where the break has occurred. Technical colleges and motoring organisations run classes in basic mechanics, and electrical wiring is included in most courses. Doing one of these courses would be worthwhile for any 4WD owner.

Batteries

Batteries, those often-forgotten and often-abused essentials, can be a major source of problems. Not keeping the electrolyte level between the high-low marks is asking for trouble. All water quality is arguable, with the additives and minerals it carries. The only guaranteed good water for a battery is distilled water. In really hot weather battery fluids usually need topping up weekly, because engine bay heat causes more than normal fluid evaporation from the battery breather holes. With dual batteries fitted, both charging off the one alternator, the safest way to be sure the electrical system is properly charging both batteries to their maximum is to have a competent auto-electrician do some tests.

As an alternative, buy a hydrometer and learn how to use it to measure battery charge condition. Despite claims of accessory manufacturers, some "isolators" favour one battery over another and/or fail to read the battery voltage properly and shut off charging before they should. Perhaps the old-fashioned manual switching between batteries still has merit, even if it is a nuisance to do. With dual batteries, a manual switch between batteries to separate them can be very useful, because if one battery is unusable for some reason, the other one on its own should be okay for the most important job — starting your vehicle's engine.

If a battery works loose in its cradle and bounces around, there is a chance that the casing could be damaged and perhaps leak. A very common "starter-motor won't work, click, click" situation is caused by dirty battery or cable terminals, or battery cable connections that have worked loose in some form. A file, wire brush and a spanner are usually what is needed to fix them. Terminals must be kept clean and tight. In some vehicles, with quite a few accessories depending on the battery (or batteries), despite individual power supply wires run to each accessory, some items won't run properly. The cause can often be ineffective earthing for the battery's negative side, where the accessories rely on earthing through the vehicle frame back to the battery. The only reliable way to avoid this, while running a normal 12V positive power wire to the accessory plug point, is to also run a return negative wire from each item back to the battery.

Electrical circuits

Twelve-volt automotive electrical systems and wiring can be a dream to work on. However, sometimes when they develop faults, finding and fixing them can be difficult and frustrating. Descriptions of the charging, starting and battery systems for your vehicle can be found in the service and repair manual. It can be complex to explain, although it isn't difficult to learn. For more information, consult a textbook about 12V electrical systems. Also, a good auto-electrician, when you find one, should be remembered on your Christmas-card list.

Most electrical trouble involves added-on accessories. Driving lights, fridges, radios, antennas, spotlights, electric fans, air compressors, trailer connecting plugs and tail lights, spare power points — any 12V electrical equipment that draws much current or is subject to weather or abuse should be properly and carefully wired for best operation. Safety and overload protection is very important, so fuses, circuit breakers and relays should be included in circuits. Even though there are only a few straightforward rules to learn, the field can become fairly complex. It is worth learning basic information about 12V systems for proper 4WD maintenance, and if you take your 4WD into remote areas, for safety you should have at least a working knowledge of vehicle electricals for problem-solving.

On page 156 is a description of a simple circuit to run a light-globe located on the back door. A normal battery has two sides, positive and negative, that must remain insulated from each other, apart from when it is controlled and used to operate an electrical device. In almost all vehicles the battery's negative terminal is directly connected to the vehicle frame or chassis, so the vehicle's whole body should carry negative current. In this case, negative current has to pass through all the metal body panels to eventually get from the battery to the light globe. (See page 156 diagram 2.)

Simply by running an insulated wire all the way to the back door, (connected to the battery's positive terminal, and therefore carrying positive current), we can provide power for a light. Connect the end of the positive wire to one terminal of the light globe. The circuit is made by connecting another length of wire from the other terminal of the light globe back to the vehicle body. When positive current flows through the light globe it passes through the filament,

A BATTERY CHARGER IS A VERY HANDY DEVICE TO HAVE IN YOUR WORKSHOP.

A trouble-free trouble light

A trouble light is an essential item to carry at all times. Make sure there is plenty of cable length, enough to reach from any power point to the furthest part of the vehicle. Don't buy a light with a globe because incandescent globes use too much current. Buy a fluorescent light, one of the tough, clear-tube protected fluorescent tube lights similar to those used in a garage or workshop. A 10-watt light output is good enough for most jobs, and it will draw almost nothing from the battery. The same light is excellent for camping, and can usually be left on for long periods without affecting the accessory battery noticeably.

which glows because of resistance, and the current completes the electrical circuit when it returns via the negative vehicle body to the battery. That's how it is supposed to work, and most of the time it does. Just about every electrical device works in this way.

However, don't trust body panels to reliably complete any 12V circuit, whether they are steel or aluminium. After even just a few months of flexing through normal driving, their electrical current carrying capability can reduce. (See diagram 2.)

Typically, a light that flickers on and off, or goes between dull and bright, has a loose connection somewhere. Loose joints in an electrical circuit cause resistance, and resistance can also cause heat and maybe even fire. Through build-up of grit on surfaces or wearing and becoming a bit loose, adjoining body panels (such as the sequence of mudguard to firewall to dashboard) may not give the best current continuity.

Using a wire that is too thin or small to carry adequate current is like trying to water the garden with the tap turned too low. It also affects the performance of electrical equipment, with the added difficulty that the longer the length of wire, the more the current carrying capacity is reduced. This is known as voltage drop. Although there is usually a small amount of tolerance built into electrical equipment to allow for power supply variations, without the full required voltage some electrical equipment won't work at all, and most won't work at the proper efficiency level or will only work intermittently. Running a full earth-return wire directly back to the battery, as well as a power supply wire of ample size from the battery out to the electrical device, may be a nuisance when first setting up your 4WD, but it certainly gives the best results. (See diagram 1.) Apart from running the direct earth back to the battery, it is wise to also earth out the device's negative side to the vehicle body at the same time.

The well-known, tough and very common 12V Engel fridge is a good example. Providing it has a good direct power supply it will work reliably under sometimes extreme conditions.

DIAGRAM SHOWING THE DIFFERENCE BETWEEN A DIRECT-WIRED CIRCUIT AND ONE USING THE VEHICLE BODY AS AN EARTH RETURN. THIS PRINCIPLE APPLIES TO VIRTUALLY ALL ELECTRICAL EQUIPMENT.

Lighting circuits

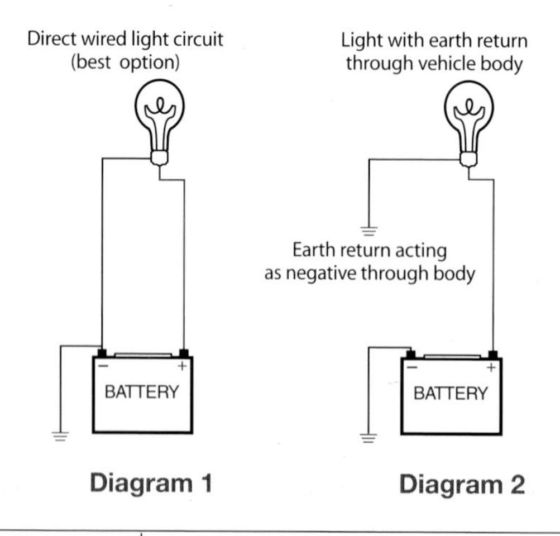

Experience has proved that to give great reliability it must have its own earth-return from the power plug right back to the battery. Depending on their age and model, when working they can draw quite a bit of current from the battery, with older models using somewhere between 4.2 and 6 amps. Regardless of where you have set the cold-control knob, without clean continuous power supply any fridge may switch on much more often than it should. In turn, this can make it draw more current or overheat. Naturally, drawing more current flattens the power supply battery faster.

Cooling systems

Radiators and the hoses that are part of the cooling system are a common cause of breakdowns, simply because they deteriorate unnoticed over time. Carry a spare for every hose, including the usually difficult-to-fit bypass hose, if your 4WD has one. Keep stones, bugs and grasshoppers out of the radiator cooling fins because if they get blocked, water cooling suffers.

Fitting a tough fine mesh screen in front of the normal radiator grille helps protect it and minimises the chances of damage. With a hot engine, never take the radiator cap straight off to check coolant level. The coolant is under pressure and at boiling point. Always keep your face out of the way when you do take the cap off. Protect your hands from steam burns, and first turn the cap only to the safety position with a thick cloth. This lets the pressure build-up steam escape before you remove the cap. Better still, let the radiator cool down for a while. Radiators get hotter for a few minutes after the engine is switched off, as hot water rises into the radiator top tank, because it is not being circulated by the water pump.

Drivebelts

Fanbelts and drivebelts can cause trouble, and just like radiator and heater hoses, a spare for each of them ought to be carried on every trip. Even though they are very tough, engine heat dries them out and they also deteriorate with age and use. Very few drivers ever take a drivebelt off and turn it inside-out to check it for cracking, but doing so could show up a fault and prevent later troubles.

Surviving in a 4WD without an air-conditioning compressor drivebelt can make life uncomfortable; and driving without a belt turning the power-

ENGINE BAY SHOWING COOLING SYSTEM COMPONENTS.

Caution

RUNNING A FULL EARTH-RETURN WIRE DIRECTLY BACK TO THE BATTERY, AS WELL AS A POWER SUPPLY WIRE OF AMPLE SIZE FROM THE BATTERY OUT TO THE ELECTRICAL DEVICE CERTAINLY GIVES THE BEST RESULTS.

steering pump can make steering very hard work. Driving without a belt turning the water pump and alternator quite often brings a 4WD trip to a stop, and could be mechanically very expensive. "No water pump" usually means a rapidly overheated engine. "No alternator" will eventually lead to a flat battery resulting in no lights, starter-motor, radio or possibly ignition. Without charge, the battery will eventually run flat, and the heavier the electrical drain on it, the shorter time the battery will last. Usually then, a 4WD trip stops and troubles begin at about the same time.

Running out of fuel

Running out of fuel is usually due to heavier fuel usage than expected, but can happen because of neglecting to check the fuel gauge before or during the trip. Carrying a backup can of fuel and a funnel or pourer-spout is an obvious need if your vehicle doesn't have long-range fuel-tank capacity. Do you know how to bleed your diesel fuel system to restart an engine that has run dry? Although service and repair manuals explain the proper sequence and parts to use, this won't give you practical experience. They don't tell you where your knuckles will get burnt on a hot manifold. They certainly don't tell you how long it will take to hand-pump the fuel through with the primer-pump when you've forgotten to switch both the fuel solenoid to the correct tank and the ignition key to the "on" position.

In a petrol engine the fuel pump normally does the work of quickly pumping the fuel back up to the carburettor, providing the diaphragms inside the pump are in good condition. Sometimes with a petrol engine, using a small amount of choke to help the engine start after running out of fuel will shorten the time it takes for the fuel pump to refill the fuel line properly. Don't leave the choke on for more than a few seconds when trying to start a hot engine, and push it off the moment there is indication the engine is trying to fire. If you are slow it may flood, and you will be no better off.

Carburettors

Tuning carburettors in petrol engines could be described as an inexact science. Incorrect adjustment can take all the enjoyment out of driving. If you are not familiar with carburettors, read the service and repair manual for your vehicle or consult a carburettor service specialist.

Early-model 4WDs can have problems with fuel delivery to the carburettor for various reasons. As only a small proportion of a vehicle's time is spent on steep ground, components are designed for general motoring conditions on average terrain.

Carburettors are designed and adjusted to feed petrol engines a specific ratio of fuel to air. Gaskets and seals are provided to keep the carburettor airtight and leak-proof, and simple lack of maintenance is a common reason for them to cause problems. If wear or damage to the carburettor allows more air than required to get in, the engine will run lean from lack of petrol. It may well lose or not develop power, and make the vehicle difficult to drive. Vibration causes bolts and other parts to work loose. Basic carburettor maintenance includes checking screws, nuts and bolts for tightness. Pink weeping and staining on the carburettor body is an indicator that fuel might be seeping out, most likely from a loose joint, or a worn or shrunken gasket. A problem not encountered with modern neoprene gaskets, that affects older cork or paper gaskets, is shrinkage. Most older gaskets rely on being damp and swollen to achieve a tight fit between the joint faces. If the joint becomes loose, the gasket may chafe, and wear or dry out and shrink, increasing the gap in the joint.

With petrol motors, low fuel-line pressure from the fuel pump can lead to insufficient fuel in the carburettor float bowl and fuel starvation. Without enough fuel pumped the engine simply cannot produce enough power to drive the vehicle, so it dies. When a 4WD petrol engine is working at top power and on a quite steep climb or tilt angle, it uses a lot of fuel. This demand can be virtually equal to the amount of fuel that is designed to be held in the float bowl. If the bowl does suck almost empty, the engine runs lean on fuel, runs roughly and eventually can starve. Although engines rarely have to work hard downhill, the descent angle itself can lead to low amounts of fuel available in the float bowl, and this could contribute to rough idling or poor running.

Pumping fuel at higher pressure to the carburettor has been tried on many 4WDs to solve this problem. Fuel pumped to the carburettor bowl, could splash out of the bowl vent pipe in rough conditions. This of course increases fuel consumption figures. Vehicle anti-pollution regulations now require systems to return the pumped but unused fuel back into the fuel tank. Carburettors are now designed with larger carburettor float-bowls to act as a buffer for higher fuel demand levels. Most current petrol 4WDs have electronic fuel injection (EFI) which overcomes the problems associated with some carburettors.

Fuel vapourisation

On hot days, another cause of starvation of petrol engines is vapourisation of the fuel. Climbing for a while in a low gear with very slow progress means there is almost no airflow across the radiator, causing the engine to run really hot or even boil. The heat build-up in the engine bay can become extreme. (Pulling the bonnet catch and carefully letting the bonnet lift up onto the safety catch when travelling at these very low speeds can help to exhaust some of this heat.) Exhaust pipes add to the temperature in the engine bay, and a turbocharger adds even more. Heat transfers to the fuel pipes or lines, and it is quite possible for the fuel inside the pipes to vapourise causing fuel-line pressure drops. The fuel pump isn't designed to pump a vapour, so the carburettor gets insufficient fuel.

One way to reduce the possibility of vapourisation is to insulate the fuel pipe in potential hot spots. Directly cooling the fuel pipe will return the fuel to liquid in a short time. I've seen a fire extinguisher or buckets of water used for this job, but spraying this everywhere can cause cracking in metal engine castings. Early Austin fire-brigade trucks, which often ran very hot indeed, suffered from fuel vapourisation. One old and sneaky way to reduce the chances of vapourisation was to virtually thicken the petrol. In about 1:15 ratio, diesel fuel or kerosene was mixed in with petrol, about four litres to sixty litres of petrol, to make it less likely to evaporate. It seemed to work!

When a motor cuts out due to fuel starvation, some things should be kept in mind before restarting. Mechanical fuel pumps are usually driven by a cam, which itself is driven by another part

DRIVEBELTS CAN BE TENSIONED BY IDLER PULLEYS OR ADJUSTING ARMS.

Drivebelt tensioning

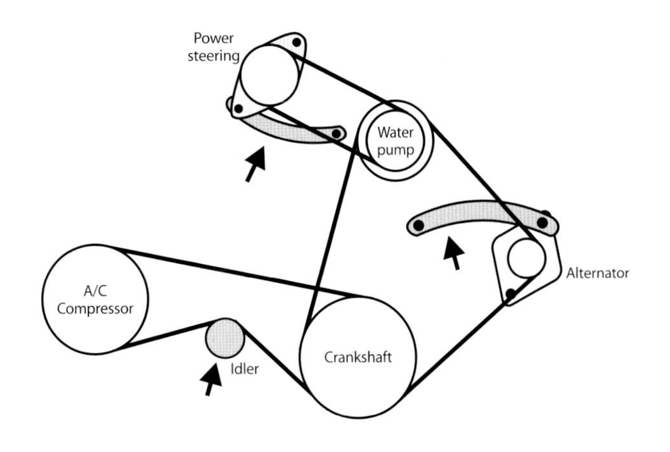

Caution

THE HEAT BUILD-UP IN THE ENGINE BAY CAN BECOME EXTREME. PULLING THE BONNET CATCH AND CAREFULLY LETTING THE BONNET LIFT UP ONTO THE SAFETY CATCH WHEN TRAVELLING AT VERY LOW SPEEDS CAN HELP TO EXHAUST SOME OF THIS HEAT.

of the engine. To get the fuel pump to work and provide enough fuel to run the engine, the engine has to spin over for a period of time. It can take a minute or two for a petrol engine to turn over sufficient times (thus driving the mechanical fuel pump) to provide enough fuel back into the carburettor so that the engine will restart. This raises the issue of how long the battery will last while supplying power to the starter-motor to crank the engine over to pump enough fuel. Electric fuel pumps have an advantage in this situation. They only use a small amount of electrical current from the battery to re-pump the fuel from the fuel tank up into the carburettor.

Flooding

Flooding occurs when the engine is overloaded with fuel, usually during starting and often because the driver uses too much accelerator. It is usually easy to tell if an engine is flooded because there is a strong smell of petrol in the engine bay and around the front of the vehicle. The engine will spin over but will not start.

Most carburettors have an accelerator pump, operated when the driver pumps the accelerator pedal, to supply extra fuel to the carburettor during heavy acceleration. When too much fuel is pumped through the carburettor by the accelerator pump, without the motor running and burning up the fuel, the petrol-to-air mix becomes saturated with petrol. The ratio is wrong and until much of the petrol evaporates the carburettor cannot suck in enough air to adjust the ratio.

When the excess petrol evaporates, the ratio automatically adjusts, and the vehicle should start. On warm or windy days evaporation might only take a couple of minutes. Sometimes when a driver is anxious and has several tries to restart but has not waited long enough for the wasted petrol to evaporate, the flooding might take a long time to clear. If a vehicle has stalled on a hill and the engine has become badly flooded from efforts to restart it, perhaps the best thing to do is to make the vehicle properly safe, leave the bonnet up for ventilation and go for a ten-minute walk somewhere away from the fumes before trying again.

BLEEDING THE FUEL SYSTEM ON A DIESEL ENGINE.

Air in fuel lines

In both diesel and petrol motors, air in fuel lines can cause engine stoppage or low power and very poor running. This can happen when a fuel tank is getting low on supply and the vehicle is working in steep terrain. If the engine is working hard it will be using all the fuel it can get. The fuel pick-up pipe inside the tank can become exposed to air, when the vehicle's descent, lean or climb angle tips the remaining fuel away from the pick-up. Air that then gets into the fuel pipe from the exposed inlet will tend to make the engine starve or hiccup. One solution is not to let your fuel tank get much down below quarter-full, before tipping the spare can of fuel into the tank, if you have a number of hills to cover.

Emergency Vehicle Starting

Flat batteries

A flat battery is always a nuisance but in some circumstances it can be fatal. In the city you may be able to call the Automobile Association on the phone for help with a jump-start. What happens if you are on your own 60 kilometres north-west of the Rabbit Flat Road-house on the Tanami Track with the same flat battery? Mobile phones don't work out there, and with a flat battery you can't use the Royal Flying Doctor Service or other radio to call for help, either. This could be getting to the "dangerous" situation. Unfortunately, this scenario has caused deaths before, and it will again. [This won't happen to you if, as part of your regular monthly maintenance, you fully recharge the battery for your satellite-phone.]

Without the correct electrolyte level, normal wet cell 4WD batteries won't work efficiently. And unless the alternator and voltage regulator do their jobs properly the battery won't receive the proper charging. If you leave items that use electricity switched on, without replacing in some way the power being drained, the battery will eventually run flat.

It is possible to drain current from a battery in a short time, to the extent that there is not enough power left for that most vital of all jobs — starting the engine. With a proper isolator battery-charging system the auxiliary battery may be used heavily without affecting the primary battery, but will charge again during normal driving. On any remote trip, by far the safest electrical option is to ensure dual batteries and isolator are fitted to your 4WD.

Some current 4WDs have complex computer-controlled ignition systems and electronic engine-management systems. Starting them with assistance from another battery, or "jump-starting" them in the wrong way can cause expensive damage to expensive components. This is where the proper workshop or service and repair manual can be invaluable — refer to it for your specific vehicle electricals. So — the problem you are faced with is — you must get the engine started, but the battery is flat. There are two practical ways to do this: jump-starting and clutch starting.

Caution

FLAT BATTERIES USUALLY RESULT FROM CARELESSNESS.

Electricity cost

Thinking technically, the replacement cost/ratio of using battery electricity is 140%. That surprises almost all 4WD users, and it might help to explain why many are caught with a flat battery. The formula we can work on is straight-forward — Watts divided by Volts equals Amps.

We can use a simple 25watt globe, in a light, to show this as:

25W ÷ 12V = 2.08A.

If you use the light for five hours then the current drain becomes:

2.08A x 5 = 10.5Ah.

That is, about ten and a half ampere hours have been taken from the battery. An ampere hour is simply using one ampere of current for one hour of time.

Therefore: 10.5Ah + 40% = 14.7A.

This amount of current must be put back into the battery to restore the original charge.

A generator or a solar panel will put the needed power back into the battery, but it does take time. For example, an 80W solar panel develops about 4A in good sunny conditions. Using one panel, it would take about four hours to restore the battery to its original level. After several hours driving, the vehicle's alternator would also have replaced the used power. Stand-alone generator output varies with size, but the concept is the same. There is no such thing as a free lunch.

Jump-starting

A vehicle battery has two terminals to which leads are connected, usually one each end. They have a positive (+) red-coloured lead and/or terminal and a negative (–), usually plain black lead and/or terminal. By connecting jumper-leads, which are flexible wire cables with a strong clamp at each end, from the rescuer's (good) battery to the flat (bad) one, electrical current can be transferred to start the engine.

As a general rule (and this is correct for the normal diesel, as well as petrol engine), all it takes is to connect two batteries together in the same way. To do this is simple, but the sequence of doing it needs to be followed carefully, as there are a few traps.

If the battery is totally flat, with not a spark of life, and your 4WD has a petrol or gas engine, leave the leads connected and carrying current for several minutes before trying to start your engine. Start your vehicle while the rescue vehicle engine is going, and then keep the engine at a fast idle as well.

In some cases the amount of life in a battery, even after several minutes of boosting, is still not enough to run engine ignition. This can happen to the extent that if the rescue vehicle engine is turned off when the other starts, the bad battery may only last a few seconds before dying again and killing the engine. If this happens, do it all again, and this time leave the good battery to boost the bad one for several minutes, with both engines running.

Diesels do not have the problem of keeping going when the battery is totally flat, because they don't use any electricity from a battery for ignition. (See pages 105-106 for more about diesel engines.)

If your jumper-leads are pencil-sized in diameter they will not be able to carry the current necessary to jump-start a big engine. If the battery clamps are cheap and simply crimped onto the cable this can cause a lot of resistance, which causes heat. Effort is lost when the cables and clamps get hot, and the needed current does not all get from good to bad battery. For safety, buy a

4X4 Tip

IF YOUR BATTERY IS TOTALLY FLAT, OR HAS SIMPLY BEEN DISCONNECTED, YOU WILL PROBABLY HAVE TO RE-PROGRAM THE RADIO, (DO YOU KNOW THE SECURITY CODE IF THERE IS ONE?), THE ALARM SYSTEM, AND OTHER ELECTRONIC GADGETS IF YOU HAVE THEM.

pair of heavy-duty cables, rated at 400 amps or better and about as big in diameter as your thumb, with big heavy-duty insulated clamps, and carry them in your 4WD at all times, especially if it has an automatic gearbox. Two pairs of thin leads in parallel may get you out of trouble, if that is all that is available. Engines of 4WDs with automatic transmission can only be jump-started with a battery. They cannot be tow-started or clutch-started.

Clutch-starting

In a 4WD with a manual gearbox, starting an engine that won't start in the usual way can be a nuisance. Information on normal engine starts is on page 104. The risk is higher when clutch-starting than when jump-starting, because in this case the vehicle depends on being mobile in some way to develop the effort needed to turn the engine over and make it start. (Note: If you have a 4WD with automatic transmission, skip this section, as you cannot clutch-start your vehicle. Your option is virtually either a jump-start, or a tow home.) There are several ways to start a vehicle using the clutch and gears — push it, pull it, or roll it, backwards or forwards. The principle is the same in each case.

When your 4WD is in gear, with the engine running and your foot off the clutch, the engine causes the wheels to turn. In essence, what you need to do to start your engine by clutch-starting is to do exactly the reverse of this, and make the wheels turn the engine. For information on stall starts, see page 31.

The simplest example to use is rolling down a hill to clutch-start your engine. Assuming your 4WD will roll forwards downhill, start with a safe vehicle, and keep a good eye out for any onlooker who might get in the way. (Remember, your vehicle is almost silent as it rolls, and others may not hear it coming.) Turn the ignition key to "on", put the gearbox into second gear but keep the clutch pushed in. Let the handbrake off, and when your 4WD is rolling about a fast walking pace, let the clutch out. The

4X4

Advice

DON'T EXPECT CHEAP THIN $10 JUMPER LEADS TO START A BIG 4WD ENGINE, ESPECIALLY A DIESEL.

Sequence for jump-starting

Checklist

- Make sure both vehicles are in a safe position and condition before beginning.
- Both engines should be turned off before connecting any cables, because electricity can cause sparks which are a hazard in an explosive environment.
- When you put the jumper-lead clamps onto each terminal, make sure that they are good and firm.
- Connect one end of the positive cable to the positive terminal on the good battery, and the other end to the same terminal on the bad battery.
- Connect one end of the negative cable to the negative terminal on the good battery.
- Connect the negative cable's opposite end to a good solid metal part of the engine in the vehicle with the flat battery.
- Check that the jumper-leads are safe and won't get tangled in the fan when the engine starts, and keep fingers out of harm's way. Start the rescue vehicle engine, and keep it at a good fast idle.
- To disconnect the jumper-leads, simply do it in the reverse of the way you connected them.
- If the bad engine stalls quickly after being started then disconnected, repeat the process, but leave both engines running and the batteries linked for several minutes to help transfer current.

Advice

FIND A HILL NEAR HOME AND PRACTICE CLUTCH-STARTING

rear tyres (assuming that your vehicle is not in 4WD) may protest a bit as they are forced to turn, but when they do they will cause the engine to spin over, and hopefully start.

The reason for using second gear is purely mechanical. In first gear the rolling-downhill motion, with tyres trying to turn in the dirt, may not be sufficient to overcome the compression resistance in the engine cylinders. (That's why some drivers leave a vehicle stationary, parked and engine off and in first gear, believing it will hold the vehicle on engine compression alone. It may, but it's risky, so do not rely on it — use the handbrake as well.) Using second gear the mechanical leverage available to turn the engine is better, and the engine will spin faster as well. In truth, you could probably roll-start your 4WD in any gear, because it simply depends on vehicle speed at the time you let the clutch out. Second gear has been found to be the best overall, as the lower the roll speed the less is the risk, yet it still gives enough mechanical advantage for starting.

You may need a little acceleration or choke to help the engine get ample fuel for starting. If it won't start cleanly push the clutch back in, and try a little more rolling speed before letting it back out, to try again. (If it won't start after three or four good tries, you may have a more difficult problem than a simple fail-to-start.)

When the engine does start, push the clutch in and brake to a safe stop, keeping the engine going at a fast idle. Most current types of alternator will usually produce charge providing your engine is doing more than 1,000 rpm. If your 4WD has a hand throttle, set the revs about 1,200–1,500, and leave the engine run for half an hour, which should give enough power to re-start with the starter-motor.

Other alternatives to rolling your 4WD down a hill to start are to be pushed from behind by people or another vehicle; to be towed from in front by another vehicle; or to do just what you would forwards, but instead go backwards, and use reverse gear.

AFTERMARKET ACCESSORY BLADDER FOR STORING WATER.

Accessories, Tools and Parts

Purchasing accessories

Spending some time in a large 4WD accessory shop, or reading 4WD magazines or catalogues can be a very enjoyable way of spending a few hours. Just like any other interest, four-wheel driving can be quite an expensive exercise. The accessory market is enormous for 4WDs, and if you had enough money, you could probably replace half of the original manufacturer's equipment on your 4WD with aftermarket gear. Often an accessory performs better or is more purpose-built than the manufacturer's item, even though there is nothing wrong with the original part. If you buy a new vehicle, the list of factory-fitted extras you can specify to be fitted before delivery is considerable, and a benefit of doing this is to take advantage of the manufacturer's warranty.

Doing your homework is vital, if you are in the market for 4WD accessories. You must know what it is you want to achieve, or you may find yourself with a problem at some later stage. It is common sense to rely on major providers and use proven products. Again, this is another reason to belong to a 4WD club, where valuable information is easily available from those who really use the items you may want to buy.

From the safety aspect, because you have to rely on recovery gear in a bad situation, it is important to buy only the best. Select proof-tested chains, shackles, snatchblocks, etc. and buy them from a reputable dealer. Use high-tensile bolts, top-quality cable and standards-approved safety equipment wherever possible.

On normal trips, the basic shovel, axe, snatchblock and shackles, snig chain, tree protector, winch of some sort, and protective clothing is usually enough. For longer trips or in different weather conditions, you may need to add a bullbar, earth anchor, chainsaw and associated gear, highlift jack, snatchem-strap, wheel-chains, winching extras, and maybe even hundreds of dollars more in other gear. Accessory choice may be influenced by personal preference, a specific need, or your budget.

Additional extras

Many of these accessory items are mentioned at other places in the book,

Tip

OFTEN AN ACCESSORY PERFORMS BETTER OR IS MORE PURPOSE-BUILT THAN THE MANUFACTURER'S ITEM, EVEN THOUGH THERE IS NOTHING WRONG WITH THE ORIGINAL PART.

A PROPERLY FITTED TOWBAR IS ONE OF THE BEST ACCESSORIES YOU COULD ADD TO YOUR 4WD.

but it's worth recounting them in this section.

Basically since the Gulf War we have had access to accurate Global Positioning Satellites [GPS] for location data. Since then, further improvements in technology have led to very sophisticated yet simple methods of easily finding out where you are, even down to just a couple of metres.

Map-plotting software linked to your GPS unit, via a laptop computer, can now direct you exactly where you want to go. If you get geographically embarrassed, your GPS can quickly guide you right back to your start point.

Worse, if you get critically lost and damaged, your Emergency Position Indicating Radio Beacon [EPIRB] can alert rescue services via satellite. The new frequency for EPIRB emergency transmission will mean much faster and much more accurate rescue response.

Electronic means to prevent rust in the many hidden parts of your 4WD, and retain value, are well proven. You can even buy a set of four screw-on devices for your tyre valve-stems to quickly deflate the tyres to a set pressure, if playing in sand is your thing. Instead of fitting dual batteries to your 4WD, if space is at a premium in the engine bay, portable booster batteries that can be fully charged from 240VAC and taken in the 4WD are plentiful. They are made in several capacities, from very heavy duty for running fridges and jump-starting big engines, to smaller types for the usual needs of camping lights and radios. Complete dual-battery installations and sophisticated electronic charging systems are at most 4WD accessory dealers. Flexible bladders to carry water or fuel, and which can fit in the rear passenger footwells, can be a really useful addition. One of the most amazing uses for plastic is the polycarbonate bullbar. As a base for a winch it has limitations, but as a general-purpose bullbar it would be very hard to beat for lightness and strength. Still in the plastic world, many top 4WD-competition entrants now use "plasma" winch rope instead of steel wire winch cable, but the benefits of much lighter weight, fantastic ease of use and strength come at a considerable price. Technology has now produced this type of plaited rope, usually much thinner than the steel wire cable it can replace, and it's claimed to have about 40% more breaking strength, at a fraction of the weight of steel wire cable.

A third player has entered the winch scene, engine-powered, hydraulically driven and very efficient. If you're looking for more absolute power from your 4WD engine, there are several manufacturers who offer plug-in replacement or additional computer-chips, to re-program or support your existing engine-management system. There is no doubt at all these amazing computer-based electronic aids work very well. Roof-racks and storage bins, bags and boxes to fit them are made by many manufacturers.

Instead of an owner going to considerable trouble to make shelves and drawers, many makers can supply just about any combination of storage method you can think of for your 4WD. They vary from overhead replacement plastic radio storage bins to wooden food- and tool-drawers, to complex aluminium four-drawer systems with slide-out fridge-trays.

In the bigger 4WD accessory suppliers showrooms, if you want an accessory, it's probably available. For those items that aren't there yet, chances are you can get it made or modified in this huge business.

Bullbars

A common accessory for 4WDs is a bullbar. They vary from cheap, bolt-over-the-front-bumperbar "dress-up" types to strongly mounted full-protection bars with integral side-rails and door steps. They are good value in the bush, but perhaps a waste of money for front-end protection in city traffic.

An effective and tough bullbar is designed to carry a winch and various types of lights and radio antennae, and provide effective scrub protection for the front of the vehicle. The age-old debate of steel versus alloy bars simply boils down to personal preference, and there are points in favour of each. Alloy weighs a lot less than steel, which can make a difference to the front-end suspension. On the other hand, if you bend a steel bullbar, getting it fixed is usually a lot simpler than straightening alloy.

One type of bullbar becoming much more common is the polycarbonate bullbar, generally coloured black but now available to match many common 4WD colours. Usually well-shaped and close fitting, and much lighter than conventional bullbars, these polycarbonate-material bars seem fairly flexible and almost unbreakable, yet they offer very high crunch protection.

Many late-model vehicles are equipped with airbags; to comply with regulations and for maximum safety it is important that the bullbar is compatible with the airbag system if fitted to your 4WD. Manufacturers seem to have taken this very much into account with changes made in current models.

Winches

An electrically powered, hydraulic or PTO-driven winch can be invaluable in a bad situation. Cost plays a big part here, with a good hand-operated cable-pulling winch costing about a quarter of the price of a good electrically driven winch. PTO-driven winches are usually more expensive than electric types, and larger-capacity winches can be very expensive indeed. Most winches carry about 30 metres of cable. On my winch I have found that 45 metres of plasma rope takes the same space on the drum as 30 metres of steel wire winch cable.

Through engineering experience, many huge and very-heavy-duty working winches are hydraulically powered, and now hydraulically-driven winches are available in several capacities for the average 4WD. "Ox" is one brand name, and in operation it is similar to most electric winches. The power source is different, because hoses for this type of winch are joined into the power-steering pump system. When the engine is running, the power steering pump provides pressure for the hydraulic winch motor, without affecting the original purpose at all.

A LARGE 4WD HAS NO MECHANICAL OR POWER TROUBLE TOWING LARGE CARAVANS OR BOATS.

Checklist

Multi-purpose items

Multi-purpose items can save duplication and using up space. For example, a solar blanket could be used for the following:

- Preventing ice build-up on a windscreen or similar overnight
- Protection when lying in the mud underneath a vehicle
- A windbreak, sun shade, or heat reflector behind a fire
- A signalling device to aircraft
- To help warm up a hypothermic patient
- A water-collection device
- A temporary shelter
- A cape in bad weather

This type of winch has a very high duty-cycle, apparently being able to work for several hours non-stop if needed.

A useful winching addition is a separate 20 metre length of cable with eyes swaged in each end. Correct D-shackles to join this cable to the fixed steel wire winch cable then give a useful 50 metre coverage. Carrying U-bolt cable clamps (of the correct internal diameter for the winch cable) can be a safeguard if a cable breaks. They will also allow another length to be bolt-joined onto the winch cable in the event of a long recovery distance. For information on winching, see page 73.

Towbars

The heavy-duty towbar on the back of a 4WD is the best anchor point for dragging or being dragged, although it has a more common and designed use. A heavy-duty towbar is one of the most useful additions to any 4WD. Towing capacity of towbars varies and safe weight limits are stamped on by the manufacturer. The regulation heavy-duty tow-hitch on most larger 4WDs is rated to pull just about anything that is practical to tow. These expensive towbars are properly engineered, and solidly mounted to the chassis of 4WDs. They are load-sharing and generally keep suspension and tyre worries to a minimum.

Some states have regulations limiting the item to be towed, according to the weight or capacity of the towing vehicle. The largest V8 sedans can be registered to tow bigger boats, vans and horse floats, but most cars are somewhat limited. A large 4WD has no mechanical or power trouble towing double horse floats, large boats, big caravans or just about any trailer.

Braking regulations in some states are quite rigid, with electric or powered brakes mandatory for any tandem-wheel trailer and for any trailer at all above a certain carrying capacity. Caravans are required to have power brakes, and there is a specified ratio of weight of tow vehicle to towed unit. Hydraulic brake over-ride couplings are becoming less common, and no longer allowable in some circumstances. Remember that regulations on towing, tow vehicles and registration of towed equipment vary between states if you are towing interstate. Check carefully with the relevant traffic authority or your Automobile Association.

Most caravan clubs run training days for new members and there are schools teaching towing techniques. For serious towing it would pay to have a towing specialist determine the best aids for the vehicle. Many accessories are very effective devices, offering good value for money. Overload springs, level-ride equipment, anti-sway hitches, anti-vibration couplings, pump-up shockers, wide mirrors, electrical plugs and looms, brake boosters, disc brake conversions — a whole service industry has grown around the humble towbar.

Towing chains

Chains are an excellent towing medium. If chains break, which is not very common, they don't usually scythe like steel wire winch cables. A six-metre piece seems to be the usual length sold by most 4WD shops, although various lengths are available. They can be interlinked temporarily with proof-tested D-shackles. Chain ends vary, and can be claws, grab-hooks, slip-hooks or bitch-links. The staff at the chain-and-sling suppliers can advise you what is the best type to buy. Like most things, the best costs the most — Hercalloy chain, or similar, has a top reputation as a 4WD drag-chain, but also has a high price. Shackles are not the best way to join chains, long-term. Devices called "hammerlinks" are a safer and better way of doing this, and proper sizes are made to fit most chains any four-wheel-driver would use.

Other accessories

A turbo-timer is often retro-fitted to 4WDs to do a simple job — to keep the engine running for a few minutes after the engine is switched off to let the turbo speed slow, lubricate properly and cool down. After turning off the engine in the normal way and withdrawing the key, the driver can lock and leave the vehicle while the timer counts down for the set amount of time (usually, one, three or five minutes) and then turns the engine off properly. Most units have switches or buttons to set the function, and are smaller than a cigarette-packet in size, with a thin wiring loom at the rear. Probably because they don't need to be reset very often once the desired time-delay has been determined by the driver, many are mounted below the steering column, screwed or glued to the housing. See page 50 for advice on stalling and turbo-timers.

An alternative to a turbo timer for non-factory-fitted turbochargers is a purpose-made turbo oiler which can be fitted as an accessory. This uses the engine's lubricating oil which is diverted, by the normal oil pump, up into a sort of pressurised container. When the engine is turned off in the normal way, the oil all runs back down through the turbo bearings and into the engine sump. One major benefit is that the driver does not have to do anything, because gravity helps the slight pressurisation put the oil where it is needed.

Think carefully, depending on the trip, about which other items might be needed. Finding space to store and carry them isn't usually difficult; it just takes a bit more time and effort. Some things that can be very valuable, don't take much room, and that could be carried include: a few muesli bars, a canteen of drinking water, a portable first-aid kit, a few metres of number-eight fencing wire and of general purpose tie-wire, and a plastic ground-sheet.

Tools

Some 4WDs are mechanically quite complex. For a long-distance trip it may be worth taking some of the manufacturer's Special Service Tools or aftermarket tools for your particular vehicle. For example, a relatively simple tool to compress coil suspension springs doesn't cost much. Trying to replace a spring without first compressing the coil can be a very difficult and dangerous job, so it is worth investing in the tool.

A relatively straightforward job like replacing a wheel bearing can take a lot less time with a suitable puller, and the correct socket to access the locknut inside the hub. Make sure that the toolkit is right for your vehicle. It is no use having AF spanners, suitable for a Ford Bronco, for a Pajero with metric fastenings. If the biggest socket in the toolkit is currently a 21 mm but you really need a 32 mm to get at some difficult part, the few dollars cost for the additional socket is cheap insurance. A 4WD club for owners of

Tip

FOR A LONG-DISTANCE TRIP IT MAY BE WORTH TAKING SOME OF THE MANUFACTURER'S SPECIAL SERVICE TOOLS OR AFTERMARKET TOOLS FOR YOUR PARTICULAR VEHICLE.

4X4 **Tip**

MAKE SURE THAT THE TOOLKIT IS RIGHT FOR YOUR VEHICLE.

your make of vehicle can be a goldmine of information and tips. Some clubs provide Special Service Tools for members on a loan basis.

Parts storage

Carrying replacement parts and tools takes up space, and in short-wheelbase 4WDs there isn't much to spare. Overhead interior storage shelves are available for almost any vehicle. These can utilise a considerable amount of otherwise unused storage. Some shelves fit overhead in front of the driver with the sunvisors usually re-fitted on the underside of the shelf. One type fits across the centre of the vehicle behind the front passengers with the dome light fitted back in the underside of the console. Others fit between or under seats, and around or over wheel-arches. Some excellent set-ups have storage drawers underneath a false floor covering the entire rear section of the vehicle. Slide-out kits are made for most 4WD fridges to allow easy access to them. Large plastic "fish-boxes" are tough and great for storage if you have room to pack them. Many types, sizes and makes of excellent and affordable plastic storage containers are available.

Soundly-engineered roof-racks in both steel and alloy are a common sight, and they have some considerable advantages. It is not advisable to carry multiple fuel containers, or any large amount of weight on the roof-rack, as this amount of weight can change vehicle handling considerably. Sometimes there is no option, but for safety roof-racks should be used to carry larger items of bulk, rather than weight.

For those replacement parts which should be carried all the time, such as radiator hoses and fanbelts, many 4WDs actually have a kind of built-in storage. Without modification, it is quite suitable to store parts in, and does not take up space. Almost every 4WD has side panels, usually made of compressed board or similar, and covered with carpet or vinyl. These are usually clipped into the metal body panel pressings using plastic press studs, and are easily removed with a flat-blade screwdriver. The side panels fit back on by pressing each stud back into its hole. Spares can be labelled, wrapped in plastic bags and put into the spaces inside the body panels, behind the side-panels.

Rubber-band or plastic-tape the bags shut, because fine dust and water condensation have a habit of getting in everywhere. Anything made of metal should be sprayed well with WD40, CRC or similar to reduce the chances of rust before you pack it away. Some padding might be needed to prevent dents in the body panels. Because it is easy to mix up drivebelts make sure you label them. Make a list of what is stored where, and what use it has.

There is actually an easier way to get access than by removing a side panel, but it costs a few dollars. Boat chandlers stock inspection ports used on small yachts to allow storage of sails inside hulls. These vary from 150–300 mm in diameter, are about 6–9 mm thick and have a circular boss with a flush screw-in lid. Fitting one of these into the side panel is quite easy, and simply by unscrewing the lid there is usually enough room to fit parts through quickly and efficiently.

A FRIDGE IS ONE OF THE BEST POSSIBLE ACCESSORIES FOR ANY 4WD TRIP.

Glossary

4WD A vehicle permanently with ability to make, or having the selectable option to make, all four road wheels in conjunction propel the vehicle.

A-BAR A towing method, using an A-shaped device, usually made of steel pipe, with means for fixing to the disabled vehicle, and a means of attachment to the towing vehicle. Being rigid, it mimics the towing vehicle's actions, acts directly on the towed vehicle.

ABS (Antilock Braking System) A computer-driven means of managing a hydraulic braking system, preventing a driver from overbraking and minimising skidding in slippery conditions.

APPROACH ANGLE The angle between the ground and the lowest foremost point of a vehicle, where it might contact an object ahead. The less overhang ahead of the front wheels and the higher that part of the vehicle, the better is the approach angle.

BITCH-LINKS A type of chain end link common on recovery or snig chains, where the outside shape of the link approximates a figure eight, with the top smaller than the rounder bottom loop.

BREATHER HOSE A thin and flexible hose commonly fitted to differentials and gearboxes, to allow heated air expansion and pressure equalisation. For hard usage, the original is often replaced with a longer and higher-positioned hose, making likelihood of water ingress much less.

CLEVIS The pin which fits through the 'D' shape of a shackle, making the 'U' shape into a 'D', sliding through one side and screwing into a threaded section in the other side.

COIL SPRINGS Typically a spiral or coiled metal spring of varying diameter metal bar, circular wound, used as a means of vehicle suspension between the vehicle body and the wheels.

CV JOINT The ball-swivel joint just inside the front wheel on the front axle, through which the jointed front drive-shaft turns, allowing the wheel to turn and the vehicle to steer whilst at the same time continuing the drive effort.

DEPARTURE ANGLE The opposite of approach angle.

D-SHACKLE A means of temporarily joining two objects, i.e., two chains, or a pulley and a cable. Made of top-quality metal, and usually proof-stamped to indicate better-quality shackles.

DIFFERENTIAL A means of turning the longitudinal and rotational drive of the tailshaft [or propshaft] through a right-angle, to drive axles which in turn rotate wheels.

DOT-3 A standardised grading for brake fluid, indicating that it will withstand a specified heat level, and is suitable for disc brake vehicles.

DRIVE-TRAIN The continuous line of mechanical connection for power transmission, from the engine providing power through to the tyres.

FEATHER [the brakes] To brake very gently, with a light on-off touch.

FULL-TIME 4WD A vehicle with all four wheels driving permanently and equally.

GLOW-PLUGS An electrical device, usually placed at the top of a cylinder on a diesel engine, to preheat the air inside the cylinder and aid in cold-starting the engine. When the engine is started at normal operating temperature this function is usually automatically minimised or bypassed.

GPS (Global Positioning System) A means of determining an accurate location on any part of the world's surface, based on data transmitted from satellites. The devices themselves may be hand-held or vehicle-mounted.

HAMMERLINK A metal device somewhat like two D-shackles facing each other, but joined together at the centre by a hammered-in pin.

HAND-THROTTLE A hand-operated means of acceleration or engine-speed control, instead of using the normal accelerator pedal.

HYPOID Normally refers to the positioning of an input shaft where the drive centreline is usually below the centreline of the driven gear. This necessitates fine machining of mating gear-tooth faces, where high contact-point pressure is normal. Such pressure requires quality lubricants, to minimise heat and wear.

IDLE-UP SOLENOID A small electrical device that applies pressure to the throttle lever to increase engine idle speed to prevent stalling or rough running when the air-conditioning is on. It operates automatically in conjunction with the air-con.

LEAF SPRINGS Typically a slightly concave-shaped spring, made up of leaves or differing length strips of tempered steel grouped together. They are attached longitudinally under the vehicle chassis, and in turn axles are attached to them, laterally across the vehicle.

LOOMS, WIRING Wiring looms are simply any number of individual wires laying parallel to each other, grouped together neatly for practicality, and branching off from the main group where necessary to connect to some item. Such a loom may be enclosed somehow with individual wires not easily visible, or merely clipped or tied together. A simple comparison is a tree, with branches running off the central trunk.

MOSAIC MAP A mosaic map is usually composed of a considerable series of conjoined photos which show the earth's surface, most commonly taken from a satellite. In general, the colour density and strength indicate features and heights or depths. Colour is commonly green for wooded areas, blue for water etc. Dependent on the photo magnification, different features and man-made objects can be seen, but in most cases, unless clearly labelled by the maker efficient use only results from effective interpretation.

NATMAP Maps produced by the Government mapping body covering the entire nation, thus National Map.

OEM (Original Equipment Manufacturer) The original equipment on a new, unchanged vehicle.

PINTLES A temporary means of joining two things together, in this case an A-bar to the front of a disabled vehicle. A pintle is usually in two parts, where one is an eye or tongue (plug) and the other is a yoke (or socket). A pin or bolt of some kind can be inserted, usually vertically, through the three parallel faces to keep them joined. This can allow swivelling flexibility but will still maintain direct contact.

PTO (Power Take Off) A means of drive whereby the engine powers a rotating shaft via a specific set of gears, usually in the transfer gearbox. The shaft provides power to operate mechanical equipment. The most common PTO use on 4WDs is to drive a winch.

SCUTTLE Usually the slotted metal grille immediately in front of, across and below the windscreen. It usually provides air from outside for the fan air intake.

SNIG CHAIN A length of good quality strong chain, commonly about 6 or more metres long, with some means of attachment at each end. Used to directly drag (snig) an item in rough conditions.

SPALLING In this case, minute pieces breaking out of the surface of a gear tooth or face, from deterioration of the metal's surface from some cause, often producing a pitted surface as more and repeated fractions break out.

SPEAR OFF In a vehicle, to rapidly fly off the side of a track or similar, most often in some place you would rather not go, as quick and straight as a spear throw.

SPIDER GEAR In a vehicle differential, the two gears which transfer drive to rotate the axles, located one each side of the central crown wheel inside the diff housing.

SPLINE In this case, a number (say 12) of longitudinal grooves of specific width and depth machined at equal spaces around the inside of a thick-walled tube, into which a shaft having the same number and size of grooves, and of the same diameter as the inside of the tube, can slide. Thus, the deleted material is a groove, and the remaining material is a land or spline. The shaft can slide into or out of the tube to a pre-determined or limited extent, whilst still maintaining the rotational drive effort.

STEERING EFFECT The extent a vehicle turns as a result of the driver turning the steering wheel a certain amount.

SWAGED A swage is a type of joining, where a short length of thick-walled tube (sometimes known as a ferrule) is compressed by some mechanical or hydraulic means evenly downwards in size. The ferrule size and material is determined by the diameter and type of cable to be swaged. It deforms sufficiently to bind integrally around the outside of whatever is being swaged i.e. cable ends.

SWAY BARS (stabiliser bars) These are designed to help reduce twitchiness in vehicle suspension, and improve body stability. Torsional twist stiffness in the bar limits or damps the amount of movement between axles and chassis without restricting suspension travel to any great extent.

TORQUE The tendency or ability to continue to turn or twist. In an engine, the sheer grunt and turning effort developed, which keeps on moving the vehicle in hard going.

TABLE-DRAIN A table-drain is usually the large, wide and generally shallow drain formed along the side of a graded and convex non-blacktop road.

WIRING-LOOM CONNECTOR These may be single, double or any combination of number and shape in multiple plugs and sockets, where the OEM has placed them as joiners for a specific electrical wire or group of wires. These metallic, plastic-covered connectors are small, typically less than 10 mm in length. Manufacturers usually try to make the one loom fit many models to reduce costs. It is common to find many unused connectors sticking out of a wiring loom.

YOKE See Pintles

Index

A

A-bar **70**
ability **51**
Aboriginal land **65-6**
acceleration **22-3**, **122**
accelerator
  footrest **35-6**, **46**
  snatch **35-36**
accessories **18**, **155**, **165-70**
aftermarket **95**, **109-13**
air
  -filter **62**, **152**
  in fuel line **160**
  intake **153**
  vents **62**
airbags **167**
aircleaner **63**
airconditioning **33**, **62**, **157**
all-wheel-drive **15-17**, **135**
alloy **97**, **117**, **167**
alternator **149**
anchor point **50**, **54**, **64**, **69**, **77-8**
antenna **53**, **81**, **97**
antifreeze **60**
antilock braking system (ABS) **29**, **48-9**
approach angle **114-15**
attitude, driver **10**
automatic gearbox **28-9**, **134-5**
axe **13**, **28-9**, **31**, **33**, **45**, **60**
axle **19**, **121**, **123-4**, **145**

B

backing *see* reversing
battery **154-5**
  dual **154**, **161**, **166**
  flat **161-2**
  isolator **154**
  portable booster **166**
beach **12**, **19**, **41**, **52-3**, **66**
beginners day **11**
bitumen **11**, **20**
  wet **56-7**
bleed, fuel system **158**, **160**
boat
  launching **12**
  trailer **12**, **19**, **96**
  body **116-18**
  construction **118**
  dimensions **116-17**
  lean **116-18**, **124-5**
bog hole **41**
bogged **41**, **68-72**
brackets, mounting **97**
brake fluid **147-8**
brakes **48-9**, **95-6**, **147-8**
  adjustment **96**
  hoses **110-11**
  power **34-5**, **48-9**
  see also handbrake
braking **28-36**, **47-9**, **53**, **111-12**, **119-20**, **122-4**
  distance **57-8**
  engine **33-4**, **48**, **59**
  power **34-5**
breather hose **150**
breakdown **152-60**
bull-bag **54-6**
bullbar **167**
polycarbonate **166-7**
bulldust **61-3**
buying a 4WD **11**

C

cable
  battery **154-5**
  electrical **154-5**
  winch **72**, **76-8**, **167-8**
camping equipment **84**
caravan **12**, **96**, **109**, **167**
carburettor **105**, **158-9**
chains
  drag **169**
  towing **72**, **169**
  wheel **56**, **58-9**
chainsaw **13**, **54**, **165**
challenges **28-91**
checklist, preparation **90-1**
checks, regular `**100**
chocking wheels **47**, **69**
choke **35**, **104-5**, **158**
clamps
  electrical **162-3**
  hose **88**, **103**
clay **53**, **55**, **121**
cleaning **102-3**
clearance **109-18**
  body/wheel **113**
  ground **114**
climb
  angle **21**
  limits **37-8**
  useless **37**
climbing slopes **42-6**
clothing **84**, **89**
  protective **76-7**
clubs **10-12**, **14**, **47-8**, **74**, **88**, **104**, **135**, **165**, **168**
clutch **42-4**, **139-40**, **146-7**
control **44**
  fluid **149**
  starts **32-3**, **163**
communication **90**
compass **80-1**
compression ratio **33**
contours **79-80**
cooling systems **157**
cornering **130**
corrosion **96**
corrugations **138**
courtesy **64**
creeks **21-3**, **25**, **80**
crossover vehicles **15–16**, **20**
cylinder damage **22**

D

D-shackle **54**, **71**, **77-8**, **169**
damage
  body **50**
  environment **65-7**
  tyre **64-5**
dead vehicle **70-1**
debogging **68-72**
deflation (tyres) **166**
departure angle **114-15**
descent **47-50**
diesel **30**, **34**, **105-7**, **160**
detour **66-7**
differential **148-51**
  breather hose **150**
  locked **150-1**
dimensions, vehicle **48**, **65**, **116-17**
double clutching **139-40**
drawers **166**
drive-train **43**, **140-1**
drivebelts **88**, **157-9**
driving skills **24**, **44-5**
dual-range 4WD **16**
dune crests **39**
dust **61-3**

E

earth anchor **54, 64, 165**
education **10**
ego **14**
electrical
- calculations **162**
- circuits **155-7**
- current **155-7, 164**
- problems **154-6**

electronic aids **166**
electronic fuel injection **159**
emergency stopping **49-50**
emergency position indicating radio beacon (EPIRB) **83, 166**
engagement, 4WD **143-4**
Engel fridge **156-7**
engine
- braking **33-4, 48, 59**
- overrun **34**
- range **18**
- -speed **34**

entry permit **66**
environment, damage **65-7**
exercises, mechanical **104-8**
exhaust **21**
experience **51**
expertise **24, 44-5**
extended breather **150**

F

family transport **12**
fans **98**
- air-conditioning **62**
- heater **62**

fanbelt **157**
filter
- air **62, 152-3**
- fuel **152**
- oil-foamed **153**
- water **152-3**

flag, safety **13**
flat battery **161-2**
flexible bladder **166**
fluid levels **103**
flooding (fuel) **160**
following another 4WD **40**
footrest, throttle **35-6, 46**
four-speed gearbox **134**
4WD
- categories **16-17**
- engagement **143-4**
- full-time **16-17, 142-3**
- vehicle choice **16**
- what is a **18**
- when to use **19-21**

fuel
- carrying **89, 99-100**
- consumption **23, 89, 98, 142**
- diesel **105**
- gauge **158**
- injection **85, 159**
- lines **100, 160**
- petrol **23, 30, 34**
- pump **158-9**
- running out of **158**
- shut-off **33**
- storage **99**
- -to-air ratio **105, 158-9**
- tanks **89, 98-100**
- use calculations **98-9**
- vapourisation **159**
- *see* also liquefied petroleum gas

full-time 4WD **16–17, 20, 142-3**
funnel **88, 158**
fuses **155**

G

gas **100**
gears **134-41**
- braking **59**
- lubrication **141-2**
- overdrive **137-8**
- ratios **135-7**
- selection **138**
- wrong **138-9**

gearbox **31, 107-8, 134-41, 163 125-7, 143**
generator **162**
global positioning system (GPS) **80-1, 83, 92, 166**
gloves **45, 76-7**
glow-plugs **105-6**
gradient **22**
gravel **52, 108, 114**
gravity **30, 42-3, 47, 52**
grease nipples **102, 106**
grease points **148**
greasy surfaces **57-8**
grooves **45-7, 55**

H

hand throttle **35-6, 46, 164**
hand-operated winch **74-5**
handbrake **49, 60, 95**
- tailshaft drum **95**

horse-float **12, 20, 168**
hoses
- brake **110-11**
- differential breather **150**
- heater **88**
- radiator **88, 157**

hubs **121, 142-5**
human factor **10-14**
hydraulic fluid **146-7**
hydrometer **154**

I

ice **58-60**
ignition **30, 42, 162**
- coil **42**
- diesel **42, 105-6**

information, local **83-4**
insurance **84-5, 113**

J

jack
- highlift **55-6, 128**
- hydraulic **106**

jacking **55-6, 69**
- -plate **55**

jerrycans **12**
- carrying **89**
- storage **89**

jump starting **162-3**
jumper leads **162-3**

K

keeping others informed **82, 90**
knowledge, technical **85, 152, 106-7**

L

light, trouble **156**
lighting circuit **155-6**
lights **18, 22, 97, 101**
load
- capacity, winch **167**
- mechanical **43**
- on/off load **140**
- -sharing **168**
- winching **77**

local information **83-4**
liquefied petroleum gas (LPG) **30, 99, 100, 104**
lubrication, gears **140**

M

maintenance **23-4, 85, 93, 169**
- routine **101-2**

manual gearbox **31, 135-7**

manuals **85**, **94**, **135**
map plotting software **166**
maps **38**, **79-80**
  reading **79**
  topographical **79**
markers **22**, **38**
mechanical exercises **104-8**
mechanical knowledge (winching) **76**
mirror **114**
modifications **93-169**
  and braking **111-12**
momentum **37**, **46**, **138**
mud **63-4**
multimeter **154**

N

navigation **79-81**

O

off-road **11**, **16-17**, **51**
oil **107**, **148-51**
  and water **149-50**
  frothing **148**
overfilling **148**
  seal **148**, **150**
oiled-foam filter **153**
outback trips **86-7**
overdrive **137-8**
overload
  electrical **155**
  mechanical **43**
  springs **168**
  winch **76**
oversteer **120**

P

packing **56**
padding **72**
part-time 4WD **16-17**
parts **85**, **88**
  broken **43-4**
  checklist **90-1**
  replacement **85**, **88**
  spare **85**, **88**
  storage **170**
passengers **14**, **31**
permits **65-66**
P.E.T.R.O.L **101**
petrol engines **34**, **107**
pitch, front to rear **10**
plasma rope **72**, **77**, **166**
point-loading **123**, **132-3**
polycarbonate **167**
power **42**
  brakes **34-5**, **48-9**
  steering **13**, **49**, **88**, **119**, **158**
  winches **74**
practice **37**, **105**, **107-8**, **141**
preparation **82**, **90-1**
priming **85**
propshaft **142**
puller, hand-operated **74-5**
pulley systems **78**
pump
  fuel **158-60**
priming **85**
  vacuum **147**
  water **88**

R

RPM **34**
radiator **60**, **157**
radio **83**
ramps **49**, **54**
rattle gun **126**
rattles **96-7**
refrigerator **156-7**, **166**, **170**
relay **155**
reversing **30**, **120-1**
rims **53**, **113-14**, **125-9**, **132**
roadworthiness **84-5**
rocks **60-1**, **64-5**
rollback **30**, **43**
rollover **11**
roof-rack **99**, **118**, **166**
rope **72**
  tow **89**
rubbish **67**
rust **96**, **166**

S

SUV *see* sports utility vehicle
safety **13**, **83**
  driver **10-13**
  driving rules **10**
  electrical **155**
  eye protection **76**
  overtaking **23**
  radiator cap **157**
stalling **28-33**
  trip planning **83**
saltpan **39**, **69-70**
sand **52-4**, **131**
  dry **52**
  dunes **39**, **52-4**
  handling **52-4**
  wet **54**
sandhills **24**, **131**
satellite phone **83**, **90**, **161**
service records **101**
services, mechanical **152-60**
shock absorbers **109**, **113-14**
shovel **13**, **45**
shudder **30**, **146**, **149**
side-slope **11**, **151**
side-slip **151**
signals **91**
single-range 4WD **16**
skidding **58**, **123**
skids **19**
skills **24**, **44-5**
slopes, climbing **42-6**
slow travel **145**
snatchblock **56**, **74-6**, **78**
  pulley **78**
snatchem-strap **71-2**
snorkel **63**, **153**
snow **58-60**
solar blanket **168**
solar panel **162**
spare tyres **106**
spare wheels **106**, **127-9**
speed **123**
split rims **125-6**, **128**
sports utility vehicle (SUV) **11**, **15–16**, **20**, **135**
springs **109-10**
  coil **110**, **169**
  kits **110**
  leaf **124**
  sag **109**
  set-up **123-4**
  overload **168**
squeaks **96**
stabiliser bars
  see sway bars
stall **28-33**, **50**
starts **31-33**
  sequences **29-33**
stops **30**
starting **104-6**
  clutch **163**
  jump **162-3**
  sequences **31**
stall **31-3**
steel versus alloy **117-18**, **167**
steep descents **47-50**
steering **30**, **119-33**, **151**, **158**
  in reverse **120-1**
  power **13**, **49**, **88**, **119**, **158**
  traction **121-2**
  wheel **45-6**
stop spots **30-1**
stopping distance **57-8**
  emergency **49-50**

storage **166**, **170**
stranded **85**
survival
  clothing, snow **60**
  vehicle kit **88-90**
suspension **109-13**, **122-5**
  aftermarket **109**
  coil **110**
  independent **124**
  weight transfer **122-3**
sway bars **124-5**

T

tachometer **34**, **107**
tailshaft **140**, **145**, **147**
  drum brake **34**
tarpaulin **89**
techniques **51-67**
technology **15**
terrain judgement **37-41**
throttle
  hand **35-6**, **46**, **164**
  footrest **36**, **46**
  control **44**
Tirfor winch **75-6**, **78**
tools **89**, **94**, **169-70**
torque **145**
tow bar **168**
tow points **71-2**
tow-rope **89**
tow-starting **164**
towing **68-72**, **96**
  dead vehicle **70**
  chains **72**, **169**
track terms **15**
trackwidth **114-16**
traction **21**, **64-7**
  control **49**
  steering **121-2**
  see also ramps
trailers **96**, **116**, **168**
training days **11**
transfer gearbox **142-5**
tree protector **72**, **75**, **77-8**
  trip planning **82-91**, **86-7**
trouble light **88**, **156**
tubes **128**
tube-patch kit **128**
turbo-timer **50**, **169**
turbo-oiler **169**
turbocharger **169**
tyre pliers **128-9**
tyres **64-5**, **94-5**, **129-33**
  changing **106**
  clearances **110**, **113-14**
  point-loading **132-3**
  pressure **24**, **52-3**, **55**, **63**, **65**, **129-33**
  repairs **128**
  sizes **132**
  spare **132-3**
  valves **166**

U

understeer **121**
universal joint **140**

V

vacuum pump **147**
vehicle placement **39-40**
vibration **97-8**

W

walking out **83**
washout **39**, **54**
water
  and oil **150**
  crossing **21-2**
  distilled **154**
  drinking **89**
  filters **152**
  flexible bladders **164**, **166**
  pump **88**, **158**
  splash **153**
wear factors **145**
weight transfer **122-3**
welding **97-8**
wet bitumen **56-7**
wheelnuts **113-14**, **128-32**
wheels **125-8**
  alloy **125**
  chocking **47**, **69**
  see also rims, hubs, tyres
wheelspin **19**, **59**, **121**, **145**
winches **13**, **73-8**, **119**, **167-8**
  buying **78**
  cable **76-8**
  electric **35**
  hand-operated **75-6**
  hydraulic **35**, **119**
  power take off (PTO) **35**, **108-9**
  powered **74-5**
  Tirfor **75-6**
winching **45**, **73-8**
  dangers **73**
  downhill **49-50**
  learning **73-4**
wiring **154**
workshop manual
  see manuals